Rudolf Schneider's The Artillery of the Middle Ages

Translated and Edited by
William Paul Dean

Publication Information

Published Independently
ISBN 9781079330557
Cover Art by William Holladay

Contents

Translator's Introduction

In 1903, Erwin Schramm began a study into the artillery of the ancient world. The following year, his work would cause him to enter into correspondence with Rudolf Schneider. A fast friendship would begin, and it would last until Dr. Schneider's death in 1911.

The year 1910, however, would see the publication of a series of books and pamphlets from the pair of men. General Schramm first published his work *Die Antike Geschütze der Saalburg* in that year. Dr. Schneider published, under the same title, his own commentary on the research process and some of the engines rebuilt for the Saalburg Institute shortly afterwards. This book was likewise released the same year.

In the 1918 edition of *Die Antike Geschütze der Saalburg*, Schramm stated that it had been Dr. Schneider's desire to publish a new, joint edition of this work. Schramm, however, decided to wait until after beginning his retirement (we would do well to note that he was an actively serving officer in the Imperial German Army); this delay would prevent the writing of a second edition, as Dr. Schneider died prior to any such opportunity.

I became acquainted with this work in 2017 while I was translating *Die Antike Geschütze der Saalburg*. After publishing the first English edition of the combined works of Schramm and Schneider on the subject of ancient artillery, I decided that this work meritted being brought to a new, wider audience as well. While I cannot present the changes that Dr. Schneider would have made in a collaborative edition, I will offer a hypothesis.

General Schramm was an engineer that enjoyed history. His work was predominately in the reconstruction of ancient artillery. Doctor Schneider, on the other hand, was a historian and a linguist with some understanding of engineering. To readers of *Die Antike Geschütze der Saalburg*, the limited number of reconstructions described and complete lack of pictures thereof in this book will come as a surprise. I strongly suspect that, had Schneider lived, the pair would have produced several engines in as close to the period manner as possible. These engines would have lent practical evidence to Schneider's theories.

If this book does not detail the reconstruction of various engines as the previous did, what, then does it do? Herein, Dr. Schneider has collected a vast array of literary sources and analyzed them for evidence of artillery. When the evidence was available, he then provided a detailed analysis of the particular engines within a document. Similarly, he provided a comparison of engines between contemporary treatises, often finding great fault or great merit with a particular author. Merely glancing at the list of accounts that he has analyzed is impressive, before one begins to comprehend the linguistic feat that this was.

The original book contained passages in eight language variants. These were Ancient and Medieval Latin; Ancient Greek; Middle and Modern French; and Middle, Proto-modern, and Modern German. The ability to compile, understand, and distill the wisdom of so many different works sets Schneider above most other scholars, even before we look at his analysis.

Modern reconstructive research has largely confirmed many of Dr. Schneider's hypotheses about the later half of the Medieval era. With a few minor exceptions, his understanding of counterweight trebuchets has withstood the trials of more than a century. I do, however, feel it necessary to clarify a point as to the construction of this type of engine. Both Schneider and the period sources distinguish between a "fixed counterweight" and a "moving counterweight." This does not mean that the counterweight in a fixed counterweight machine was permanently attached the arm and did not move in relation to the arm. Rather, both types had a pivot point between the arm and the counterweight, but the moving counterweight was pushed forward of the arm as far as possible in addition to being raised in the air. The additional momentum from the rotation would impart additional power to the shot.

However, I believe that there are some serious issues with Schneider's analysis, particularly as concerns the early Medieval era. The first is not obvious from the text of this book and only becomes apparent after reading his *Die Antike Geschütze der Saalburg*. In that work, he asserts that Heron's *Cheiroballistra* is merely a scrap from an engineering dictionary. Further study of it in the 1960s revealed that the document is, in fact, a treatise on constructing a torsion engine. This strongly indicates that the tradition of torsion artillery lasted for quite some time in the Eastern Roman Empire. As this book does largely restrict itself to Western Europe, this is not a significant problem, but it is enough to raise some questions.

Secondly, Dr. Schneider pays little attention to the traction trebuchet. This engine could quite easily bridge the gap between the early and late Medieval eras. Depending upon the interpretations of documentary evidence from the Sieges of Paris and Orleans, a traction engine would potentially resolve the issues derived from the quite reasonable assertion that torsion had disappeared from the Western half of Christendom. Additionally, the restriction to Western Europe creates a problem here. An Arabic treatise from the early XII century details the construction of three forms of traction trebuchet, including one that it refers to as the "Frankish model". If the Franks in the Levant used a traction trebuchet sufficiently distinct from the two asiatic styles as to warrant being called Frankish, then the Crusaders likely had a fair amount of experience with the engine prior to the writing of this treatise.

As to the translation itself, there are a few points that I must address. First, I have generally rendered the word *Geschütz* as engine. While from a purely technical perspective, the word gun may have been a more accurate choice, the word gun has connotations in contemporary English that are somewhat problematic. In military and technical language gun means a projectile weapon requiring two or more individuals to crew for it. However, modern English commonly uses it to mean any form of firearm. The German word is far closer in intent to the military meaning, thus I have chosen to avoid gun, with a few exceptions for either flavor or textual clarity. Further, while the word *Hebelgeschütz* does refer to trebuchets, I have often used the term lever-gun or lever powered engine. This is due to both the traction and counterweight engines being powered by a lever arm. Hopefully this literal translation of the German word will add clarity, particularly when distinguishing between the two sources of power.

An absolutely necessary portion of translation work is getting inside the head of the original author. Doing so with Dr. Schneider was somewhat difficult, but highly rewarding. His command of multiple languages clearly influenced both his writing and his thinking. In order to improve readability, I have made changes to some of his sentence structure. Nowhere did I alter his content, and, wherever possible, I have used language as close to his original. However, I do feel that the book is improved by breaking some of his sentences into more manageable portions.

Doctor Schneider also provided significant amounts of information in quoted evidence supporting his claims. Whenever possible, I have attempted to translate the quoted material into English. If Dr. Schneider provided the original language, I translated from that; however, he sometimes provided the material in German translation and did not include the original text. When that occurred, I had to work from the German.

There were several pictures taken from period manuscripts at the end of the book originally. Sadly, I have not been able to find extant copies of all of them in North America. I have included the majority of them. However, I have been unable to locate a copy of the first table of images. All of the others are present.

Finally as regards the document itself, Dr. Schneider included the full text of the relevant portions of several ancient and medieval manuscripts as appendices to the book. At first, I had considered either leaving them out entirely or attempting to translate them into English. However, the more time that I spent with Dr. Schneider, the more I realized that that would be contrary to his aim in including them. His intent was to make the primordial language of his research materials more readily available to the general public. Therefore, in order to honor his wishes, I have simply included a transcribed copy of each of them as appendices to this book.

There are some people to whom I owe thanks, for this work would not have happened without their aid. To those readers familiar with my previous book, many of these names will be familiar. My parents Paul and Jenette Dean deserve my thanks. My father instilled a deep love of history in me, as well as a working knowledge of carpentry and the rudiments of the German language. My mother has been a great supporter of this project. This book would not exist were it not for the tireless efforts of Herr Professor Ron Cates. His careful and patient instruction in German truly built a marvelous foundation for the further study of languages. Elizabeth Duncanson was kind enough to assist me with the brief section in Middle French when I got somewhat out of my depth. David Carr likewise helped me with the section in proto-modern German. The word Nidsichfahrung was quite a puzzler. William McCole assisted with a tricky Latin passage. Sarah Budai did not directly contribute to this work, as she passed away more than a year before I learned of the existence of this book; however, her assistance in locating a copy of General Schramm's *Die Antike Geschütze der Saalburg* and her "gentle nudging" to translate and publish it eventually led to this project. Lastly, Ruairi Hutchison has been absolutely critical to this piece. In addition to double checking problematic passages and generally reviewing my grammar, he has provided invaluable assistance, both in terms of research and as a sounding board for this project. Doctor Marsden states that no student of artillery can long study engines without building them. I would hate to estimate how much time Ruairi has spent helping me build experimental and functional pieces.

To the many others that provided me with a bit of emotional support, a gentle nudge, or a swift kick in the pants when I needed it, thank you.

Dr. Schneider was a brilliant historian and linguist. His philological work is of the highest possible caliber. The quality and depth of research that he presented is second to none. While a few of his hypotheses have been disproven over time, he knew that most of his ideas would require testing with reconstructed engines and many of his conclusions have been supported by modern reconstructive archaeology. I strongly recommend watching the NOVA special on the medieval siege to see how many of Schneider's ideas play out in the realm of the physical world.

It would be a lie for me to claim that I never complained of Dr. Schneider's writing style. His style was difficult to read and even harder to translate well. However, the truth is that he clearly enjoyed playing with language, and he occasionally took things a step too far. Nowhere is his joy more palpable than at the very conclusion of the book. He clearly wanted to see these engines rebuilt and his hypotheses tested.

I consider this man a friend. He was not a part of my life for as long as his friend General Schramm was, but I do sincerely regret never having had the opportunity to meet him. One of his contemporaries asserted that science was deprived of a great mind by his early death. Perhaps no one can say it better than General Schramm did when he called Schneider “irreplaceable.” I can only hope that my work here has brought a little bit of the man to life.

Chattanooga, 19 March 2019
William Dean

Forward

If one considers only the predominately used guns of each era, then the history of artillery can be divided into three periods corresponding to the three periods of world history. Antiquity had torsion engines, the Middle Ages had engines made of levers and counterweights, and the Modern Era saw the development of gunpowder artillery. There is not the slightest doubt about the artillery of antiquity and the modern era, and for the second half of the Middle Ages, the views of the military authors of the era agree as well, yet for the first half, i.e. from the Migration Era until about 1200 AD, there are two fundamentally different views that are mutually exclusive, and thus should be brought to a decision. Napoleon III places the end of torsion artillery in the Migration Era, whereas Köhler asserts that torsion engines persisted until 1200 when they were replaced by trebuchets. The campaigns of Charlemagne fall in the disputed period, and the battles of Frederick Barbarossa for northern Italy, then the Crusader siege of Acre (1189-1191), halcyon events, wherein the artillery is so debatable that it becomes almost incomprehensible if one does not know the form and capability of the engines. Our newer depictions attempt to force the issue by unceremoniously joining with Köhler, ignoring Napoleon, and throwing around the slogan "Tradition of Antiquity." However, we cannot permit ourselves to accept the weight of this assertion until it has been confirmed by the available source material.

Thus, it was the task of the following investigation in turn to identify and explain these sources, which may provide information about the period; as these sources can be difficult to obtain and are often in poor printings, they have been added as supplements to this text. My work is not conclusive, for it lacks the reconstructions of the engineer, nor does it address Eastern cultures, and, lastly, it does not include the strange machines and giant crossbows, which though the appeared after 1300 people take as characteristic of the entire Medieval era. Hopefully, however, this study will present a clear and true picture of the stated period; at the very least, no effort has been spared in clearly and precisely presenting and explaining everything, both in words and pictures. The results will likely only be surprising to those confused by today's illusions. To the impartial reader, they will likely be quite simple and almost self-explanatory. Further, those that wonder that these conclusions, as simple and obvious as they are, have never been thought of by anyone previously, will be pleased to learn that almost everything contained herein has been stated by the now all but forgotten experiments of Napoleon.[1] For me, at least, this unsought coincidence is most pleasing as confirmation that the results are correct.

Thereby, the conflict over the dating of the curious writings entitled "Anonymi De Rebus Bellicis Liber" is settled. No one was seriously concerned about the, at best, shallow contents, and the anonymous source had been dated to the IV Century AD, for Anonymous's writings were considered to be an appendix to "Notita Dignitatum." In my edition (Berlin, 1908), which is printed at the expense of the Saalburg Institute, it has been proven that the writings of Anonymous should be placed for technical reasons at no earlier than the XIV Century. In opposition to this, however, are the views of O. Seeck, in Pauly-Wissowa's Realencyclopedia I 2325, who dates the document from 366 to 378 AD based on reasons of paleography, which are expressed in an article in Deutsche Literaturzeitung 1908, No 50, wherein he "warns the reader against my little book." As a result, I was obligated to trace the handwritten tradition of the Anonymous work, which I have published in a detailed essay (New Journal for Classical Antiquity, 1910 XXV 327-342) stating that O. Seeck had arbitrarily published

[1] Translator's Note: Napoleon III of France conducted several experiments in counter-weight powered artillery.

the results for “Notita Dignitatum” as those for “De Rebus Bellicus”; he is entirely unfamiliar with the handwritten versions of Anonymous, having only studied the flawed printings of the Basel edition. Therefore, there is nothing from the perspective of tradition to object to the later origin of the manuscript “De Rebu Bellicus.” The following treatise will establish that the author in question had no knowledge of the torsion engine, instead relying on the elasticity of the bow arms for an arrow-shooting engine, whereas the ancient and early Medieval eras utilized the former but did not exist by 1300.

Heidelberg, 15 February 1910
Rudolf Schneider

The Era Without Artillery
1: The Sixth Century, Procopius

The Teutons that served with the Roman Army were praised for "their great achievements in siege warfare," because many cities that had been defended tenaciously in earlier centuries fell quickly into their hands.[2] These achievements must be explained by deeper reasons, which may be found easily enough, for "without artillery and engineering soldiers," no one can achieve anything great in siege warfare. Yet, as the Germans had by this time long been in the service of the Roman Emperors and fought on the side of their well-equipped armies, it is only natural that the Germans should have learned many things from Rome. Certainly the "Tradition of Antiquity" cannot be denied to the independent Germanic armies following the Migration Era, but the significance thereof must be determined in isolation for each army and certainly should not be taken as wholy proven. The military structure, warrior culture of the individual fighter, and the civilization of the people as a whole all vary greatly from place to place, and all of this must, therefore, be considered in order to avoid erroneous conclusions. For this reason, it seems questionable to assume that the Germanic armies carried forth with the use of torsion engines. These reservations intensify to a contradiction with an understanding of the well-known positions of Procopius, which is, surprisingly, not taken into account by the other military writers of the era.

Procopius, born in Caesarea, Palestine, was a lawyer. In 527 AD, he was assigned as legal advisor and secretary to General Belisarius. In this position, he participated in the campaigns against the Vandals, Ostrogoths, and Persians, even

---

[2] Max Jahns, Handbuch einer Geschichte Kriegswesens. Leipzig, 1880, p 448 and 451.

being an eyewitness to the Siege of Rome (Dec 536-Mar 538), which he describes in detail in his *History of the Gothic Wars*. Here, we only need to take from his long description of the siege the section dealing with the mutual preparations for the storming of Rome's walls, and then we need to look briefly at the course of the day of the assault itself in order to understand properly how the Germanic tribes would have conducted siege warfare during the VI century.

Immediately upon their arrival, the Ostrogoths crossed the Milvian Bridge and routed Belisarius and his cavalry before the gates of Rome. Confident following this initial success, Vitiges believed that the city was already lost and demanded its surrender. His envoys, however, returned with dismissive answers. The following is a faithful translation[3] from Procopius's *History of the Gothic Wars*, Book I Chapter 21:[4]

"When Vitiges heard this, he decided to take the walls by storm, and he prepared to assault the city walls. He built wooden towers as tall as the city walls of the enemy, for he had previously learned their true height by counting the individual layers of stone. These towers stood on wheels, which were attached beneath each corner, and, when these wheels turned, then the towers rolled easily toward wherever the assaulting men desired, and for this purpose, oxen where harnessed to them. But he also had made a great number of ladders that would reach the battlements, as well as four machines called rams. Such a machine has the following form: Four wooden posts, all of the same length, are placed vertically opposite each other and connected by eight cross beams, four above and four below. Thus the whole takes on the shape of a rectangular house. Only the workmen give it neither screens nor walls, instead covering it with animal hides on all sides so that the machine is easy to pull and the crew finds adequate

---

[3] Cf. Appendices

[4] Translator's Note: I have translated this from Schneider's German translation rather than the original Greek. Please see the ancient Greek at the end.

protection from enemy projectiles inside. Within the machine, they hang from the top, approximately in the middle, a horizontal beam, attached by loose chains, that tapers towards the front and has either, like a lance, a mighty iron spike at the tip or a broad, anvil-like head. The entire machine rests on sixteen wheels, four at each corner post, and, in order to move them, at least fifty men must work inside. Once these machines have been rolled up to the city walls, the beam is then drawn rearwards by means of a winch, and then it is allowed to swing back against the wall with a rapid, mighty strike. And, if this machine strikes again and again, it loosens every structure, tears through everything without the least difficulty, wherever it hits; this machine got its name in this way, for just like a real ram, the head of this beam shatters whatever it hits. Thus are rams made for use in attacking a wall. In addition, the Goths also stored up a large supply of fascines made from rods and reeds to throw into ditches so that the paths before these machines would be smooth, thus easing their transport. So equipped, the Goths set off for the assault.

"Belisarius, however, placed upon the towers those machines known as ballistas. These machines have the appearance of a bow, but on the lower part, they have a grooved, wooden slat that is slidable and sits on an iron bar. When one wishes to shoot at the enemy with it, one pulls back a short string between the two wooden arms - just like that between the arms of an ordinary bow - and thereby move the heads of the arms simultaneously, and then place the projectile in the grooved slat. The projectile is only about half as long as the arrow for a bow, but four times as thick, and it does not have, as per usual, feather, but rather in the place of feathers, thin wooden fins based on the style of the projectile in question. Additionally, it has a large (as appropriate for the thickness) iron head on its end. The machines crew then pull on both sides with greater power via the winch, and thereby is the string drawn back. They then release the string,[5]

[5] At this point, the text of the original is corrupted. Compare this to the Greek

and the arrow the flies force with such enormous force that a range of at least two bowshots' length is achieved and the arrow easily punches through whatever it strikes, be it wood or metal. This is the design of the machine that is known as the ballista due to its great shooting power.

"Behind the parapet of the encircling walls, they placed other engines which served to throw stones; these were like slings and called Onagers.

"On the outsides of the gates, they attached "wolves," which are made in the following manner. First take two beams which reach from the ground to the parapet, then lay across them overlapping planks, nailing these planks together so that there are no gaps between them. A barb protrudes from each point of intersection, like a strong spike.[6] Now, fasten these crossplanks to the two beams so that they hang down from the top to the middle, and then lean the beams backwards against the gates. And when the enemy approaches, the defenders grab the beams and push them over so that they fall on the enemy, inevitably killing whomever they strike with their sharp spikes.

"Such were Belisarius's preparations for the defense."

On the eighteenth day of the siege, the assault took place. Though the citizens awaited with trembling and hesitation, they saw Belisarius's firm confidence in his superiority. And rightly so: the wooden towers of the Ostrogoths remained immobile in the fields once the oxen had been shot down, and likewise the rams must have remained at a great distance, for at the very least they were not successfully put into action anywhere. In fact, the Ostrogoths succeeded in penetrating the fortifications in only one place, and that without contributions from their machines, for the

---

text in the Appendices.

[6] This toothed grid forms a sort of harrow.

weak walls of the *Vivarium*[7] were east of the actual city wall. Even there, the walls were not actually pierced, but only cut off from the main wall, which requires little engineering. Incidentally, this partial success brought only sorrow to the Goths, as a vigorous sally by the defenders drove the invaders back with heavy losses.

From this account of Procopius, it seems evident that the superiority of the Byzantine army, apart from the prudence of its leader and good morale of the soldiers, is essentially due to the use of projectile weapons and artillery. Procopius names (in the second section) the large, slinglike stone-thrower called the Onager, the one-armed torsion engine whose exact form Ammianus XXIII 4.5 gives us. The other engine, the heavy arrow shooter, is called a ballista and is often also a torsion engine, as Marquardt[8] has correctly asserted, even though Procopius never mentions the torsion springs in his detailed description. It lacks any mention at all of the motive force; however, that should not prevent us from establishing that the Byzantine army utilized both main forms of ancient artillery, i.e. two-armed torsion engines partnered with one-armed engines, as we are given by Ammianus and Vegetius. Therefore, the traditions of antiquity are clearly uninterrupted in the Eastern Empire.

The matter is quite different with the Germanic tribes. Procopius's report indicates that they did not use artillery at all. This can only surprise those that do not understand the artistry required to build a torsion engine or that do not realize that such engines are useless if the best materials are not used for the spring bundle, which even then must be skillfully tightened by learned hands using a tension ladder. And whoever believes that the Teutons would have been able to absorb gradually the

---

[7] Translator's Note: The *Vivarium* was large stabling area for the animals of the Coliseum.

[8] Joachim Marquardt, *Römische Staatsverwaltung,* (Roman State Administration). Leipzig, 1884. II, 254, Anm. 1.

engineering feats of their enemies and that they would have made, with the aid of defectors and captured engines, artillery of the same design (with weaker, though still sufficient power) can perform a personal experiment in the imitation of the engines, like that demonstrated in 1865 by the Heidelberg Philologen's Conference.[9] The Germans could not have done more with their limited means. Either they never attempted to develop such engines, or they abandoned the attempt very early on, for such weak engines are not appropriate for war.

Yet still the Germans dared, as Procopius teaches us, to to make wooden towers on wheels and ram machines in the Roman fashion. Since these constructions require little more skill than that of a mere carpenter, the Germans were able to build them. However, they were lacking in sophistication, for the towers required oxen to pull them, and these hand no cover from the shots of the enemy. Thus, when all of the draft animals were shot away, the Goths were left standing in their immobile towers. The ram machines were rolled forward by teams that found cover within them, but these machines likewise did not reach their objectives. Apparently, the Goths failed to smooth the ground before them, which while a great deal of work is absolutely essential to the successful use of both of these types of war machines. In addition, one must select exactly the point of the wall that will be attacked in order to build this road correctly. Because the Goths did not fulfill these necessary preconditions, their war machines availed them not. It should be remembered that the tower and the ram only attained their full importance after the development of the torsion engine (after 400 BC). Suppressing fire from them was absolutely required. The Goths lacked catapults, but the Byzantines had them and knew how to use them skillfully.

---

[9] Proceedings of the 24th Conference of German Philologens in Heidelberg, 1865. Leipzig 1866. p223.

The above statements, based upon the reports of a knowledgeable eyewitness to the operations of the Ostrogoths in 536-538, apply equally well to all of the Teutonic armies that acted independently from the time of the Migration Era. Despite frequent contact with the Roman Army, the Germanic armies were merely acquainted with the techniques and technologies of siege warfare: both the tower and the ram they built, but failed to deploy effectively. Of torsion artillery, the best tools of the siege, they were completely lacking.

2: The Tenth Century- Richerus Remensis

At this level of advancement in the art of the siege, the Germanic peoples held fast for several centuries, as reports from the X Century indicate. The difference between Richerus Remensis and Procopius is that in Richerus' account, neither the attackers nor the defenders possess artillery; therefore, the attackers could conquer with less than perfect means. It was by these means that Louis IV, in 938, built a four-wheeled siege hut that protected a dozen warriors during the siege of Laon; the crew therein undermined the walls, causing the garrison to surrender once a breach had been effected.[10] Yet the same city mounted a successful defense in 989 against a force of 8,000 men while Hugo Capet threatened the walls with a huge battering ram. However, this war machine became stuck on its approach, and a fortunate sortie by the defenders forced the king to withdraw.[11] The siege of the city of Verdun, undertaken by the King Lothair III in the year 984 with an army of 10,000 men, deserves an in-depth consideration for Gottfried of Verdun and Hainaut prepared his defenses with great care in order to resist the attacks of the king.

---

[10] See the Appendices.

[11] See the Appendices.

As a result, of course, the initial, violent assault failed, and Lothair was compelled to begin a traditional siege. About this siege, Richerus reports the following:[12]

"Following this assault, the Gauls ordered a traditional siege from all sides, and dug deep trenches around their camp so that if the enemy should make a sudden sortie, the approach would be difficult. They then gathered tall oak trees, cut down at the roots, to construct a siege tower. Four beams, each 30 feet in length, were laid upon the ground so that two rested beside each other at a distance of 10 feet, and the other two were fastened at equal intervals across the first pair. The area thus enclosed measured 10 feet in length and as much in width, with the beams extending 10 feet out from the square. Above the places where the wood was joined together, four beams, each of 40 feet in length, were erected by winches, so that they were equidistant from each other, thereby forming a vertical quadrangle. And in two places, at the top and the middle, 10 foot long cross-beams were placed through all four sides, thus connecting the corner posts firmly together. However, from the ends of the beams on which these posts stood rose four supports that ran obliquely almost to the height of the uppermost crossbars and were then fastened to the vertical posts; in this way was the framework supported so that it would not sway. Planks were then laid over the cross-beams, which held the tower together in the middle and at the top, and these planks were covered with braided hurdles for the warriors to stand upon, thereby being able to fling down spears and stones from great height upon their enemies. Once construction was completed, the Gauls considered how to move it towards the enemy's position. Yet, as they were afraid of the enemy's marksmen, they had to consider a way to approach the enemy without casualties. After much thought, they found a very good way to bring the tower to their enemies. They ordered that four logs of immense thickness be sunk into the solid earth so that 10 feet were buried beneath the ground and eight feet projected up from the ground. These

[12] See the Appendices.

trunks would then have been firmly connected to each other on their four sides by the strongest cross-beams available, and these cross-beams would have ropes looped about them. The ends of these ropes would have been faced against the enemy, with the upper ends fastened to the tower and the lower ends tied to oxen.The lower ends must be longer than the upper ones, and the upper ones must be shorter and connected to the framework, so that the tower will come between the enemy and the oxen. If this is done properly, the framework will move towards the enemy as the oxen move away. By means of this innovation, the tower, which had rollers placed beneath in order to ease its movement, could be advanced towards the enemy without exposing any of its crew to attack. While their enemies built a similar framework, it did not match that of the attackers in height or strength. When both were finished, the combatants climbed both towers directly. Both sides fought bravely, but neither would yield. The king, who had approached the wall, was wounded on his upper lip by a shot from a sling. This embittered his followers, who fought all the more violently as a result. Because the enemy, defiant with their towers and their weapons, refused to give way, the king ordered that iron hooks be brought forward. These were tied to ropes and thrown at the platforms of the defenders, so that they hooked upon the cross-beams. Once these were hooked firmly to the scaffolding, other warriors grabbed the ropes and began to pull them so that the scaffolds were soon pulled completely over. The defenders began to abandon the tower, as some climbed down the beams, other leapt to the earth, and still others, overwhelmed by ignominious fear, sought to save their lives by hiding. When the defenders saw that they were all in danger of death, they gave up their tower and humbly begged for their lives."

Having thus established, by the testimony of irrefutable witnesses, that the Ostrogoths had no artillery in the VI century and that artillery was completely absent on both sides (despite extensive preparations) in France during the X century, we now must consider why it is today commonly accepted that the armies of Charlemagne used artillery and establish that there is continuity from the ancient torsion engines to the introduction of gunpowder artillery.

3: The End of Torsion Engines

According to Napoleon III, torsion engines disappeared from western Europe after the time of the Great Migrations; however, there is a strong counterargument in the contemporary community that says that they existed for the entirety of the Middle Ages and were in use that whole time.

Napoleon, who had practical training as an artilleryman through his service with the military of the Canton of Thurgau in 1830 and later designed an improved artillery piece, wrote an extensive history of artillery during his captivity in Ham. It is published under the name *Études sur le passé et l'avenir de l'Artillerie* from Liége (1847) and Paris (1851).[13] Even W. Rustow,[14] who loves to disparage the French Emperor deliberately for the sake of his furious hatred, has not failed to acknowledge the worth of this book; the judgement of Prussian artillerymen can be found in the General Military Journal (3 December 1853). It is available in a German language translation by the recently deceased Hermann V. Müller, who as an officer and historian was held in the highest regards by artillerists. During his years as a Lieutenant he described it as "a work of the most careful historical research that performs the most difficult, artful examination of the past in greatest detail, that required so rare a union of science and scholarship with pure power of the spirit and certainty of estimation, in short all of the best qualities of both the writer and the thinker." This was also the opinion of the contemporary

[13] Translator's Note: "Studies of the Past and Future of Artillery"
[14] Wilhelm Rustow, *Julius Caesar's Commentaries*. Stuttgart 1867.

military, as given by Moltke, Roon, Brandt, Goeben, and other high-ranking men of military literature.

On the other hand, it is difficult to comprehend how Major General G. Köhler[15] could say of the same book, "As brilliant as the work of Napoleon III is, it is equally superficial." However, that author's pride, given that he claims to have demolished all of Napoleon's results, may serve as an explanation. Yet it is also equally incomprehensible that, following Köhler's verdict, Napoleon's book has been largely forgotten; now it is only mentioned infrequently in hidden and fleeting notes. Presumably, however, these notes must be derived from some source; otherwise, writers about medieval military science, such as Viollet-le-Duc,[16] would have most certainly renounced what would be arbitrary drawings of trebuchets, as Napoleon provides a reasonable description of a reconstructed engine in his writings. The behavior of Köhler does, however, give us one advantage: we need not worry about him and his followers, rather, only dealing with those that are reckoned against his opinion.

> Köhler writes on Volume III, page 9,
>
> "My results as regarding the shooting and throwing machines are quite surprising. As I will prove, the onager, under the names mangonel and later "Rutte and Poler,"[17] for the entirety of the Medieval era; further, the catapult, under the names Tarant (Scorpion) or Mangonellus, was still in use during the XIV Century. In the XII Century, the *funda balearica* appeared, a new machine unknown in

---

[15] G. Köhler, *The Development of Military Science and Warfare in the Knightly Era*. Breslau 1886.

[16] *Dictionnaire raisonné de l'Architecture française* Book V, pg 224. Paris 1861.

[17] Translator's Note: The term "Rutte und Poler" from Köhler's book appears only on the given page in that book. I have found no other trace of the term. It does not translate from German to English. I firmly believe it to be a fabrication of a pseudo-historical nature on the part of Köhler.

> antiquity. They were then given the name *petraria*, which had previously been applied to all throwing machines. The artillery system peculiar to the Middle Ages, of which the *funda balearica* is only a precursor, thus truly begins at the start of the XIII Century. This system is typified by machines with a sling and counterweight, the trebuchet and trebucket.[18] Simultaneously, the giant crossbow came into use."

The astute reader will have already noticed the absolute certainty with which Köhler assigns names to the different types of engines. This has been an otherwise especially difficult problem. In antiquity, so little is comprehensible that the terms *catapulta* and *ballista* should no longer be used; rather, only the term *onager*, as a name for the one-armed engine, is given with absolute certainty. However, that term can only be applied with certainty to the latest part of that era, despite the fact that the one-armed engines was already in use. The uncertainty in these names can also be easily explained. One can only give a particular name to a special weapon if one is an expert in the mechanics or use of special weapon if on is an expert in that weapon; the historians of antiquity were as incompetent in this skill as are those of modern times. Even today's historians like to pepper their descriptions of battles with terms such as howitzers, carronades, and culverns in order to delight both themselves and their readers with colorful words whose technical differences are meaningless to both. And so it was in the Middle Ages, where the Chroniclers wrote in semi-skilled style, using with particular preference the expressions of the Latin authors upon whom the Medieval writers modelled their language. It is in such work that insecurity or apathy[19] of language

---

[18] Translator's Note: At this point in the text, Köhler uses the phrase "der Tribock und die Blide." Both of these words mean trebuchet in English, but are distinguished in German by their etymology and gender. This is roughly comparable to the two spellings used above. More commonly used is the term "Hebelgeschütz."

[19] Jacobi Malvecii *Chronicon Brixianum*: *Erexerant quoque petrarias, quas nos*

stand out the most clearly! Equally uncertain are the names given by the Middle High German poets, such as tarant and blîde. And, if Köhler wants to weld these names together in pairs, such an act is only a piece of artistic license in which a great deal of effort will be wasted to no good purpose. Thus, we shall leave Köhler and what he derives merely from the names to study with greater attention those sources that may give more substantive grounds for the continuation of torsion artillery into the Middle Ages.

In the chapter "Der Tarant"[20] Köhler cites the following passage from the *Gesta Friderici* by Otto von Freisingen:

"Ferunt quadam die lapidem vi tormenti ex ballista, quam modo mangam vulgo dicere solent, propulsum ad superiora moeniorum loca conscendisse, ex collisione parietum tribus factis frustris tres simul milites armatos inter maiores civitatis iuxta principalem ecclesiam de suae reipublicae statu consultantibus stantes uno ictu percussisse necique dedisse."

A modern English translation of this passage yields the following:

"It is reported that one day, a stone shot from a catapult or ballista, which we have already seen are often called *mangeniq* by the common people, so that the stone was propelled towards the highest parts of the walls and it struck against the battlements. The stone caused, by this clash against the wall, three splinters of rock to be dashed from the wall. These fragments flew forth, striking three of the soldiers stationed in the cathedral's courtyard, and cheated them of their lives."

And Köhler concludes the following:

"Again, as with its derivative *mangonellus*, the mangeniq is only intended a stone throwing engine, not a palintone (i.e.

---

manganas aut trabuccos dicimus. "Erected there were catapults, also named mangonels and trebuchets."

[20] Translator's Note: The Scorpion

with a sling arm). Of particular interest is that the engine in question is termed a ballista, and Otto von Freisingen, who calls it such, expressly notes that it moves the stone by the power of tightened cords, so the engine had no bow. Additionally, the way that he describes the effects is most informative. He says that after the battlements were shot, three shards of the wall fragmented off, killing as many of the defenders who were standing at the main church, likely some distance away. All of this indicates a direct strike."

However, it does not necessarily follow from this description of the shot's effects that the passage refers to a flat-trajectory weapon; under particular circumstances stone balls have produced comparable results when thrown by a mortar in a high, arcing trajectory.[21] A high-angle shot, therefore, is not impossible here either. Despite taking caution here, we must also be careful to reject false translation: the phrase *vi tormenti* means to "through a gun." The word *Tormentum* is the term for all forms of artillery, whether they use torsion springs, counter-weighting, or gunpowder to provide their motive force. Torsion springs are called *nervi torti*, or simply *nervi* or *funes*.

Of course, this refutation only addresses a single point, and one could commit this error without renouncing the continuity of torsion artillery at all. In fact, Köhler places his main emphasis on "the presence of hand-drawn sketches," which he reproduced in the second plate, Figure 4 and 7. They will be found on page 154 of Köhler, introduced with the following passage, "there exists a drawing of the onager in a late XIV century picture manuscript from the court and state libraries of Munich (Cod. Germ. No. 600), as well as drawings in a fireworks manual from the XV century which give us an image of this engine. However, the name, as such, is not given."

---

[21] One should compare this to the reports of the Siege of Orlean, 1428-1429.

Although the name is missing, Köhler asserts with absolute certainty that the drawing from the Munich manuscript is a true depiction of the ancient onager; he writes on page 162,

> "As far as the drawing from the end of the XIV century, it is quite clearly in agreement with the writings of Ammianus. We have the two posts, even down to the curved shape suggested by Ammianus, with the same stretched cords of tendon between them, and stuck in this latter, an arm or rod in the form of a tiller. In place of the sling, however, a spoon for holding combustible materials is attached, and at the front of the machine, instead of there being spread a mattress beneath the torsion spring, there is a stretched, strong rope which the lower end of the rod strikes after firing, thus bringing the rod to rest. The drawing also reproduces the "antwerc"[22] by which the rod is pulled downwards for loading. When viewed from the side, one would come to a similar understanding of the rear of the machine."

That is a serious mistake. The Onager, which Colonel (later Lieutenant General) Schramm reconstructed exactly according to Ammianus's treatise,[23] is completely different from Medieval artillery in construction and shooting power. The force of the ancient torsion springs is so strong (in Schramm's Onager, approximately 60,000 kg) that only the strongest wooden frames can endure it, but the freely rising wooden parts of this device are much too weak to bear the force of the torsion spring. So, if these

---

[22] Translator's Note: The word antwerc is from Old to Middle German.

[23] Translator's Note: Ammianus's treatise is far from clear as to the exact construction of the onager. Some debate persists in the historical community over its exact form. Schneider and Schramm disagreed on some of the particulars (see my earlier translation: *The Ancient Artillery of Saalburg* for a full description of their differences). E. W. Marsden came to a somewhat different construction based on his interpretation of the phrase "sublimis adstans" in Ammianus. My own experimentation leads me to agree with Marsden's conclusions.

miserable machines were ever used, they could never have accomplished anything. And whoever wishes to stiffen in defense of the conventional opinion and to discover herein nevertheless even the least trace of the ancient traditions will be forced to abandon his position if we can provide the testimony of an expert man from the XIII century who, despite the most penetrating study of Vegetius, does not have the faintest understanding of the torsion engines described here. Such testimony would be a sure sign that every trace of the ancient tradition was extinct by 1300.

Yet Köhler still brings special proof in word and picture to attempt to refute Napoleon. In his first plate, Figure 1, Köhler reprints the drawing that Justus Lipsius has handed down to us. In his explanations of the plate, Köhler states, "Scorpion or Mangonel (Catapult, Ballista per Vegetius)," and in his text on page 153, "It was only in the following manner that J. Lipsius gained an idea of the ballista of antiquity: he found in the arsenal of Brussels a real ballista, which must have been stored there a long time." And it is further attributed to, "J. Lipsius, *Poliorceticon Antverpaie* 1605. The writings of Heron and Philon first made the reconstruction of ancient artillery possible, for Vitruvius is incomprehensible without them, only became known through the publications of Thévenot, Paris 1693. The ballista of the arsenal of Brussels, therefore, cannot be a new construction from the time of the Renaissance, as Napoleon implies."

Here, Köhler has forgotten that learned people often read manuscripts, even before they are spread by the printer. And, he overlooked the fact that J. Lipsius, in his caption for his sketch, quite clearly describes this ballista as a new construction with the phrase, "skillfully crafted (*affabre factam*)," and dispels any doubts in the text: "Cleverly devised and quite pretty, much like an ancient engine (*ingeniosam et pulchellam, nec longe a prisca*)." Thus, Napoleon is right, and the engine in Brussels is not a scorpion, but a reconstruction rightly praised by Lipsius, the designer of which we should look for in the circle of Moritz of Nassau (died 1625), where Roman military science was most eagerly studied with the intent to imitate it.

A detailed examination of all of the individual pieces of evidence has shown that Köhler, despite all of his efforts to do so, has failed to prove the use of a torsion engine anywhere in the Middle Ages. This result is of the utmost importance, for Napoleon's opponent has found, with astonishing attention to detail, everything that could possibly serve Napoleon's purpose. Despite his overarching failure to prove his point, it remains to Köhler's undisputed merit that he has, from the vastly abundant material of all of the medieval chroniclers, collect all of the important notes on siege warfare; it is in this respect that his book retains its lasting value.

4: The Era of Charles the Great

As to the era of Charlemagne, Köhler has limited himself to a few, casual remarks, and I do not wish to describe their errors. I will merely content myself with the remark that the author, in stark contrast with his previous behaviour, unquestioningly cites the sources for the false quotations of his predecessors. His sole contribution is the apodictic assertion that the *fundibula* is the ancient Onager.

But what for Köhler, who wanted to depict the age of chivalry, appears to be merely secondary, is of the highest importance to us: the time of Charlemagne. The military campaigns of the first German Emperor are only to be understood properly if one is familiar with the equipment of the soldiers of the era, and the image of siege warfare is different if artillery is used or not, for it has been shown that a more skillful utilization of the engines or an improvement in either their construction or projectiles, can provide either the besiegers or defenders with a significant advantage. Moreover, the army of Charlemagne offers us a very sure means of verifying the conclusions previous drawn from Procopius and Richerus. For as Charles himself informed us in detail in his *Capitulares* of the equipment of his armies, so it should be possible for us to determine with absolute certainty whether or not any torsion engines remained by the year 800. The actual artillery of the Medieval era, trebuchets with counterweights, will not be considered for the time being, for they did not appear until after the death of Charlemagne, as we will establish later. Therefore, if it can be proven that Charles had no torsion engines, it will follow that he did not possess artillery at all.

As representative of the prevailing opinions, I will present the comments of an officer and a historian: Max Jähns and Gustav Richter.

Jähns[24] wrote of the Frankish army,

> "The siege train followed the soldiers in wagons. As to tools, the following are mentioned: *cuniadae* (wedge shaped axes), *dolaturiae* (wall hammer/mason's hammers)[25], *taratri* (wall drills/masonry drills), *assiae* (mortise axes), *fossorii* (shovels), *palae ferreae* (hoes, mattocks), etc. The positioning of the carts and the fresh horses was the particular duty of the clergy. The counts had to procure the camping equipment (tents and fencing piles) as well as bridging material. Food was considered part of the levy, and it fell to each individual warrior. Everyone had to provide their rations (*utensilia ciborum*) for three months, as well as

---

[24] *History of Military Science*, pg 530

[25] Translator's Note: Mason's hammers would be far more correct here. I have intentionally left this error in because of Schneider's discussion of it in a slightly later paragraph. The term "wall drills" should likewise be translated as "mason's drills". A full discussion of this point will be made after Schneider has hypothesized about their meanings.

the necessary draft animals and carts. Tracking of war machines: throwing machines and mills, remained the province of the blessed leader."

Gustav Richter, however, states,[26]

"In addition to the throwing machines, rams, armored roofs, and all of the other equipment necessary for the conquest of fortresses, each departing army was followed by a not inconsiderable train of pack animals and wagons for the transportation of camp equipment and food."

On the whole, as we can see, Richter has the same concept as Jähns; however, by going into more detail he makes an error that indicates a lack of definite military knowledge. Rams and armored roofs were not carried with the army, but rather were built on the spot. The necessary wood could be procured everywhere, and therefore, only the ropes and nails would need to be carried on the carts. It would be unreasonable to impose the same error on the soldier Jähns, for he would certainly have understood "war machines" to only mean artillery pieces.[27] But what does Jähns mean with his term "wall hammers"? Such an instrument is unknown to me from either antiquity or from the Middle Ages, and I cannot imagine, even in my deepest flights of fancy, the form of such.

However, as regards the "Wall Drill," the matter is quite different. There is the following evidence.[28] The "Wall Drill" is described and pictured in both "Apollodorus's Siegecraft" and the Byzantine "Instructions on the Art of Siegecraft." Compare this with "The Greek Siege Engines, Volumes I and II with Hand-Drawn

---

[26] Gustav Richter, *Annals of German History*, Vol II. Halle, 1885. Pg 646.
[27] Translator's Note: This is a somewhat interesting interpretation by Schneider given that Jähns used the word *Mühlen*, or mills, in his original piece.
[28] Translator's Note: This was originally a footnote. I felt it to be of sufficient importance to Schneider's argument to merit being in the body of the work.

Pictures," published and translated by Rudolf Schneider. Vegetius does not mention the "Wall Drill." However, Vitruvius treats it in detail. One predominantly wonders that it is found in the siege train of Charlemagne. In order to come to terms with this, we should look at passages from the original text.

In the *Capitulare Aquisgranense* of 813, Charles commands,

> "*Ut regis spensa in carra ducatur, simul episcoporum, abbatum et optimatim regis: farinam vinum, baccones et victum abundanter, molas, dolatorias, secures, taretros, fundibulas, et illos homines, qui exinde bene sciant iactare. Et marscalci regis adducant eis petra in saumas viginti, si opus est. Et unusquisque hostuluter sit paratus, et omnia utensilia sufficienter habeant.*"

> In modern English, this translates to:

> "And the army of the King shall so be supplied. From the storehouses of the King, as well as from the bishops, abbots, and nobles of the King: flour, wine, bacon, and abundant food; as well as mauls, hatchets, axes, drills, and slings; and men skilled their use. And for the King' service, a mule should be given for every twenty men. Thus should every freeman be prepared to do, and have equipment enough."

> From a decree to the Abbot Fulrad of 806:

> "*Ita vero praeparatus cum hominibus tuyis ad praedictum locum venies, ut inde, in quamcunque partem nostra fuerit iussio, et exercitabiliter ire possis; i. e. cum armis atque utensilibus, necnon et cetero instrumento bellico in victualibus et vestimentis. Ita ut unusquique cabalarius*

habeat scutum et lanceam et spatham et semispathium, arcum et pharetras cum sagittis; et in carria vestris utensilia diversi generis, i.e. cuniadas et dolaturias, tarratros, assias, fossorios, palas ferreas et cetera utensilia, quae in hostem sunt necessaria. Utensilia vero ciborum in carris de illo placito in futurum ad tres menses, arma et vestimenta ad dimidium annum. Et hoc omnino praecipimus, ut observare facietis, ut cum bona pace pergatis ad locum praedictum...hoc est, ut praeter herbam et ligna et aquam nihil de ceteris rebus tangere praesumatis."

Again, in modern English:

"You shall come to the aforementioned place, and so there be drawn up with men under your service, so that you may be dispatched to any part of our realm and there execute our mandate. Each should have weapons and tools, as well as the other instruments of war, and food and clothing besides. Each man must have a shield, a lance, a sword, a dagger, a bow, and a quiver full of arrows. Your carts should have equipment of different kinds, i.e. axes, hammers, mauls, drills, shovels, and other iron implements which are necessary in war. There is to be in the wagons enough food, stored up against my future request, for three months from the time of request and the correct clothing for half of a year. You must do so in peace, so as to be ready at the place mentioned... this in addition to the fields, forests, and waters, thus touching upon greater matters."

Only through the above, definitive paragraphs can the meanings of Charlemagne's ancient baggage train, especially as concerns the term "*Mauerbohrer*" be understood. Because in both documents, the word *taratrus* is listed with other tools of the carpenter, we may conclude that like the hatchet and axe, *taratrus* describes the carpenter's drill. In general, these two decrees show that the military equipment of the Frankish army of 800 AD was at a fairly low level. The primary baggage carried by the wagon train was foodstuffs: flour, wine, and ham, as well as hand mills. Then came equipment for wooden buildings and earthworks. Finally, there was only one actual piece of siege equipment, the *fundibula*. However, the *fundibula* is neither the ancient onager, as Köhler has asserted quite arbitrarily and without the least justification, nor even truly an engine at all, but rather the staff-sling, well-known in both the Middle Ages and in antiquity, as Vegetius describes:

> "The *fundibula*, is the staff-sling for the throwing of stones. The staff-sling's rod is about four feet long, to the end of which is attached a sling made of leather. The wielder then takes it in both hands, and flings the stones like those tossed by wild donkeys."

This is clearly a hand weapon. For this, one needs round stones (Vegetius III 24: *funditores cum fustibalis et fundis rotundis lapidibus destinatis*), and the best stones are pebbles from a river bed (Vegetius IV 8: *saxa rotunda de fluviis, quia pro soliditate graviora sunt*). Since there are areas in which one cannot find these stones, it will be necessary "under certain circumstances" to carry in the requisite ammunition.

The Aachen Capitulare, therefore, proves precisely the opposite of what our commentators[29] wish to derive from it.

If Charlemagne had used torsion engines in the field, it would have been absolutely necessary to provide for spare torsion spring material in the instructions for preparing for war. This self-evident conclusion is further confirmed by Vegetius IV 8, where he reinforces an earlier assertion: "It is profitable to collect for the

---

[29] This regards other testimony provided by G. Richter, which shall be addressed later.

onager and ballistas cords made from sinew and tendon, for without those cords, all of man's artillery is of no use."

Therefore, the siege equipment of the Carolingian era are exactly the same as those we found in use by the Ostrogoths of the VI century and in France during the X century. Projectile engines are out of the question. However, siege towers, rams, and armored roofs were present, or rather could be constructed on site with the aid of the tools in the baggage train. Of course, not much can be done with these small means, but the same can be said of many reports of Charles's military campaigns. Only weak fortifications fell into his hands without difficulty: as soon as he approached a well-defended city, Charles was almost helpless. Pavia, Barcelona, and Tortosa all withstood years long sieges, and were only reduced to surrender by hunger.

5: Review

Now that we have established, using the most reliable sources, that there was a long period from which artillery was entirely absent, it may be implied by the end of this section that this result fully corresponds to the general course of Medieval history. At the same time, the colossal break caused by the Migration Era marked the end of torsion engines. Further, anyone who accepts the continuation of ancient artillery into the late Middle Ages will seek in vain to justify its disappearance from the later epochs. A gradual decline of the ancient tradition does not exist anywhere else in the Medieval Era; quite the contrary, a connection with the old world was always growing. Unfortunately, much of those traditions had so long disappeared from the eyes of man that even the most learned and smartest minds were unable to grasp them. Thus did the torsion engines not merely go out of use, but they were so completely forgotten that writings of the ancients describing these weapons became unintelligible. Only this complete ignorance of torsion power can explain the development and diffusion during the Middle Ages of a new system of artillery that cannot be in the least way compared to the ancient torsion guns. For just as far as the technology of the XIII century is behind that of antiquity (particularly the Diadochi era), so to is the trebuchet behind the artillery of the ancients. These artillery pieces no longer had to compete against the torsion engines, for that, older system of artillery had long since vanished by the development of the trebuchet. Thus, the way was clear for this second system, which at least ameliorated the total lack of artillery. The poor performance of the trebuchet results from the principles of the technology, as well as the fact that they soon had to make room for the third form of artillery, gunpowder. However, this successful competitor from the third era of artillery development should not be judged by its present performance, for it first appeared with only weak firepower, and it took a long time for it to win the undisputed acceptance of warriors. As late as the year 1595, according to the testimony of Justus Lipsius, scholars and soldiers argued seriously over whether it would be better to reintroduce the ancient torsion engines, as opposed to the "bombards" of the day.[30] Even further, we have that the reconstructions of ancient engines by Colonel Schramm actually surpassed the gunpowder artillery of 1600 AD.

Finally, the army's composition should be addressed. Under the Merovingians, there was only a standing bodyguard, consisting of armed servants to provide security for the king and to perform policing duties. Presumably, they also served as a standing garrison for guarding fortified places. The real army was made up of people who were only obliged to military service for the summer campaigning season. Naturally, skilled artillerymen are lacking in this structure, and no one can reasonably assert that the bodyguards could have remedied this deficiency. Remember that

---

[30] Lipsius does not mention trebuchets in this passage, even though he knew of them both from drawings and models.

artillery also includes the guns themselves, the production of which requires weapons factories, such as antiquity possessed: who would have done this work? And since the army of Charlemagne did not deviate from that of the Merovingians in its basic features, the lack of artillery in this later period is explainable, or perhaps even self-evident.

What has been cited by the authors of the above sources as counter-evidence will be presented and evaluated in the following section

6: Incorrect or Dubious Testimony

The Chronicles of the Carolingian era do not have the same evidential value as do the decrees of Charles, and, moreover, caution must be exercised when using them, for it is possible to show in places in them both the deed and desire to falsify. Both of these dangers come together in a position of Köhler's, in which he relies upon a citation of General von Peucker.[31]

The *Annales Laurissenses et Einhardi* (*Royal Frankish Annals* attributed to Einhard) reports, "*Inde pergentes (Saxones) voluerunt de Sigiburgi similiter facere: auxiliante Domino Francis eis viriliter repugnantibus nihil praevaluerunt.*" In English, this reads, "From Sigiburg they, the Saxons, wanted to do the same; yet, with the help of God, the Franks resisted them manfully, and they achieved nothing."

It then goes on to state,

[31] V. Peucker, *German Military Science through the Ages*, 3 Volumes, Berlin 1860-4.

> "*Dum enim per placita eos, qui infra ipsum castrum custodes erant, inludere non potuissent, sicut fecerunt alios, qui in aliud castellum fuerant, coeperunt pugnas et machinas praeparare, qualiter per virtutem potuissent illud capere, et Deo volente petrarias quas praeparaverunt, plus illis damnum fecerunt quam illis qui infra castrum residebant.*"

In English, this is roughly,

> "For the Lord was moved by the pleas of those beneath him, particularly the guardians of the castle, the foe was not able to assault it as they had other castles. Therefore, they began to prepare a siege line and machines to throw stones. And, just as it is possible through courage to capture such machines, so did God's grace permit the defenders to do, and thus the stone throwing machines did more damage to the attackers than to those who remained within the castle."

Now follows the description of a miracle, and this heavenly appearance gave heart to the Christians whilst striking fear and terror into the heathens. This entire passage, beginning with "*Dum enim*" and closing with the words, "*christiani confortati omnipotentem Deum laudaverunt, qui dignatus est sum manifestare potentiam super servos suo*"[32] is missing from many of the best manuscripts, and, in the remainder, it appears in differing positions in the text. Therefore, this pious legend is a later addition. It is, in fact, set in parantheses by Pertz, and G. Richter has removed it entirely in his edition.

The same fate is met by a proof presented by Paulus Diaconus, as cited by Justus Lipsius and Köhler. In Waitz's[33]

---

[32] The Christians were strengthened, praising almighty God, who deigned to reveal His power over slaves.

edition we cannot find the following passage, "*Deicitur lapide emisso ex mangone et contritum est caput eius et facies.*[34]" However, I have found another section in the named edition that shows the lore in a different light. VI 20 p.171, 14 states clearly in the text, "*Bergamum obsedit (rex Arpert) eamque cum arietibus et diversis belli machinis sine aliqua difficultate expugnans mox cepit*[35]. " A later transcriptionist (codex Bambergensis E. III. 14) derived the following from it, "*cum arietibus et diversis belli machinis, id est cum manculis*[36]." And we find this same copyist at work a second time in V 8 p.148,19. The manuscript gives us here, "*Cumque hoc dixisset, iussu imperatoris caput eius abscisum atque cum belli machina, quam petrariam vocant, in urbe, proiectum est;*[37]" it states further, "*petrariam (quam vulgo dicimus mancolam).*[38]" *Mancola* (as an artillery piece), therefore, can be eliminated as an XI century addition; yet the *petraria* (stone thrower) cannot be blamed for this emendation. However, it is most remarkable that there is no mention anywhere else in the extensive works of Paulus Diaconus any mention of a gun, nor is there any reason to suppose the use of artillery from other sources, such as in the battles of King Desiderius. If the Lombards had had a catapult, even as a mere, crude amusement, then they would certainly have used this marvelous device of war, at least in cases of extreme

---

[33] *Pauli Historia Langobadorum. Mon Gemania Historica. Scriptores rerum Langobardorum.* Hanover, 1878. Presumably, the above mentioned citations can be found in the so-called *Hostoria Miscella des Ladolfus Sagax* (circa 1000 AD), but I have been unable to locate them in the edition published by Fr. Eyssenhardt (Berlin 1869), despite a long and thorough search.

[34] Translator's Note: "A piece of stone launched from a mangonel struck his head, smashing his face."

[35] Translator's Note: "Bergamo was besieged by King Aripert, who, using all manner of diverse engines and machines of war, overcame its defenses with no difficulty."

[36]Translator's Note: "...with engines and diverse machines of war, such as the *manculis*."

[37]Translator's Note: "And when he had spoken thus, enforcing the commands of the Emperor, the city was cut off [surrounded], and the chief machines of war, the *petrariam*, were directed at the city."

[38] *Petrariam*, commonly known as the *mancolam*.

emergency, for it is especially useful in both attack and defense. Without such evidence of use, it is justifiable to deny strongly the existence of this device; all the more so as from the time of the Great Migrations to the death of Charlemagne, there is nothing to establish the existence of this *petraria.*[39]

We have just become aware of, through an emendation from the XI century, the new term *mancola*, which is already known by the word *mangonellus* and the other names related to it, *manga, mango, manganum, mangena*, which are all descended from the Middle High German word *mange*, which itself is derived from the Old French *manganeau*, as well as all of the other names that come with a grounding in Medieval languages. Naturally, the words *μάγγανον* and *manganîq*, the terms for catapults according to the Byzantines and Arabs. However, we do not permit ourselves to study the reciprocal relationship between these two, for in this investigation we only consider these two cultures when they come into direct contact with Western Europe. Thus, if we only consider the Western peoples, we find that *manga* and all of its related terms can only be found after the beginning of the second era of artillery development, or, in other words, the terms *manga*, *mango*, and so forth actually only refer to the trebuchet. Later, with the help of an eyewitness, we shall learn of the beginning of the new form of artillery. We shall have straight from his mouth that both the machine and the word *manganum* are entirely new to him; yet, we shall see that following the Chronicles of the Crusades, both the machine and the word are completely familiar. That cannot be a coincidence. Further, an exacting examination of the only witness to use *mango* in reference to the Siege of Paris in the year 886, Abbo Cernuus, who described the siege in detail, will nullify the worth of his statements.

---

[39] Köhler cites III S. 201 Anm 2 of Turpinus, "*Septimo mense aptatis iuxta murum petrariis et mangonellis et troiis.*" However, the *"Historia de vita Caroli Magni et Rolandi*" was not written by the Archbishop of Rheims, but is rather a "poor imitation from the XI/XII century" (Potthast).

In the year 811, King Ludwig campaigned with his strong army in front of Tortosa, and of his successful campaign, Vita Hludovici reports in 811 MG. SS. II 615, 15, "*Quo perveniens adeo illam arietibus, mangonibus, vineis, et ceteris argumentis lacessivit et protrivit muralibus, ut cives illius a spe deciderent... et clave civitatis traderent.*"[40]

However, if we accept this wording, then G. Richter (compare to pg 32 above), is entitled to assign artillery to the train of a Carolingian army. For torsion artillery - and only these engines should be considered, for trebuchets did not yet exist - cannot be easily made upon the spot, but rather were normally carried along or, as was often the case in Antiquity, borrowed from a friendly town near the theatre of operations. Nobody will seriously consider the neighborliness of the towns nearby, so Ludwig must have transported them from home. However, this assumption is contradicted by the Aachen *Capitulares*, as previously presented in the text. Consequently, Ludwig cannot have had any artillery. His offensive tools must have been restricted to the limits of the era's science of the siege: rams, towers, mobile shelters, ladders, and portable bridges as well as spades, shovels, hoes, and other tools for undermining the foundations of city walls and ripping out their stones. And we have already seen that even these feeble means were often sufficient to overcome the equally feebly equipped defenders. If we are not dealing with a later addition to the Vita Hludovici, then there would have to be a textual version thereof; both are quite possible in my opinion. However, it has alway been impossible and remains so, that torsion engines could have existed in the year 811 AD, for the *Leges Caroli Magni* absolutely denies such, and the weight of this document is fully

[40] There arrived there such a quantity of engines, mangonels, and all the other implements of war to entice the city to surrender, and they shoot forth darts and stones against the walls in the hopes that they would collapse. And from lack of hope, the men of the city gave in.

inviolable. Further, just as there are laws with retroactive powers, so too may this conclusion be extended to an earlier period in order to definitvely rule out the *petraria* from the Lombards. The influence of artillery upon fortress warfare was so strong, that even if we assume the weakest capabilities of the engines, the effect upon the townspeople of a severed head flung over the walls would certainly be perceptible if a catapult had ever done so.

The Era of the Trebuchet

1: The New Engines

In the second half of the Middle Ages, there appeared a type of artillery entirely different from the ancient torsion engines in both construction and motive force. The power of the new engines was derived from a two-armed lever, the fulcrum of which was supported between two posts of considerable height, so that the shorter arm of the lever could swing freely between the posts and below the level of the fulcrum. Assuming that the lever is straight and that the end of the short arm is drawn downwards so that it is directly below the pivot point of the lever, then at the same time the tip of the long arm will rise so far that it stands directly above the fulcrum. The endpoints of both arms will have traversed a quarter circle; however, since the radii of the circles are unequal, the speed of the ends of the arms will be unequal. In other words, the speed at the tip of the long arm will be five times that of the end of the short lever arm if the long arm is five times as long. The simple, core principle of the trebuchet can also be made clear as follows. Wherever a country road crosses a railway, to the side of the intersection there stands a vertical beam that rotates around a bolt and that can be pulled down to close the crossing. Yet to remove the barrier easily, gravity is utilized: one reinforces the shorter arm of the lever with a heavy weight, so that when the long arm is allowed to swing freely, the short arm will drop and pull the long arm back to the vertical position. Now one needs simply to imagine that a sling has been fastened to the long arm of this lever, and then one will be perfectly picturing the fundamental design of the trebuchet. Of course, this example is only sufficient to demonstrate the basic principle, that is to explain the nature and form of the new catapults. In particular cases, there will be remarkable differences in the various forms of this new, Medieval artillery, through which it can be clearly seen that the master artillerists of the era expended much thought and labor upon improving the effects of their machines. Yet despite all of this, it is clear from the outset that the lever and counterweight must always be inferior when compared to the power of torsion; the divide between the shooting capabilities of ancient artillery and the Medieval trebuchets is most evident in the fact that engines using the new principle could, at best, be brought up to the shooting performance of the ancient onager, which was the most artless engine of Antiquity.

The end of this second form of artillery coincides exactly with the end of the Middle Ages: the appearance of gunpowder artillery is the landmark that denotes the dawning of the Modern Age. For the beginnings of the lever-engine,[41] whose chief representative is called the *trabucium* in Latin, *trabocco* in Italian, *trébuchet* in French, and *tribock* in German, one can refer to the following passages from the year 1212 in order to place their invention at about 1200 AD.

From the *Chronicon Sampetrinum*, dated 1212, as published in *Historical Sources of the Saxon Provinces*, Halle 1870:

"Otto came into Thuringia, bringing with him a *tribracho*, also called a tribock, where besieged and assaulted the castle of the Land Graf [Count] of Salza."

> The *Annales Marbacenses,* also dated 1212, states, "And from there (Salza), he proceeded to Wiznense (Wei□ensee),[42] where he similarly besieged the town and carried the castle by storm... Present there for the first time, was a device that had just come to be recognized as an

[41] Translator's Note: The German word *Hebelgeschütz* translates literally as lever-gun. It is one of the more common equivalents for the English word trebuchet.

[42] Translator's Note: White Lake, a small town in Thuringia.

instrument of war, the machine commonly known as the tribock."

Finally, the *Magdeburger Schöppenchronik*, 1212, published in *The Chronicles of German Cities*, Leipzig 1869, gives us the following.

"It was not until now that the device known as the *tribock* was well known."[43]

It appears from the last passage quoted above, that the tribock was already being used in siege warfare elsewhere, outside of Germany. And further, the evidential value of the above passages only applies to the engines known as tribocks, not to counterweighted artillery as a whole. The duration of these engines must have been strikingly short, only lasting about 200 years until 1326 and the first documented gunpowder cannon. However, we do not wish to continue to raise such concerns and objections, for we may reach an exceedingly positive conclusion. First, however, we must abandon our chronological account for the time being, and jump forward to the year 1300 in order to visit an arsenal, in which all of the engines of the period are to be found. If we have on hand a knowledgeable guide to these models of engines, we may then be taught by an expert in the military science of the day about the details of construction for these machines. By using this view, we shall examine the evidence of the Chroniclers of earlier times in order to ascertain the truth of the use of these counter-weighted engines, as well as their structure and the materials used in their construction. We shall also evaluate what types of projectiles they launched, and what their shooting capabilities were.

Finally, we should call upon the oldest witness to the existence of a trebuchet, for, if we can interpret the words of the poet correctly, we may learn the homeland of this new invention.

---

[43] "Dar wart erst bekant den Dudeschen dat werk triboc heitet."

The witnesses from roughly the year 1300 are Aegidius Romanus and Marinus Sanutus.

2: Aegidius Romanus

Aegidius (Fr: Gilles de Rome) was born into a prominent Neapolitan family, the Colonnas; however, he is more commonly known by the place of his birth, Rome. In his youth, he travelled to Paris, where he studied under the holy Saint Thomas Aquinas, and, in the manner of the XIII century, Aegidius came to earn the honorary title of "doctor fundatissimus" through his erudition and multidisciplinary studies, as demonstrated by his lectures and numerous writings. Thus, King Philip the Bold became aware of the Augustinian monk, and gave him the responsibility for training the future King Philip the Fair in the virtues and duties of a ruler. Aegidius later became the superior-general of his Order and then the Archbishop of Bourges. He died, much advanced in years, on 22 September 1316[44] in Avignon.

Philip the Fair ascended the throne in the year 1285, at the age of seventeen; therefore, the essay "De regimine principum," which is dedicated to the Crown Prince, must date from about 1280.[45] Numerous copies of the Latin manuscript, as well as the

---

[44] Translator's Note: Other sources place Aegidius's death on 22 December 1316.

[45] As Thomas Aquinas also authored an essay entitled "De regimine principum" and the two works are often considered to be identical, some scholars have constructed an intimate relationship between the two documents. However, the real truth is easy to establish, as the older document is printed in the collected works of Thomas Aquinas, such as the 1634 Parisiis edition. This essay was intended to serve as a gift to the King of Cyprus, to whom St. Thomas dedicated this gift; yet the author did not quite finish as he planned and got stuck at the beginning. Perhaps, therefore, this fragment is merely a draft, and, in any case, the surviving sections of the older document are of far lesser value than the corresponding chapters of Aegidius. Echos of Thomas can be found in Aegidius (for example, on the privileges of the Monarchy and on the healthy layout of

translations into French, Spanish, and Italian which followed shortly thereafter, demonstrate most clearly the impression that this "Prince's Mirror" made upon its appearance. This impact has been long maintained, for we possess a whole series of incunabula with the Latin text of this essay, as well as German manuscripts contemporary with the Latin under the description, "From the Prince's Regimen." Thereafter, though, the similarity visibly suffers, and as Friederich Hahn begins in his "*Collectio Monumentorum Veterum et Recentiem Ineditorum,*" the works in their proper condition can still offer something new and unknown to the reader. After finding a parchment manuscript that chance led to his hands, Hahn reprinted the conclusion from the work of Aegidius under the title, "*Libellus de re militari veterum ad mores praesertim medii aevi.*" This booklet is difficult to find nowadays, but it is also not worth the effort to seek it out. The text is no better than that in the incunabula, and those are quite complete. Great impact should have resulted from Hahn's assertions, yet even at the time it enjoyed limited acceptance. Further, Herrmann Müller was unable to win any friends for the forgotten text of Aegidius by asserting that it was a "frivolous and unoriginal epistle" by an Augustinian monk from circa 1400 AD, with the full armor of critical apparatus, yet without any explanation being offered.[46]

From this review, it is clear that it is necessary to go back to the original manuscripts in order to properly assess the works of Aegidius. And this work will be fruitful in many ways: for the historian, to come to understand the ideal Prince of the XIII century; for the philosopher, to see the knowledge and works of a perfect scholar; and for the historian of literature, to aid in

---

cities), but they are also a continuation on Ptolemy Lucensis, and thus probably go back, at least in part, to a common basis in the writings of Aristotle. In the skillful use of Aristotle and the philosophical basis for his thesis, Aegidius far surpasses his teacher and his forerunners.

46 Herrmann Müller, *Aegidii Romanii de regimine principum libri III abbreviati*, per Leoninum de Padua, from the Journal of Collected Political Science, 1880. The "Critical Edition of Aegidius Romanius's De Regimine Principum" promised by the author did not appear within this text.

measuring the exact state of knowledge during the era. However, it takes a great deal of effort and patience to endure the long-windedness of the presentation, the partitions, enumerations, recapitulations, etc.; however, these are common flaws of the scholastic discipline of the period, which one must accept in order to preserve the golden nuggets. In order to clarify the piece, we must not shy away from the work of properly sifting away all of foreign material, such as the reminiscences of old authors, which they have interjected, and we must accurately eliminate.

To carry out this task for the entire essay would be a rewarding task for someone, if they wished to do so for one of the viewpoints indicated above. Yet, for the purposes of the current investigation, it will suffice to restrict our rigorous treatment to a narrow perimeter, to establish only a basis of and guidelines for the whole work in order to see what Aegidius intended and by what means he worked. In order to understand the plan and layout of the book *De regimine principum*, one merely needs to skim through the titles of the individual chapters, as these headings completely contain the majority of the content, or at the least summarize it clearly.[47]

This method, however, is only sufficient up to the point where the section on military science begins. From then on, however, it is essential to bear in mind the text of Aegidius in order to ascertain through thorough examination what the author has borrow and what are his own ideas. In fact, as regards the artillery of the Middle Ages, only a single chapter enters into consideration, and that is why newer military writers have merely elaborated upon it in greater detail. However, that is the highest analysis permissible if the information contained within this chapter is accepted unconditionally; but if Köhler, as well as M. Jähns and Alwin Schultz after him, wish to contest the validity of an extremely important sentence, then they would have had to justify their

[47] See the appendices.

opposition to the credibility of Aegidius from other sources. Therefore, in order to understand the eighteenth chapter, it is necessary to delve deeper to determine Aegidius' point of view: his relationships with Aristotle and Vegetius will reveal how we should assess the personality of our current author.

The focus of scholastic philosophy centered around the writings of Aristotle, which by the XIII century were well-known due to high quality translations from the Greek texts. Thus, the writings of Aegidius are thoroughly permeated, from beginning to end, with ideas and notions that are derived from the study of Aristotle. The development of moral concepts rests upon a foundation of Nicomachean ethics and that of the state stems from politics. In addition to these lines of thought, which may be found in the same form in Aristotle, there are other, unexpected reminiscences which spring forth from lesser known Aristotelian texts, or echo his thoughts, thus making one notice how Aegidius wove in Aristotle. In his dependence upon the ancient master, however, Aegidius never forgets what separates him and his time from Aristotle: Christianity and the changed character of the state. That is why he includes a special chapter in a presentation that otherwise follows Aristotle (lib. III, p. II cap. 20), "In addition to human and natural law, it is necessary to give evangelical and divine law."[48] Further, after having established the Monarchy as the best form of government over the course of two chapters, he asserts (lib. III p. II cap. 5), "This method of accession by the King's sons to the government through heredity is superior to election by nobles."[49] Aristotle concludes otherwise in Politics III 10,9, "How shall it be maintained with the children of kings? Should the royal dignity be forcibly inherited? Experience has shown that this would easily cause harm."[50] It will be seen that Aegidius knows how to

---

[48] *Quod praeter legem humanam et naturalem oportuit dare evangelicam legem et divinam.*

[49] *Quod melius est regimen regni et principatus ire per hereditatem et successionem filiorum quam per electionem aliquam..*

supplement Aristotle where his execution seems incomplete. What's more, Aegidius has the courage to offer direct opposition and vigorously defend the political principle of his own era against the words of the great master.

For the conclusion of the book, which deals with warfare, the authority of Aristotle takes a back seat, though it never completely loses its influence. Here, Aegidius adheres closely to "De Rei Militaria" by Vegetius, which Aegidius has apparently studied for the particular purpose of his treatise, learning much from the celebrated military writer.

In this way, many things have passed into the writings of Aegidius which do not correspond to the state of military science of the era; however, one must be careful not to declare the author merely an unthinking copyist of Vegetius. This reproach is only accurate in one place and, because it is near the beginning, it has given rise to this false accusation. It is clear that the Kings of France in the XIII and XIV centuries were only able to muster their soldiers from the temperate zone; it was, therefore, entirely superfluous for Aegidius to repeat what Vegetius (in the manner of Aristotle) had said about the warlike natures of people from hot and cold climes. However, it is different with the rules copied from Vegetius for the training of recruits and the setting of camp fortifications. To be sure, neither of these fit with the prevailing paradigm of the day, but they could and should serve as a model. With a firm resolution, one could successfully implement those methods that had already been proven by the ancients.[51]

On the other hand, Aegidius adamantly refuses to follow Vegetius into recommending the use of "dishonorable" weapons (a

---

[50] Aristotle's *Politics*: πῶς ἕξει τά περί των τέχνων; πότερον χαί τό γένος δεὶ βασιλεύειν; άλλά γινομένων όποϊοί τινες ετυχον, βλαββερόν.

[51] Vegetius III 10, *Unum illud est in hoc opere praedicendum, ut nemo desperet fieri posse quae facta sunt.*

temptation to felony), for such is contrary to morality.[52] The same "Knightly Spirit" is evident in the fifth chapter, concerning peasants and city-dwellers. In his description of peasants, Aegidius follows the model of his intellectual forebear, but he goes his own way when handling city-dwellers. Under the term *urbani*, he does not include all of the artisans and merchants that live within the city's walls, but rather, he means solely the *nobiles*, those men who serve on horseback. These are not the equal of the peasants in terms of physical strength or endurance, but they are far superior to the peasant through moral courage and intellectual power. He thus comes to the conclusion, quite different from that of Vegetius, that one should draw their foot soldiers from the peasants, but the cavalry, which was the decisive factor on the Medieval battlefield, should be drawn from the city-dwellers.

The differences in siege warfare, which Aegidius treats with the greatest breadth, extend far deeper, however; this difference corresponds exactly to the changed objectives of offensive warfare. The proper siege of Antiquity required bringing the ram against the wall, and, if it succeeded in shattering the wall with its reinforced striking beam, then the besieged city was considered lost.[53] Yet in a Medieval siege, while the ram still functions alongside all of the other siege machines, it no longer is of such decisive importance. The main assault was no longer directed against the walls themselves, but either against their foundations, which the attackers sought to undermine, or against the battlements, which they would attempt to gain via ladders and drawbridges. Accordingly, the ancient tools of the assault in Aegidius's account, though externally quite similar, appear in a very different light. As regards artillery, however, Vegetius and

---

[52] Lib III p. III cap. 14: *Sed haec cautela, licet ponat eam Vegetius, non multum est apprettianda, quia videtur repugnare bonis moribus.*

[53] Caesar BG II 32, 1: *se magis consuetudine sua quam merito eorum civitatem conservaturum, si prius quam murum aries attigisset, se dedissent.* Cicero refights a traditional siege with the words, "*ii, qui armis positis ad imperatorum fidem confugient, quamvis murum aries percusserit, recipiendi.*

Aegidius contradict each other sharply: Vegetius only names torsion engines, while Aegidius only discusses counter-weighted engines, and that neither of the two authors had any clue as to the existence of the other type of engine is easily proven. For Vegetius, it is sufficient to reference the history of ancient artillery, which over the course of almost a thousand years makes no mention of a trebuchet. For Aegidius, we will extract our proof from the book, *De regimine principum*.

Closely connected to Vegetius, Aegidius requires that a city, whenever threatened by siege, be amply provided with animal sinew, and he takes from his source, as well, a story of how Roman women cut the hair from their heads to be donated for the repair damaged torsion springs. One would think from this passage that Aegidius would have had to be aware of torsion engines, but he has so thoroughly misunderstood his Vegetius that he asserts that all of these tendons are merely to be used on crossbows and bows (*propter ballistas et arcus*), as does Christine de Pisan (circa 1400). Further, the detailed descriptions of the individual engines in Aegidius does not appeal to Vegetius: construction, motive force, name, everything is different with these Medieval engines. Here, Aegidius stands entirely upon his own two feet, and everything that he reports corresponds to the artillery of the period.

Thereby does Aegidius preserve his independence from Vegetius, for where the altered conditions of his time do not coincide with the logic and conclusions from his source, Aegidius has both supplemented and even outright contradicted Vegetius. Certainly, he has also treated Aristotle in this manner, and for the same reasons: in places supplementing and in places contradicting him.

However, since Aegidius's independence is only apparent within definite and narrow limits, demonstrating clear insights into the military science of the day but with no practical experience of warfare, we must be cautious. We shall take as our example the warm-hearted patriot Napione, both a clever scholar and a military writer of the first-order, who placed Aegidus between Vegetius and Montecucolli, who likewise wrote in Italian, “our Vegetius of the XIII century,” and “extending, so to say, one hand to Vegetius and the other to Montecucolli.”[54] Aegidius has no claim to comparison with the war hero Montecucolli, and he can only be called “the Vegetius of the Middle Ages” if this appellation from Napione has its implications markedly reduced. Conversely, however, we must object equally adamantly to denigrating unduly Aegidius’s knowledge of military science, for his great task of educating the Crown Prince required the author, in addition to his scholarly studies, to pay great attention to the details of warfare; therefore, the manuscript has value as source material, which many researchers have ignored, to their own detriment.

In the appendices, the third part of the third book is provided, taken from the manuscripts of Aegidius. Here, however, the 18th chapter is translated verbatim.

> “On the form and numbers of different types of engines that shoot stones, with which one can attack besieged fortress and conquer cities and castles.
>
> “Often the besieged fortress stands on extremely hard rock, or is surrounded by water, or possesses a particularly deep moat, or is protected in some other way so as to prevent one from taking them via mining or underground passages, or at least make it extremely difficult. And, if one is able to take the fortress via mining, it still happens often enough

---

[54] See Conte Gianfrancesco Galeani Napione di Cocconato, “Della scienza militare di Egidio Colonna.” Memorie della R. Accademia della scienze di Torino, 1824. P 56 and 58. *“Il nostro Vegezio del secolo XIII.”* and *“Stendendo, a dir cosi, una mano a Vegezio, e l’altra al Montecuccoli.”*

that the besieged locate the miners and harass them, so that they cannot be taken by treachery and tricks. How to do so is covered in the following chapters, which are concerned with the defense; therein, we will discuss how the besieged should defend themselves, and how the besieged must protect themselves against mines and other techniques of the besiegers. Therefore, art is as necessary as nature, which always makes things easier to develop: if, therefore, it is less easy to take a fortress through mining rather than stone throwers or wooden buildings pushed against the walls of the beleaguered castle or city, then it is necessary to use such means to achieve one's purpose. Therefore, we must see how many forms of stone throwers there are, as well as how many types of wooden buildings for fighting against fortresses.

"The engines for throwing stones can be traced back to roughly four basic forms. For in every such type of artillery, there must a force applied to the arm of the engine, to fling it upwards, taking the sling attached to the arm up with it, causing the stone to be shot out. This acceleration of the arm is sometimes caused by a counterweight; sometimes, however, the counterweight is insufficient and the acceleration of the arm must be supplemented by ropes: when the arm has flung up, the stone is launched.

"If this launch is achieved solely through the counterweight, then this counterweight is either fixed or mobile, or even some combination of both of these two types of attachment.

"Fixed refers to the counterweight, in which a kind of box is attached to the arm, and hangs immovably from the arm and is filled with rocks and sand, or with lead, or with any other heavy material: this type of engine was christened "*Trabucium*" by the ancients. This engine shoots more accurately than the other guns, for the reason that the counterweight always performs consistently, and, therefore the engine shoots consistently: you could thread a needle with it, so to speak. If one wishes to hit a particular target and the engines shoots too far to either the right or the left, then one must rotate the engine to the point against which the stone is to be shot; if it shoots too far, one must either move the engine further from the target or place a heavier stone in its sling, so that it cannot hurl the stone through such a high arc; if, on the other hand, the engine's shot fall short, then one must further advance the gun or use a lighter stone. Therefore, the stone balls must be weighed, if one wishes to hit a particular target with precision.

"In the second type of engine, the counterweight hangs loosely from the pole or arm of the engine, and it turns about that arm. This type of engine was called "*Biffa*" by Roman warriors. This is different from the *Trabucium*. As the counterweight is loosely attached to the end of the arm of the engine, it has a stronger effect due to its momentum, but it is not as uniform. As a result, the engine shoots farther, but it does not strike as accurately or as consistently.

"There is yet a third type of engine known as the "*Tripantum*"; it uses both forms of counterweight: one is firmly fixed to the end of the arm, and the other is loosely attached to the arm, which it rotates around. This type of engine shoots more precisely than the *Biffa* due to its fixed counterweight; the loose, rotating weight causes the engine to throw the stone farther than does the *Trabucium*.

"The fourth kind of engine has no counterweight, but rather ropes that are pulled by the power of human hands. Such a machine, of course, cannot throw stones as large as those thrown by the three types of machines described above. However, it does not take as long to prepare this engine to shoot as the engines above; as a result, this engine shoots more often and can achieve a higher density of fire than the aforementioned engines.

"Thus anyone who wishes to besiege a castle or a city and desires to attack it by throwing stones must carefully consider whether his assaults on this fortress will be best served by exacting precision, distant shooting, or a combination of the two. He must also decide whether he cannot cause the besieged more harm by shooting more often with the density of hail. He may then use, as the circumstances dictate, all of the aforementioned guns and all of the types of shooting described, or some of them, or even just one type in order to effectively combat the town. Quite simply, if one understands the machines herein described, then one will truly understand how to attack a town via stone-throwers.

"Any form of stone-throwing machine is either one of the previously described machines or is derived from these types of machines.

"Incidentally, it should be noted that with stone-throwers, one can bombard the besieged position both by day and by night. However, in order to see at night where the stones launched by your machines fall, it is always necessary to attach a flaming brand or some other glowing material to the stone, for by this luminous material, one can see how the engine shoots in order to determine the type and weight of the stone that one must load into the engine's sling."[55]

---

[55] Translator's Note: This is a description of how to make a Medieval tracer round.

This portrayal of Medieval artillery does credit to the wise philosopher. He has correctly grasped the basic character of lever-based artillery and accurately described the differences of the individual types, so that the pictures that we occasionally find handed down in the various manuscripts from the Middle Ages, including the many without the names of the engines, descriptions from Aegidius come immediately to mind. It is also of particular merit to the author that he has, in contrast to the practices of his era, dispensed with the ancient terms *ballista*, *catapulta*, *onager*, etc., and he has bestowed the new engines, which had nothing to do with the ancient machines, with their own names. While he does nevertheless invoke “the ancients” (*veteres*) and “Roman warriors” (*Romani pugnatores*) as the sources for the names *Tribucium* and *Biffa*, with his notoriously incomplete knowledge of Vegetius, it is obvious that this cannot be true in a literal sense. Instead, the author is attempting to ennoble the beginnings of these weapons via a Classical origin. It is striking that the great godfather of military theory never uses the word *Tribucium*. In fact, it occurs nowhere else and defies all attempts at etymological explanation. It is quite likely that Aegidius simply invented the word.

Aegidius lavishes his *Tripantum* with high praise: “This type of engine shoots more precisely than the *Biffa* due to its fixed counterweight; the loose, rotating weight causes the engine to throw the stone farther than does the *Trabucium*” that is unjustified. This contradicts practical experience. If the counterweight is formed of two parts, the weapon does not combine the advantages of the moving and the fixed counterweight. Rather, it gains the disadvantages of both weapons with uniform counterweights: the precision of aiming is disturbed by the inclusion of the moving counterweight and the range is reduced by the presence of the fixed counterweight. Through this false theory, we find tangible proof that Aegidius had no practical experience in the use of artillery.

However, this admission that Aegidius lacks practical knowledge of this subject, we are still far from conceding to those that wish to accuse this teacher of the French prince of the grossest ignorance. Aegidius clarified at the end of this chapter, "All agree that every kind of machine is either one of the aforesaid stone throwers or takes it or origin from one of them."[56] These statements resolutely excludes the existence of any kind of arrow shooting engine around 1300. As the newer writers of historical military theory, particularly since the contributions of Köhler, have generally assigned arrow shooting engines to this era and the preceding centuries, it is obvious that they ignore this testimony. In truth, they have invalidated their own portrayals of Medieval Artillery. However, no one has any other explanation for what might have caused the otherwise painstaking and detailed Aegidius to neglect the other half of available artillery - or no, the term is wrongly chosen - to deny the existence of this other half with a drought of words. The urgent insistence for evidence, upon which the methodical examination of history must be based, is not fulfilled herein, nor can it be fulfilled, as a second witness from the same time (circa 1300) will confirm that there were only lever-powered engines, that is stone throwers. Arrows were only shot from the common crossbow, or perhaps a strengthened crossbow (*arbalète à tour*), which was simply an improved hand weapon rather than an artillery piece.

[56] *Nam omne genus machinae lapidariae vel est aliquod praedictorum, vel potest originem sumere ex praedictis.*

3: Marinus Sanutus

The Fall of Acre marks the end of the Crusades: in the year 1291, the Christians abandoned their last possession in Palestine, and since then, the Holy Land has remained in the hands of unbelievers. This abandonment would become difficult for some, and when neither the Pope nor Princes knew any longer how to inspire the Christian peoples to the sacred struggle, a whole host of learned men came forth to present, in a succession of well-crafted tracts, the necessity, viability, and utility of renewing the Crusades. Ignorance of the conditions on the ground and disregard of the myriad difficulties led to many strange ideas being put forward, which must certainly have met by the experts with shaking heads. However, one can nevertheless find much that is necessary and proper hidden within the fantasies: initial points of attack, improvements to transportation of food and supplies, and commentaries on unity of command and the disciplining of armies. It will be demonstrated that the authors had benefited from drawing on their experiences with their own armies and that they had gone to great lengths to familiarize themselves with the people and lands of the intended future theater of operations. In these points, Marinus Sanutus touches upon his predecessors, and, as he regularly argues against foreign proposals, he may have gained some of his knowledge tacitly. On the whole, however, he stands quite on his own two feet, and his well-preserved memoir is the result of many long years of study and experience, as well as a collection of the information he gathered on five trips to the Holy Land.

The finalized plan for a new crusade, dating from 1321 and as presented in *Liber secretorum Fidelium Crucis,* can only have taken shape during the later part of the author's life, for as long as Sanutus was still dependent upon Philip the Fair, he could not possibly have portrayed the Pope as the supreme warlord, nor could he have granted all of the fruits of victory to his father-city of Venice. Apparently the French had previously been utilized predominately and were, therefore, thought of better. Their cancellation forced the limitation of the plan to Italy. In fact, Sanutus had to give up much more in the end, and, at the end of his life (1329), he saw his plan, to which he had constantly sacrificed his time and energy, fail under the tepidness and self-serving natures of his contemporaries. In spite of these failures, which worldly individuals might immediately have prophesied, it would be wrong to place Sanutus amongst the fantasies, for is work is so thoroughly grounded in reality that the real events of a later time, e.g. England's sea and trade policies, are exactly in line with the policies that Sanutus had demonstrated to the Venetians.[57] Further, this example is neither isolated, nor is it merely the result of a game of chance, for it is, among many other examples, the mature fruit of many long years of work. History and geography, trade routes and movement patterns, transportation and control, recruitment and divisions of soldiers, food and supplies, hospitals-in short, everything that is required for a well-prepared campaign, Sanutus has thoroughly studied and applied his own experiences; therefore, he was able, in the year 1321, to hand over to Pope John XXII a memorandum which, in its entirety and detail, coincides perfectly with the work of a Chief of Staff today.

Lineage and residency place Marinus Sanutus in the Orient from an early age. While he was not part of the branch of the Sanuto family that established a principality in Naxos, the gaze of the whole family lay upon this splendour; additionally, the entirety of Venetian policy was directed at the Levant. The loss of the Holy Land, which had paralyzed the activities of others, served to arouse in him a thirst for action, and so, he gave of his services to the Church so as to eradicate this ignominious stain from Christendom. His plan for a Crusade is portrayed as a service to

---

[57] Saint-Marc Girardin has elaborated in depth upon this concept in *Revue des deux mondes* 1864, LI 40.

the Church, and therefore he names the Pope as the supreme warlord, who should therefore pay the initial costs, which have been most carefully and precisely calculated. The Pope, however, is strongly shifted to the background: recruiting, equipping, and transporting the soldiers is to be handled by Venice. Further, the goal of this calculated, three year campaign is to establish a new lagoon city in the Nile Delta. This second Venice would exclude Egypt from world trade. This exclusion was absolutely necessary to achieve, and if the founding of a new city were to fail, the goal of starving Egypt would be achieved by "Continental Blockade." Here Sanutus shows with great skill that Egypt could not stand without exports and imports and gains its supremacy via the transit of goods. He further shows that the goods of the East could just as easily be transported to the West through Persia or Syria. Thus, by directing the importation of Eastern goods through other ports, Sanutus is far more realistic than Napoleon who attempted to embargo colonial goods completely; whether or not, however, the other powers would have quietly submitted to the intervention of Venetian naval policing is highly questionable. The plan is dubious, yet it is far from being adventurous. The same judgement stands for the proposed alliance with the Mongols as well. In both of these proposals one recognizes the true Venetian, combining the routine of the merchant with the far-sighted gaze of the politician in order to make his native city into the queen of the sea.

These highly ambitious plans are only feasible if you have a war-ready army at your disposal, and, therefore, Sanutus paid the greatest attention to the supplying and equipping of the soldiers. With the brash droves that had flocked to the flags of the various, independent lords in the earlier Crusades, nothing could be accomplished. The army of this new Crusade required professional soldiers: hired mercenaries subordinated to salaried officers with a single, paid commander-in-chief at the head of the army, all in service to the supreme warlord, the Pope. The Pope would take over the costs, and the plan provides for the procurement of liquid capital at low interest rates in Venice. Venice would also provide the ships for transportation and was the primary source concerned with the production of all of the equipment. In return for these services, the city of Venice, according to Sanutus, would be awarded a tariff, the values of which he had set for all individual types of items that it covered. In this way, he would fund the total cost of the three year long campaign. In this way, we obtain the most accurate knowledge of the calculation and gradation of wages, the types and quantities of food, the weapons and their components, the ships and oars, etc. On the whole, this is not merely the work of bureaucracy which bases its calculations on mere paper, but rather it is founded upon the author's own personal knowledge and experience. Where these fail, the author has sought the advice of experts. Sanutus cites both of these heavily. After he had calculated the necessary amount of food per day (ship's biscuit, wine, cheese, and vegetables daily, but meat only thrice each week), he feared that these portions could be considered too meagre; therefore he added that he himself was well fed on this menu and that even less was sometimes required.[58] Further, he refers to an advisory board of experts in a matter that is of particular concern to our study, in the introduction to the chapter covering artillery.[59]

Marinus Sanutus's *Liber secretorum Fidelium Crucis* Book II Volume IV Chapter 22 reads, in translation:[60]

> "For the construction of an ordinary engine, one must first determine the height of the support point[61] (of the two-armed lever or rod) lies above the ground with said engine;

---

[58] Lib. II p. IV cap 10: *et ego fui in armata, in qua non dabantur nisi novem unciae cuilibet praedictorum, sed illud est ultimum extremorum.*

[59] Lib. II p. IV cap 22: *Idcirco aliquid tangam quam potero breviter de praedictis cum aliquorum ingeniatorum consilio sapientum.*

[60] Translator's Note: This passage is translated from Schneider's German translation. Compare this to the original Latin in the appendices.

[61] Translator's Note: The fulcrum of the engine.

for from this, one then determines the needed strength of the supporting longitudinal beams, and these posts must support the arm at that height. This height determines the width between the posts, for the space beneath the arm must be a third shorter than the height. Thus, if the aforementioned engine has a height of twenty-four feet, measured to the support point, then the distance between the support posts must be sixteen feet wide.[62] For the arm, the masters have prescribed the following rule: one must first measure the entirety of the arm from the pivot bolt of the weight box to the extreme end, then divide this number by five, then divide it by six. The support bolts for the arm[63] between these two numbers, i.e. between a sixth and a fifth from the end of the arm. For example, if the arm in question is thirty feet long from the pivot bolt for the weight box to the tip of the arm, then the fifth is six feet and the aforementioned sixth becomes, as one can see, five feet. Thus the pivot bolt of the arm [i.e. the fulcrum of the whole arm] is placed five and a half feet above the pivot bolt of the weight box.

"On Constructing the Long-Ranged Engine

"Here it is necessary to move the above mentioned pivot bolt (of the two-armed lever) to only five feet from the pivot point of the weight box for an arm of thirty feet, i.e. one-sixth the length of the arm, the arm in turn being measured from the pivot pin of the box to the far tip of the arm. And one must then do the following: divide the rod by a fair line into two equal parts, and across this line...[64] One must then place the pivot pin of the weight box, cutting

[62] In Bongar's edition the word *altitudinem* is used.

[63] Translator's Note: The point at which the arm rotates.

[64] Translator's Note: Dr. Schneider was unable to translate the remaining words of this sentence, *versus latus mannettae*. He referred to them as ununderstandable.

through the center line, and, likewise, cut through to both sides of the support pivot pin, also along this line. Now reinforcements must be attached to the sides of the bolts of said engine, and then at the top of the box, a traverse connection of two feet in length is attached (this may be shorter or longer, depending on whether or not the engine is smaller or larger than the example) for the purpose of adjusting the position of the counter-weight, thereby changing the burden upon the arm. Additionally, the box must be longer and larger, as much as possible the master insists, for the deeper the load hangs, the higher that it can be raised into the air, and the heavier that it is, the more powerful it is, thus allowing it to shoot farther and with a larger stone. Therefore, all of the components, particularly the box, the arm, and the bolts must be built more strongly in this machine. The arm must be of sufficient thickness in the middle (at the pivot point) and taper towards the tip; the box must also have a mighty plank that forces it higher into the air when it is raised. The bigger the engine, the bigger the stone that it shoots and the farther and higher that it shoots the stone. And the farther and higher that the engine launches the stone, the stronger and more powerful the effect of the shot.

"If one wishes to mount a long-range engine on a ship, then one allows the support beams to extend sideways and make the arm so long that it reaches to the quarterdeck and the gutter for the stone extends almost to the forecastle of the ship, and design the box so that it reaches almost all the way down to the gutter.[65] Of course, this whole machine, as well as the ship as a whole, must be made extremely strongly if it is to hurl a stone as long as an

---

[65] Batholomaei *Scribae Annales Ianuenses* ao 1241 MG. SS. XVIII 200,32: *Tune parata fuit in civitate quaedam bricola in navi una.*

equally sized machine with the same sized arm would on the land.

"Incidentally, it must be remembered that the precision and range of the engines is based entirely on measuring the weight of the stones properly, such as the size of the engine and the counter-weight box require, as well as forming the stones into balls. Moreover, the shot depends upon the correct positioning of the iron hook at the tip of the arm,[66] to which the eye of the sling attaches: this hook must be bent differently, according to the desired angle of shot, such as a high arc for a short range or a relatively flat arc for distance.

"The master artillerist and engineers must direct their attention to all of these things in order to maximize the precision of the previously described engines.

"The Manufacture of the Long-Ranged Crossbow

"To manufacture long-ranged crossbows, be they made of wood or horn, you need both good master craftsmen and good wood, yet they have been found to be better made from horn, which is produced via glue composed with horn and sinew. These crossbows made of horn prove to be better in arid regions rather than in humid areas, and they shoot further when the temperature is cold than when the weather is warm. This has been proven quite often. Wooden bow arms should be made from the type of tree that is commonly known as the Nassus, but you will find the best variety of these on the island of Corsica. It is found in good quality in many other places as well, but one

---

[66] Translator's Note: Most other sources recommend a pin rather than a hook, as the angle of the pin can be adjusted in the field with a hammer. A hook requires more advanced metalsmithing to adjust properly.

must always take the wood from the forest at the same time as when other wood is cut, as mentioned previously. If one makes the wooden bow arms longer and with only moderate curves, then they are more resilient and shoot their projectiles further; however, this only applies within certain limits. For the shot's range, it is also beneficial that the string on the crossbow is as thin as possible while still able to withstand the pressures of drawing and shooting; therefore, one must make the string out of good, carefully worked hemp. Further, the long range of the crossbow, however, is based upon the previously mentioned arrows as ammunition. Therefore, it is absolutely necessary to make the tips and shafts of the arrows fit well to one another, as well as to the crossbows themselves. Moreover, the shafts of said arrows must be feathered to the highest quality, for such arrows are particularly suitable for shooting at long ranges, directly towards the target.

"As to the various other components of the crossbow: the stock, which is also called the handle, in addition to the nut and the trigger, I will only make the quick remark that all of the pieces must be well-made and perfectly formed, as well as the bow arms of the crossbow. One must use good, workable wood that will simultaneously be resistant to fire.[67] It is also recommended to facilitate the drawing of powerful crossbows by good, wide tensioning hooks, and the tensioning hooks must properly interlock, particularly at the rear of the crossbow. You must train the soldiers to use these tensioning hooks, as well in other techniques of drawing and shooting. Remember that familiarity will give the wielders great strength to draw the

---

[67] Whoever wishes to learn more about the crossbow and its individual components will find the best information in the excellently written book by Payne-Gallwey, *The Crossbow*, London 1893. Translator's Note: Even more than a century after Dr. Schneider wrote this advice, it still holds true. Payne-Gallwey's work is the definitive work on the medieval crossbow.

crossbows, because, after well-founded experience, practice will make perfect.

"Incidentally, both types of crossbow, those made from horn as well as those made from wood, must be well protected by the shooter from the sun and rain, from the wind and the dew, and, thus, these crossbows should always remain in a protective case, unless the wielders need them for shooting. Therefore, every man must have a sheath for his crossbow whilst shipboard, and each man should have an assigned place to hang his crossbow, not so high that it cannot be reached, according to regulations.

"It must also be noted that the crossbows are more readily drawn with both feet than with only one, and this is better for the bow, as well. And for this reason, whenever they attack from a fixed position, be it on a ship or on land, the shooters must have a designated place where they may draw their crossbows with both feet. This was mentioned in chapter 8.[68]

"With these crossbows, if necessary, you can fire the type of projectiles known as Muskete;[69] however, these Muskete are properly the ammunition for the so-called *ballistae a pectoribus.*[70]

"The battle-hardened leaders of the army will have prepared every type of crossbow, and they will require the commanders of the archer units to make proper use of

---

[68] Translator's Note: Dr. Schneider's references to Chapter 8 pointed to nothing in the original work.

[69] Muschettae appears to mean small stone or lead ball.

[70] This statement is still unclarified. In all probability, the *arbalète à tour* is meant. This is what the letter of King Edward II to the city of London in 1307 reads, "*centum ballistas unius pedis, quadraginta ballistas duorum pedum, viginti ballistas de turno.*"

them, particularly ensuring that they use those crossbows that best suit the army of the Christian Crusaders. Likewise, they will maintain the other type of strong crossbows, as has already been discussed in chapter 8.

"And so, Most Holy Father, the General appointed by the Holy Church must devote his full attention to the construction of the above detailed war materiel, the artillery and the crossbows, and, as he will have already noted, he must also take care of all the other needs of long-range projectile weapons. For once the above-mentioned projectile weapons have been installed in a manner that will permit them to perform their duties properly, then they will frighten the enemy so that they will have to flee the road and field in fear and terror."

This testimony of Marinus Sanutus is the decisive element. As this memorandum concerning Venetian war preparations describes all of the weapons and military preparations in great detail, there cannot be the least doubt that it is quite complete. And thus, this second testimonial clearly and absolutely confirms what Aegidius has already stated: *Nam omne genus machinae lapidariae vel est aliquod praedictorum, vel potest originem sumere ex praedictis.* Therefore, there were no arrow shooting engines at that time. The only arrow shooting was done via hand weapons. That is why Aegidius does not mention arrow shooting at all in his chapter "Artillery Engines." Although Sanutus described arrow-shooting weapons in extensive detail in the relevant section, he starkly distinguished it from the "guns" (*machinae*). It is clearly a hand weapon, and its name *ballista* is merely the common Medieval abbreviation of the word *arcuballista* (crossbow).

The sum total of artillery around the year 1300, therefore, amounts to but a single genus with only a mere handful of species. Common to all of them is the lever (the arm), the projectile (stone balls), and the trajectory of the round (a high and arcing path). The only difference is how the lever is set in motion. Sanutus distinguished two forms, both with counterweights. Aegidius mentioned three different types of engines by name that are propelled by counterweights, and the fourth type, which is put in motion through the strength of human hands, he does not give a name. For the moment, we shall leave the exact details undiscussed because it is important for us to confirm the statements of these two witnesses with information from the chronicles.

4: The Time of 1100 AD

We now go backwards to the time around 1100 AD so as to determine from the reports of period historians as to the nature and functioning of the artillery of that day. Albertus Aquensis[71] did not participate in the First Crusade, but he faithfully utilized the reports of the crusaders. Guilelmus Tyrius (William of Tyre), born in Syria and living and serving at Tyre, lastly as its Archbishop (until his death circa 1190), knew the country and its people; further, he moved in the inner circles of leadership. Anna Komnene heard much from her father, Emperor Alexios I (1081-1118), as regarding the military campaigns of the day, as well as having interviewed many of the participants of those campaigns as to military affairs for her history, *The Alexiad*. From these three sources, we obtain definite information about the artillery of the crusaders and the Saracens, and it can be concluded with a fair degree of certainty that at this point the Byzantines possessed the same form of artillery, i.e. only the trebuchet. This strongly implies that, even in Eastern Europe, the torsion engine had been entirely forgotten.

---

[71] I cap. 1: *Sed cum minime ob diversa impedimenta intentioni meae effectus daretur, temerario ausu decrevi saltem ex his aliqua memoriae commendare, quae auditu et revelatione nota fierint ab his, qui praesentes adfuissent.*

While we have already seen from Procopius that there were two types of artillery, namely the *ballistra* and *onager*, both of which had continued in use from antiquity, Anna Komnene speaks only of a single form of engine, and these engines are only capable of being used for throwing stones: λιϑοβόλα (πετροββόόλα) ὄργανα (μηχανήματα). As regards the arrow-shooting engine (βαλλίστρα in Procopius), we find nothing. These stone-throwing engines employed by the Byzantine Emperor Alexios may have been copies of the ancient onager, torsion engines; one can well imagine that, by the year 1100, the technology of the ancient was no longer fully available, so that the construction of the two-armed torsion engine could not be performed, but that at least the power of torsion was well-enough understood for the considerably simpler mechanics of the one-armed engine (giant sling) to be used. A complete break with the ancient world, as was caused by the Migration Era in Western Europe, did not occur in the eastern half of the ancient Roman Empire; and it can be proven that the Byzantines knew and understood the theory of torsional force in the X century.[72] So here are two highly important events that occurred in the West against the continuation of the ancient tradition of torsion artillery.

However, there are serious concerns about this view. Anna Komnene uses the same names for the artillery of the Byzantine army[73] as those that she uses for all of the other armies to which she refers in her history: the Normans[74] under King Robert,[75] the

---

[72] Compare with Greek Politics II. pg 253, 20.

[73] I 269, 18: τὰς γοῦν ἑλεπόλεις καὶ τὰ πετροβόλα μηχανήματα ἔξωϑεν καταστήσας (Alexios).

[74] I 188, 22: οἱ δὲ ἐντὸς (the same Dyrrhachium at Robert besieged the Byzantines) ὁρῶντες τὰς ἔξωϑεν ἑλεπόλεις καὶ τὸν κατασκευασϑέντα ὑπερμεγέϑη μόσυνα (storming the city walls)... καὶ τὰ λιϑοβόλα μηχανήματα

Crusaders,[76] and the Saracens.[77] Their guns, however, were lever powered engines, as can easily be proved.

If you wish to employ torsion artillery, then you must bring the engines into the field with you; however, he that uses counterweighted engines can save himself the trouble of transport, for if he has iron and rope in the camp with him and can procure wood from the local neighborhood, then such weapons can be built for immediate use without difficulty. Only under the utmost need would an army occasionally be compelled to transport a trebuchet on the march, such as when moving on a city where there was no wood to be found, like on the treeless coasts of Palestine or if one feared the approach of a relief army, thereby compelling the acceleration of the siege.[78] In general, the transportation of them was omitted simply because guns of such dimensions - we shall accept Sanutus's length of 30 feet as the normal length - are difficult to transport, and they can be prepared from easily procured materials. Further, nowhere are the torsion spring cables mentioned, merely the wood, ropes, and iron.[79] For

---

κατὰ κορυφὴν τούτου ἱστάμενα

[75] Translator's Note: This is Robert Curthose. In English, he is more typically referred to as Duke Robert of Normandy. While he was the eldest son of William I of England (the Conqueror), Robert never inherited a king's throne.

[76] II 184, 5: τειχομάχοις μηχανήμασι καὶ πετροβόλοις ὀργάνοις τὴν ὅλην πόλιν (Epidamnus) παραστησόμενος (Bohemond).

[77] II 260, 8: ἑάλωσαν δὲ καὶ τινες τῶν περὶ τὰς χελώνας ὄντων, ἓξ στρατιῶται τὸν ἀριθμόν, οὓς ὁ Τύριος ἐκεῖνος θεασάμενος ἀρχηγὸς καὶ τὰς κεφαλὰς ἀποκόψας διὰ πετορβόλων ὀργάνων τῷ στρατεύματι τοῦ Βαλδουίνου ἀπεσφενδόνησε.

[78] Alb. Aquensis III 25: *Baldewinus... ad obsidionem urbis Sorogiae proficisci disposuit cum mangenis.* Guil. Tyrius XVIII cap 12: *Noradinus... convocataque militia et machinis comportatis ex improviso ante urbem (Paneas) consistens.* XXII cap 28: *(Saladin) revocat cohortes, congregat legiones, comportat machinas, et eorum omnium, quae urbes obsidentibus usum solent praestare necessarium, curam gerit diligentem.*

[79] Guil. Tyrius VIII cap 8: *Nam et artificium eet instrumentorum fabrilium, ferri quoque et aeris et funium et ceterorum, quae ad huiusmodi solent esse*

this reason, the arrival of ship repeatedly remedied the lack of artillery, for their remains could provide the engineer with everything that he required, provided that only trebuchets were to be constructed.[80] Therefore, the Crusaders had only lever powered artillery, and, by all reports, the Saracens were perfectly their equal in artillery.

On the other hand, of course, all of the Crusaders were on an exactly equal footing with the Normans under Robert, and, therefore, if Anna Komnene equates their artillery with that of her father, we may then conclude that at that point the Byzantines had no more torsion engines. Furthermore, it would also be strange if the Crusaders did not take note of such a machine carried out according to the ancient pattern, for such were by far the superior engine, as they otherwise discovered that which was new and different in the Orient with open eyes, exploiting such for their benefit. If one considers that the Crusaders began to study the Oriental knowledge of Greek Fire, and that they independently formed an understanding, from this rather incomplete means, a new form of firearm using the entirely new gunpowder, then one is compelled to believe that the Byzantines knew nothing better than the trebuchet.

Of course, if lever artillery had done all that which is described in our chronicles, then one would not have had to search for better artillery. It is natural to take much of their contents with a grain of salt.

It is merely a pious legend that during the siege of Jerusalem a single stone ball killed five people standing together

---

necessaria, multo maiores habebant intus (in Jerusalem) *quam nostri deforis copias.*

[80] Guil. Tyrius XVII cap 24: *At nostri* (before Ascalon) *interea emptis multo pretio navibus sumptiques ex eis malis, vocatis artificibus castrum ligneum* (by assault) *ingentis erigunt celsitudinis... Ex reliqua autem lignorum navalium materia machinas instruunt iaculatorias.*

upon the battlements; two sorceresses and their three maids, who desired to banish the power of the Christian artillery via the devil's power, were shot and dashed to pieces before being swept from the walls (William of Tyre VIII:15). Yet this wonderful shooting performance is nothing compared to the following selection, which I must reproduce in the original language. William of Tyre describes the following occurence from the Siege of Ascalon in XVII 29:

> *"Accidit eadem die, ut quadraginta fortibus ex eis trabem ingentis magnitudinis ad locum, ubi necessaria videbatur, deferentibus, lapis ingens de nostra emissus iaculatoria casu super trabem decideret et quotquot oneri suberant deportando omnes simul cum trabe contereret."*

In English,

> "On the same day that the ram of such magnitude that it took forty men to move it was brought against the gates of the place, a stone was thrown against the walls and made a hole as large as the ram would have done. As the ram was a large burden for the men to carry out, they forced the breach and caused the evacuation of the place, just as if the ram had crushed the gates."

Belief in miracles cannot serve as an excuse here, but this is the rather brazen invention of a glory-seeking artilleryman that fooled the inquisitive historian. The fact that the two spiritual leaders did not know the effects of their engines and, therefore, overestimated them (just as do the laity tend to do today), is readily proven.

Both chroniclers repeatedly report that the engines had been successfully shot at the strong walls of a city, but Albertus Aquensis, in his own idiom, expresses himself vaguely and mildly, "the guns weakened the walls."[81] However, William of Tyre does not merely leave it this,[82] but he paints with full clarity the scenes at Nicaea and Tyre, where he claims that even the strongest walls could not withstand the continuation of such a prolonged and powerful bombardment, until finally the walls threatened to collapse.[83]

Such a feat is beyond the power of a trebuchet, as well as that of a torsion engine; it is also a mistake to assume that even early gunpowder artillery could accomplish it, for such was not possible until recent centuries. If one desired to effect a breach in the wall during the Middle Ages, one was forced to employ a ram or resort to spade and hoe to undermine the walls - either via mines or underneath the protection of constructed roofs. The balls from the engines were not directed at the curtain of the wall itself, but rather at the battlements or over the wall entirely at those portions of the city near the wall. As regards the battlements, fire could clear the tops of the walls, thus preventing the defenders from disturbing the work and actual means of attack; the bombardment of the city proper caused various kinds of damage and loss, but its chief effect was that of terror.[84]

Incidentally, our chroniclers only give way to such exaggerated flights of fancy on rare occasions; often, they will

---

[81] Albertus Aquensis II cap. 29: *Cum… principes, alii iactus et tormenta lapidum ad minuendos muros et turres aptarent.* In folio X cap. 40: *Boemundus… diebus multi moenia et turres crebo ictu lapidum minuebat.*

[82] Guil. Tyrius X cap. 14: *magnorumque molarium immissionibus turres et moenia debilitant.*

[83] Guil Tyrius III cap. 8: *Unde, ne ab incepto quasi victus desisteret (Raimund von Toulouse), instantiam ingeminans, torment etiam multiplicat et contortis maioribus saxorum molibus et mirae soliditatis cautibus immissis, rimas coepit agere (turris) et in pulverem ictibus fatigata resolvi.* In folio XIII cap. 6: *tantis viribus tantoque conamine ingentia torquebant saxa, ut muris illisa vel turribus universa concuterent, et paene traherent in ruinam.*

[84] Guil. Tyrius XIII cap 6: *Machinas nihilominus iaculatorias fabricari praecepit, quibus magnis molaribus turres et moenia concutiantur et civibus terror inferatur.*

admit that the guns could accomplish nothing and that other, better means of attack were commonly adopted in their stead. The Christians shot, for example, at the Warfaru Gate with three engines in vain,[85] and finally they were forced to admit failure against the enemies reinforcement of the gate with tree trunks and giant stones. The Saracens could not penetrate the protective coverings of an approaching siege tower with their shots.[86] At the Siege of Paneas,[87] the heavy bombardment led to nothing. The Crusaders resorted to constructing a siege tower so that they could use ranged hand weapons, such as bows and slings, to rain down fire "from above" in order to effectively combat the defenders.[88]

The end goal of all siegework in the Middle Ages was chiefly to mount the battlements and overpower the defenders in close combat. In this final struggle, personal courage and chance determine the outcome. A purposeful command of the battle is not possible; that is the attackers were expelled as often as the defenders were thrown back from the walls. Thus, the success of the offensive works of the Medieval siege, if collapsing the wall with shovel and pick was not possible, was a poor, miserable result when compared to the certainty of sieges in antiquity. Those led to victory as well, even when not decided by storm. And by this very different state of the aims and means of siege warfare, we may establish a yardstick for comparing the engines of both sides. One must not demand too much of lever-powered artillery, but,

---

[85] Alb. Aquensis III 41: *sequenti die instrumenta trium mangenarum opponunt (Franci barbicale vocant) ponti… Sed nec sic in contritione portae valuerunt.*
[86] Alb. Aquensis VI 17: *Saraceni milites videntes, quia impetus mangenarum crates vimineas penetrare non poterat.*
[87] Translator's Note: Modern day Banias on the Golan Heights.
[88] Guil. Tyrius, XV cap. 9: *et machinis iaculatoriis, quas petrarias vocant, immissis magnae quantitatis molaribus moenia concutiunt et infra urbem conterunt domicilia - His igitur per dies aliquot tractatis videntur omnino non proficere, nisi castello ligneo moenibus applicato, obsessis desuper bellum inferatur.*

within particular limits, they performed not insignificant service on both the offense and the defense.

With the help of twelve engines, Tancred drove the citizens of Vetule from their city following a month long bombardment.[89] At the siege of the particularly strong fortress Gerez, he positioned his engines in an uninterrupted ring about the city and ordered them to fire constantly, both day and night, until the city forcibly surrendered.[90] Before the walls of Jerusalem, three engines were positioned alongside the rams, in order to drive the defenders from the point of assault.[91] They brought fourteen engines into action; nine of them bombarded the siege tower of Count Raymond with such a ferocity that the war machine had to be withdrawn beyond their range and remained, therefore, unused as no one would venture back into their field of fire.[92] The remaining five engines were directed against Godfrey's tower, and they had less success, for the visible hand of God (*Deo protegente*) stretched out over this attacking tower that carried the Crucifix on top as a sign of the piety of the builder and the leader (Godfrey). However, things still went badly enough that even this tower had to be brought out of range of the guns. In this case, however, it happened in the opposite direction: the pushed the tower up to the wall. This placed the tower underneath the guns: they could not be relocated either backwards or to the sides at the correct distance, and, therefore,

---

[89] Alb. Aquensis XI 47: *Tankradus... obsidionem magis firmans, mangenas XII ad urbis moenia applicuit, donec barbicanas et turres spatio unius mensis quassatas usque ad interiora praesidii perforavit.*

[90] Alb. Aquensis XI 43: *machinas et tormenta lapidem fieri constituit, quibus undique in XII partes suos circa praesidium constituens nocte ac die turres et muros comminuens oppugnabat.*

[91] Alb. Aquensis VI 9: *ex consilio maiorum instrumenta trium mangenarum ordinata eriguntur, quarum priori assultu et impetu Christiani Saracenos civis a muris et moenibus arcentes absterrerent.*

[92] Alb. Aquensis VI 15: *Cives... et ipsi instrumenta XIIII mangenarum erigere. - Ex his vero XIIII mangenis VIIII comitis Reymundi machinae opponuntur. - Unde quia tot creberrimos lapidum ictus sustinere non poterant, et machinae protectio defecerat, procul a moenibus machina seducta est; nec ultra inventus, qui hanc iterato ascenderet ac cives impugnando lacesseret.*

from their positions on the wall their shots passed over the tower and into the blue.[93]

The gate of Antioch, where a weakness in the defenses threatened to become extremely dangerous, was brought under the fire of three engines, and as long as they were engaged, the denizens of the city dared not fight there.[94] Whenever possible, one bombarded the inner city, smashing buildings and bringing not only terror to the citizens, but also inflicting casualties upon them.[95] The dust thrown up by the smashing of the battlements would produce a cloud to block the view of the defenders.[96] However, even the best-directed artillery attack did not always lead to the desired goal. Sometimes, the soldiers would bravely man the walls, their losses would be replaced, and they would hold the place until their own artillery could be constructed. An artillery duel would then provide some relief to the weary defenders.[97] Experienced master artillerists taught the younger crews how to

---

[93] Alb. Aquensis VI 17: *Tandem harum V mangenarum assidus ictibus dux suique gravati applicuerunt machinam in virtute Christianorum comminus moenia et muros, ut sic tutiores adversus machinas obsisteret, et mangenae propter aedificia domorum turrium abduci in loco spatioso non valentes, minus iacerent et machinam ferire non possent.*

[94] Guil. Tyrius IV cap. 15: *sequenti die tres iaculatorias erigunt machinas, ut saltem eorum iactu continuo et saxorum contorsione muros et portam debilitare et civibus per eam exitum possent impedire. Fiebat itaque, ut, quam diu se in iaculando continuarent machinae, nemo per eam portam auderet egredi; remittentibus vero illis operam, iterum cives ad solitas recurrebant irruptiones, castris vicinis multas inferentes molestias.*

[95] Guil. Tyrius XV cap. 1: *Hic demum machinis congrua provisione dispositis, turres ac moenia et infra muros civium domicilia gravium immissione molarium incessanter concutiunt, et crebis ictibus et vicaria immissorum cautium repetitione non sine multa inhabitantium strage funditus deicunt… aedificiorum munimina.*

[96] Guil. Tyrius XIII cap. 6: *Excitabatur de collisis lapidus et caemento dissoluto pulvis tam immensus, ut his, qui in moenibus et supra turres erant, quasi nubes interposita negaret adspectum.*

[97] Guil. Tyrius XX cap. 16: *Hoc videntes oppidani (von Damiata), ut arte artem deludant et nostris moliminibus eadem subtilitate obvient, e regione nostri castellum (Turm) educunt in sublime, armatos imponunt, qui nostris renitantur a pari et eis aequipollenti conatu respondeant: tormenta nihilominus tormentis obiciunt.*

work the guns properly.[98] Furthermore, just as in the early days of gunpowder artillery where there were renowned masters who could, for a considerable amount of money, be brought into an army's service, there were men in this period who enjoyed the reputation of excellent artillerists that would be summoned in cases of urgent need. Thus it was when the Christians were in dire straights before Tyre, for they had no experienced men to silence the artillery of the defenders. As it is well known that the courage of even the best men sinks when they are struck from afar by the shots of the enemy, without either recourse or protection, the Christian army breathed a collective sigh of relief when the Armenian Havedik arrived at the camp to assume command of their artillery. He was preceded by a great reputation, and, though it is all but certainly exaggerated that "he hit every target with the first shot," he must certainly have been a true master, for the position of the attacker improved immediately.[99]

At the above-mentioned Siege of Tyre, one can best understand the importance of artillery in fortress warfare. Even the most rudimentary artillery grants one party such an advantage that his adversary must despair if he cannot raise the same weapons, for only then is the game equal. However, this must not lead to an overestimation of the importance of artillery.[100] While the decision does not solely fall to the artillery, artillery is such an important element of siege warfare, that one may not truly speak of sieges during the era without artillery. Until the time of King Philip of Macedonia, the other means of siegecraft (towers, rams, and

---

[98] Guil. Tyrius XIII cap. 6: *Qui autem in machinis erant, docentibus his, qui iaculandi peritiam erant assecuti.*

[99] Guil. Tyrius XIII cap. 10: *quodque non esset in castris, qui dirigendi machinas et torquendi lapides plenam haberet peritiam, vocantes quendam de Antiochia, Armenum natione, Havedic nomine, qui in ea facultate dicebatur inctrictissimus, subito receperunt eum; qui tanta arte in dirigendo machinas et ex eis missos molares contorquendo utebatur, ut quiquid ei pro signo deputaretur, id statim sine difficultate contereret.*

[100] Translator's Note: With the advantage of more than a century of hindsight, I find this statement of Dr. Schneider's to be darkly hilarious.

protective canopies) availed the attacker little, for it was only when artillery intervened that these means were able to achieve anything. In the Middle Ages, too, these same implements were of but the merest value until the trebuchet lend them its support. That is why the art of siegecraft around the year 800 was far behind that of the year 1100. Despite their inability to compete with the performance of torsion engines, trebuchets still lifted the art of siege warfare to a new level.

The engines mentioned by Albertus Aquensis and William of Tyre correspond exactly to the description of counterweighted artillery which we have come to know from the writings of Aegidius Romanus and Marinus Sanutus, despite the engines going by different names. Either they are generally called *tormenta, tormenta lapidum, machinae iaculatoriae, petrariae,* or they were named *mangenae (instrumenta mangenarum)*. In addition, Albertus Aquensis speaks repeatedly of a *mangonella*, which William of Tyre never mentions. Some passages almost seem to indicate that it was a hand weapon that shot small stones,[101] but others clearly suggest that it was a lever-powered engine of smaller dimensions powered by traction rather than counterweight that could be loaded quickly.[102] Regardless of this, it remains in any case, that the actual engines of around the year 1100 were lever powered and bore the name *mangenae*. This name is extremely important for us, as it leads us to the birthplace of the lever-powered engine.

---

[101] Alb. Aquensis VII 1: *urbis defensores in sagittis et fundibalis et mangonellis circumquaque impugnantes.* VII cap. 3: *ab intus mangonellis, ballistis et sagittis viriliter resistentes.* VII cap 56: *tam manganellis quam sagittarum grandine fessi et victi.* IX cap 20: *subito mangonellae impetu lapis emissus illi in verticem venit.* In these references, the word *mangeneles* appears to equate to the Latin term *fustibula* in the dictionary of Alex Neckam, "*De nominibus utensilium*". Compare with Augustus Scheler's *Lexicographie Latine cu XII et XIII siecle*, Leipzig 1867, p 95.

[102] Alb. Aquensis VI 17: *qui assidue moles lapidum fundibulis aut parvis mangonellis in machinam iacerent.* X cap 45: *obsedit tam mari quam terra (Sidon) in mense Augusti mangenellis et machinis muro a terra in circuitu applicitis.*

5: Abbo

Shortly after the death of Charlemagne, the Normans began to invade the empire, and in the year 886, the city of Paris was sorely pressed when the Normans laid siege to it. Abbo, a devout monk from the Abbey of St.-Germain-des-Près, details it for us in an expansive poem,[103] which historians consider to be a valid historical reference, as the poet took part in the defensive fighting himself and the portrayals within it are singularly lifelike. However, one must not overlook that in the poem "De bello Parisiaco", the quirkiness of the composer is readily apparent in the third book and that, in both of the first two books, the realistic depictions of events immediately turn into something miraculous when the Blessed Saint Germain intervenes in the fight. Therefore, it is quite understandable that Abbo did not limit himself to realistic terms when attempting to render the scenes of battle in poetic terms. Here the poet looked to example of his master Vergilius, and, in order to enliven the descriptions, Abbo has applied colors drawn from his vast wealth of literary knowledge and added in objects which we would call anachronisms, but which the poet and his learned audience would merely think of as beautiful embellishments. The miracles worked by Saint Germain will excite no special interest today, and the reminisces of Vergilius and other ancient authors have only captivated an extremely narrow readership. However, it is impossible not to find one's heart warming when Abbo himself, with the Crucifix in his right hand, ascends the walls to encourage his brothers and strengthen their will to fight. With open eyes, he spies where the enemy intends to assault, and he rushes to the most troubled spots, where the sight of the enemy's war machine strikes at his heart. Above all, his anxiety is excited by the "framework of two, lofty poles of equal length, launching enormous stones":

[103] De bello Parisiaco, libri III. MG. SS. II 776f

I 363: *Conficiunt longis aeque lignis geminatis.*
I 365: *Saxa quibus iaciunt ingentia.*

These were something completely new, and so it haunts even the most courageous men with its tremendous horror. For these machines, Vegilius provides no names, and so the poet must thus call the barbarous guns with a barbarous name:

I 364: *Mangana quae proprio vulgi libitu vocitantur.*

Did Abbo forget that the *catapultae*, of which there were one hundred standing on the city walls,[104] so that he should not have to fear these *mangana*? No, for the Parisians had no guns at all, and he expected that no one would take this mere poetic ornamentation seriously. Yet, the *mangana* are real, and Abbo is an eyewitness to this. From his vantage point upon the walls, Abbo sees above all the two towering posts, which, according to Sanutus may have had a height of twenty-four feet, and this tall structure is, in fact, characteristic of a lever-powered engine, which was called *mangena* during the time of the Crusaders. It is in Abbo, therefore, that we first find a mention of a gun after the Migration Era, and it is, indeed, found with a people who had never come into contact with the civilizations of antiquity. It may be supposed that the Normans were also the inventors of these new engines, for a ship's carpenter, well-versed in the functions of both the lever and the crane, can most easily come up with the idea of using this powerful force to hurl a rock, as has been demonstrated in ancient times by seafaring peoples when they conducted sieges, thereby needing artillery.[105] In the IX century, Abbo had to

---

[104] I 156: *Tunc centena quium* (=quorum) *pepulit cum sanguine vitam Centeno catapulta nimis de corpore pernix.*

[105] Viollet-Le-Duc, Dictionnaire raisonné de le'architecture française du XI au XVI siècle. Paris 1861, volume V p. 220: *Les engins inconnus jusqu' alors" dont parlent les annales de Saint-Bertin, et qui furent dressé devant les murailles d'Angers occupée en 873 par les Normands, avaient probablement été importés*

apologize for the peculiar name *manganum*; however, by the year 1100 it was familiar to everyone.[106] From the year 1300 onwards, it would live on in the transformations found in various modern languages. In addition, there were all sorts of special names that suggest the existence of the different variations upon the basic type of engine, as we have previously learned from Aegidius Romanus. In this respect, the names reflect the development of Medieval artillery during the given period, and they happily confirm the assertions proposed by rejecting the common naming conventions.

6: The Time of 1200 AD

If the artillery of the year 1100 coincides with that of the year 1300, the sieges of 1200 must then have been conducted with lever-powered artillery. In other words, even in the time of the Hohenstaufens, there were no arrow shooting engines or torsion engines. We could spare ourselves a lengthy search through the Chronicles in order simply to find the natural, self-evident answer. However, so that this important period does not remain without period evidence, we shall take as an example a siege that falls almost exactly upon the year 1200, in which both sides employed all of the customary means of warfare for the day, that displays the valor and gallantry of combatants from both the Orient and the Occident, and that continued with the utmost exasperation to both sides so long as the defenders held -until they were defeated, not starved- the Siege of Acre (1189-91).

---

en France par ces artistes que Charles le Chauve faisait venir de Byzance. How far, however, the influence of these Byzantine masters may have reached the learned scholars may overstate. In any case, the previous artillery system is entirely eliminated. The passage in *Reginonis Chronicon* MG. SS. I 585, 39 states: *nova et inexquisita machinamentorum genera applicantur.*

[106] One will miss here the attractiveness of the Greek word μάγγανον. However, nothing can be done based merely upon this single word. Its history and meaning can only be determined once Byzantine and Arabic military science have been drawn into the light.

While Saladin remained in the interior of the country during the spring of 1189, in order to wrest from the Christians the last of their possessions in that area, King Guy, encouraged by the arrival of new Crusaders, desired to conquer the important port city of Acre. However, his coup de main failed due to the valiant resistance offered by the garrison, who also kept it well supplied, both with provisions and all means of defense, until Saladin was able to approach with a relief army. In a two-day battle (14 and 15 September) Saladin repulsed those of the Crusaders, who had established themselves in the north of the city; entered the city by force; and reinforced the garrison. He then also established new lines of supply for food and organized everything quite well, as was necessary for continued defence. On the fourth of October, King Guy made a bold attack upon his enemies at the River Belus, but his initial success ended in defeat. The Crusaders must have been happy to withdraw behind the entrenchments of their camp, and, as they were no longer sortieing out on new attacks, on the fourteenth of October Saladin was able to move his camp from the marshy plains onto the heights of Charuba.

In the spring of 1190, Saladin retired to his former camp, but it made no difference in the campaign, for the Christians had turned their camp into a fortress in the meanwhile. Additionally, Saladin had had to detach part of his army to interdict the march of the approaching Crusader army, which was already nearing the borders of Syria. Naval operations had a minimal influence on the course of events, so the first half of the summer was quiet, until an action on 25 July. Then, a failure by the Christian sailors in an attack cost half of them their lives. It was against the orders of their leaders that the starving men took up arms. That’s why Saladin was able to relocate his camp to Charuba again in August of that year. Yet his heart was filled with great anxiety, as his letter to the caliph shows,

> "All of the Christian princes have allied themselves, sending men and weapons to the army. For every one Christian that dies on the land, a thousand come by sea to replace him. The seeding exceeds the harvest, and the tree sprouts more branches than the iron can cut."

And thus it happened. Duke Friedrich of Swabia, of course, died on 20 January 1191, but others landed in the spring. King Philip of France, Philip of Flanders, the Marquis of Tyre, Leopold of Austria, and the Landgrave Ludwig of Thuringia all appeared at that place. On 8 June, Richard the Lionheart arrived with twenty-five ships, to the jubilation of the Crusaders. From that moment, the siege was given a renewed start, and, a mere month later, the city fell on 12 July. Richardus provides an exceptionally detailed account of the end of this siege in his "*Itinerarium Ricardi*", and, since he includes a separate chapter on the utilization of artillery, let us take a closer look at his information on artillery.[107]

The besiegers constructed three mobile towers, and when they advanced these against the city walls, engines were positioned on both sides of each tower to ward off the attacks of the enemy and to bombard the wall.[108]

However, the besieged were also well versed with artillery. Further, one of them was of especial size and strength, so that the balls that it shot buried themselves a foot deep in the earth when they missed their target, but when they did strike the target, it would be dashed to tiny pieces.[109] Perhaps, however, this monster

---

[107] Compare to William Stubbs, *Chronicles and Memorials of the Reign of Richard I.* vol 1, London, 1864. "*Itinerarium Peregrinorum et gesta Regis Ricardi*".

[108] Itin. I cap 36: *Singulis autem castris* (Towers) *suae applicantur petrariae et lateratim assistunt, quibus et machinae productae defendantur et moenia deiciantur adversa.*

[109] Itin. I cap. 47: *Petrariarum hostilium, quarum fuit in civitate copia, una fuit incomparabilis et magnitudine compactae machinae et pro voto torquentium inaestimabilis molis lapides iaculando efficax... Lapides nihilominus, quoties*

gun was not so dangerous after all, for Richardus reports that one of its shots bounced off of the back armor of a warrior.[110]

King Richard's first concern was the procurement of guns, the construction of which he organized, even during his illness.[111] And in describing the assault which King Philip undertook before Richard had recovered, the chronicler tells us that the main engines fired one at a time, working at all times to prepare for the assault and hinder the foe.

Itinerarium III cap. 7 reads:

"The King of France recovered somewhat more rapidly from his illness; he then ordered war machines to be built and guns (*petrariae*) to be emplaced in suitable locations so that they could shoot at night almost as well as by day. Amongst them was an especially fine engine that he named "The Bad Neighbor." But the Turks in the city also had such an engine, which they had named "The Bad Base," which, with its powerful shots struck "The Bad Neighbor" repeatedly. However, the King had it repaired again and again, until it had, after a particularly animated bombardment, it had successfully collapsed a portion of the city wall and smashed "The Accursed Tower" (*turrim maledictam*). Here, the engine belonging to the Duke of Burgundy works, and not in vain, and there the gun of the Templars used to

---

nullo retardarentur obstaculo, unius pedis longitudine agebantur in terram cadentes. Nonnullas petrariarum nostrarum percutiens in particulas dispersit, vel certe inutiles effecit; machinas quoque alias plures vel ictu dissolvit vel particulam, quam attigerat, abscidit.

[110] *Haec igitur talis in quendam ex nostris hominem lapidem enormis magnitudinis dedit a tergo. Aversa quippe facie steterat nihil suspicans, sed nec tam procul aestimans posse lapidem pervenisse; sed nec hominem quidem vel in minimo laesit, immo nec loco movit, sed resiliens a tergo tamquam a monte ferreo decidit haud procul inefficax.*

[111] Itin. III cap. 4: *Nihilominus vero petrarias suas interim et mangunellos et castellum* (Towers) *ante portas civitatis fecit erigere.*

belong to the Turks, and even that of the Hospitallers did not stint in firing, thereby giving the Turks a shock. In addition, there was an engine that had been built at the cost of all named “The Lord God’s Gun.” There was a priest, an extremely righteous man who preached diligently to the people, and he gathered from them a great amount of money from which the gun could be repaired quickly and from which the men who brought throwing stones for the gun could paid. Through the working of this engine was the wall near “The Accursed Tower” was brought down for a breadth of twenty feet. The Count of Flanders had had a special (*electam*) engine, and, after his death, it passed to the ownership of King Richard, who had one like it, just smaller in size. These two guns fired without ceasing at a tower next to the gate in which the Turks had gathered, until the tower was half demolished. In addition, King Richard had had two new engines built, of exquisite craftsmanship and from the best materials, and these struck, unbelievably, every target that was assigned to them. He also had constructed a tower of very solid timber with ladders for ascending, a so-called “bercfrit;”[112] strong iron bands held it tightly together, and it was covered in skins and mattresses and the strongest possible boards. Thus, no shot could damage it, nor could Greek Fire, nor could any other form of attack. Further, he had two smaller engines (*mangunellos*) built, and one of them shot so skilfully and powerfully that its rounds landed in the courtyards of the city’s slaughterhouses. These guns of King Richard’s shot continually, both day and night, and it is certainly true that one of them killed twelve men with but a single stone ball. This stone was brought before Saladin for his inspection, and the messengers spoke to him thus, ‘Behold, the King of

---

[112] Translator’s Note: There is no good English equivalent for this particular word. The closest would likely be the Greek “Helepolis,” or “city taker”. This referred to a particular type of large, mobile siege tower.

England, who is the Devil incarnate, has brought with him from the city of Messana, which he has conquered, sea-pebbles and smooth stones such as this in order to punish us, for nothing can resist these stones. They smash everything they strike or grind it into dust.'"

This last described feat of shooting belongs clearly in the realm of the anecdote, the sort of lies that soldiers would tell one another around the guard house (a sort of "Artillerist's Latin"), which the other branches of service would have been wont to counter with similar boastfulness. And that our Chronicler himself tends to exaggerate is well-proven by his repeated comments that an engine had brought down a tower or a wall. What is far more likely true, is that the breach, which was made by undermining, was far too narrow, and that it was widened to a practicable breadth via concentrated artillery fire. However, Richard took another path, which was most expensive in both human lives and money. He had proclaimed by a herald, "He whoever shall pull a single stone from the wall shall receive two ducats!" Later, he increased this wage to three and then four ducats.[113] Obviously, artillery is not needed for this. Yet it served by maintaining a continual fire until the end of the siege, in order to keep the defenders away from the point of assault, as well as frightening and shocking the defenders, thereby softening their positions.[114]

The guns used in the Siege of Acre are called *petrariae* and *mangunelli*, which are the lever-powered artillery that we have come to know, simply in large and small scales. In the other Chronicles, we find all of the other common names for engines, such as *biblia*, *briccola*, *chadabula*, *troia*, *etc*., and it is certainly possible that these are different forms of engines. However, it is

---

[113] Itin. III cap. 13: *Praeconem igitur statuit clamare, ut quisquis unam petram a muro iuxta praedictum turrim extraheret, duos a rege aureos perciperet. Post promisit tres aureos, demum quattuor.*

[114] Itin. III cap. 16: *Iterea nocte et die Christianorum non cessabant petrariae muros iugiter conquassantes.*

more likely that these are only expressions of soldier's jargon.[115] In any case, all of the engines of the Hohenstaufen era certainly belong to the genus of lever artillery. The fact that their performance could not have been superior to that of the engines discussed above,[116] one needs only to study the sieges of Crema and Milan. To defeat the small town of Crema in the year 1159, Friedrich Barbarossa required six months, and Milan only succumbed to hunger, not the attacks of the Emperor.

Thus, the Hohenstaufen period becomes another link in the chain of the second era of artillery: the time of the trebuchet. This period began in the IX century and extended until the dawn of the modern era. The other portion of the Middle Ages, the time from the Migration Era until the death of Charlemagne, certainly saw no artillery in Western Europe.

---

[115] This is almost certainly the case with terms such as *petraria turquesia*, as used by Guillaume der Ormes in his letter of 1240 to Queen Blanche. Napoleon, Etudes II p. 55.

[116] These engines were used in the campaigns of 1229. *Annales Placentini Guelfi* MG. SS. XVIII 448,3: *Bononienses circa duodecim plaustra, super quibus manganellos et trabucos constituerant, in proelio duxerunt.* 448,23: *plaustra cum bobus et manganellis.* See as well the above discussion of artillery on ships.

The Hand-Drawn Images

1: The Value of the Drawings

From the consistent testimonies of Aegidius Romanus and Martinus Sanutus, we have found that they each knew only of a single genus of engines, and a thorough examination of the historical sources has confirmed for us that the period from 886 to 1300 saw only the use of lever-powered artillery. Our two informants, however, are not in agreement as to the species: Sanutus knew of only two types, yet Aegidius described four. Sanutus does not provide any special names, merely making a distinction between the *machina communis* (common machine) and the *machina lontanaria* (long-ranged machine). However, Aegidius leaves only a single type unnamed (that which is powered through the force of human hands); the other three are named the *trabucium* (with fixed counterweight), *biffa* (with moving counterweight), and *tripantum* (with both forms of counterweight). The last name given, *tripantum*, occurs nowhere else, and the word *biffa* is only found in isolation[117] and in such an obscure way that one can not be truly certain that whether or not Aegidius is actually defining different forms of engines. Thus, only the name *trabucium* remains, the first provided by Aegidius. This name probably deserves its position first on the list, not only because it is the most common of all of the names, but it also appears in the same general meaning as *petraria* and *machina lapidaria*, terms often given to the entire genus of lever-powered artillery.

It is not, therefore, advisable to use the names provided by Aegidius as a starting point for further research, particularly as to

---

[117] *Le Chroniche de Viterbo*, 1243 in Boehmer's *Fontes rerum Germanicarum*. Stuttgart 1868. IV 711: *et fecero una buffa grande et una piccola.* IV 712: *et le due buffa continuo gectavano per lo campo, e tutti li nimici facevano fuggire per paura di quelle pietre.*

find other examples of engines that fit into the rubrics given by Aegidius. Otherwise, a great many difficulties which cannot be solved immediately arise. However, these difficulties are really based simply upon the fact that the machines are given different names, for Medieval authors freely distributed new names throughout their works.

Incidentally, the doubts concerning Aegidius are not confined merely to his names, but extend also to the factual information presented. In theory, he praised his *tripantum* as having the advantages of both the *biffa* and the *trabucium*, as it had both a fixed and a mobile counterweight; in reality, it combined the disadvantages of both types of weight. And thus, it is not outside the realm of possibility that the joy of neatly categorizing things led the scholar to remodel things so as to force them into well-conceived categories. On the whole, Aegidius's depiction of artillery, as much of his other work, in *De regimin principum* is that of the true scholar: first, he clearly defines the genus of the engines, then he names and describes in fine detail four species, and finally he subsumes all of these into the established genus. Transitional forms from one engine type to another are not described, yet this strict taxonomy does not always fit with actuality: for example, it is known that there was a form of engine that was powered by human hands that was also complemented at the short end of the lever in order to facilitate operation of the engine. We actually have this machine depicted in some of the images.

For these reasons, it is decidedly better to reject the particular names of the engines, and perhaps even to leave Aegidius on the shelf for now. This way, we may first gain a clearer and more complete concept of lever artillery from the descriptions of Sanutus, as he presents several details that are lacking in Aegidius. By doing so, we place ourselves upon even firmer ground, because Sanutus, by his own assertion, consulted with technical advisors for his representations. Admittedly, this does present a serious difficulty for the modern day writer, as Sanutus adopted artistic expressions from these master craftsmen, artistic expressions that were best understood by readers of the day if they had such an engine available. However, without the aid of an engine being present, these words often defy explanation, for they are not present in the Latin dictionary or, if they are present, they are so loosely defined that the aid of the dictionary fails us. If we were to do so, we would then be forced to reject Sanutus altogether - this and this alone offers explanation of why our predecessors in military history have used these weighty witness, perhaps the weightiest of them all, little or not at all - particularly since neither Sanutus nor Aedigius have made their descriptions particularly vivid or supported them with drawings.

Luckily, however, this deficiency may be remedied. There are all kinds of representations of trebuchets on stone and ivory, as well as illustrations that are sometimes included with the manuscripts or in the occasional book on military theory, works actually intended to be used in the profession of war. Alwin Schultz has performed a great service by collecting a great amount of this pictorial material in one place. As searching through such collections still often yields results that are less than successful, it was not through chance but the friendly support of Mr. Rudolf Sillib, head of the manuscript department in the Heidelberg Library that I found much of this collection.

2: The Heidelberg Military Manuscript

The depictions of two trebuchets in the Heidelberg Military Manuscript of 1496 are almost two centuries younger than the writings of Sanutus (1321); additionally, they date from a time when gunpowder cannons had come into general use, lever-powered artillery being, at most, an emergency measure.

However, that does not genuinely matter, for the "military manuscripts" are not limited to depicting merely the common weapons of the day, but rather show drawings of the entirety of the inventory. It was the intention to show rich, detailed illustrations (the relevant text is almost always minor and often completely absent), and therefore long-forgotten war machines continue to be most faithfully traced by one hand and eventually the next. Further, the fact that the model shown in the Heidelberg Military Manuscript readily conforms to the description of Sanutus permits only insignificant changes: the size and counterweight are variable, and the way in which the lever is set in motion allows for a few different options. Yet, on the whole, lever powered artillery must have remained largely the same.

On the reverse side of the first page of this manuscript (Pal. germ Nr. 126 Pap. XV century), the following is stated in a caption:

> "*1496, Dys buch der stryt uñ bůchssē ward gemacht in der vassnacht als man zalt von crisstus geburt 1496 jar, dar uff soellen die buchssenmeister haben grossacht fer war. G.f.z.b.f.m philibs mönch der pfalcz buchsēmeaister.*"

These hand-drawn pictures, which rarely contain even a few words of explanation, offer two large illustrations of lever artillery on consecutive pages. One illustration takes up two full pages, the reverse of folio 30 and the obverse of 31. The other illustration is a single page on the front of folio 30. One can tell, even at first glance, that the original drawings were done by an intelligent man and that the slightest error will not have entered them until they were later reproduced via tracing.

The machines rest on a base made of strong beams, wherefrom the vertical posts rise, as well as struts to further support the posts. Above these, one can see the head of an iron bolt about which the arm rotates. On both engines, the box, which is filled with heavy stones and pieces of lead, is attached to the short lever arm by an iron rod that is threaded through the arm and from which the box hangs. The box hangs from the bolt via planks, and the square box (on reverse of 30) hangs significantly lower than the triangular box pictured on the obverse of folio 30. The triangular is deliberately drawn open in order to show the filling. About halfway up the long lever arms, there are iron rings to which an iron hook is attached; a rope runs downwards from this hook around a winch by which the arm is brought down in order to load the engine. The ring for the rope is then connected to a trigger lug; this alone holds the gun in tension once the hook of the drawing rope is unhooked from the arm. Another rope is tied tightly to the engine a short distance from the extreme tip of the arm; this rope extends to the end of the gutter-like projectile-trough, where it contains the stone ball. The other end of the rope then is run to the very tip of the arm, where an eyelet on the rope is hooked over an iron prod. This rope forms the sling of the engine: it pulls the ball through the projectile-trough when it is discharged and then it grips the ball firmly through the air, until the arm nears the vertical position. As the arm reaches the vertical, the end of the rope slides off of the prod, and the round is released, allowing it to fly free, arcing towards its target.

Apart from the idle wheels present on the larger drawing, which probably served to wind the engine and were almost certainly not for locomotion,[118] the two engines actually differ only in the weight box. Even its shape is different. More importantly, however, the square box does not hang vertically immediately beneath its pivot bolt, but rather is pushed up far beyond its natural center of gravity. It is pushed into that position by a strong, thick

---

[118] Translator's Note: Research in the late XX and early XXI centuries has shown that these wheels are actually intended to improve efficiency. They act to allow the weight to drop in a straighter path, thereby converting more of the weight's potential into kinetic energy applied to the projectile.

plank that extends from the weight box to the lever arm. On the weight box, this beam is firmly attached, but it is not so on the long arm of the engine: here it merely leans with its tip rested against the underside of the long lever arm. In the pictured position of the long lever arm, the plank has already pushed the weight box outwards, and as one pulls the long arm down even further, the weight box will be pushed even further forward. At full tensioning of the engine the weight box will reach its peak.

Conversely, as the engine is released, the tip of the beam that is aligned with the underside of the long lever arm loses its point of support as soon as the arm is released and swings up. This frees the weight box (so that it is no longer held forwards), allowing it to swing to its natural center of gravity. Thus, the weight box acts on the short arm not merely by it great weight but also through this sudden, sharp momentum. The force of this swing is stronger in proportion to the length of the swing, i.e. the deeper below its pivot point the box hangs, the more powerful the swing will be. And this is why Sanutus wrote: "*Et debet fieri maior capsa et longior, quae fieri potest a magistris, quia, quanto onus bassius est, tanto ipsa melius supinatur.*" In English, this reads "The box should be bigger and longer, as can be demonstrated by the masters, for the burden of the load is much, much greater than that of a low load." He wrote further, "*Ac capsa bonum debet habere gamelum, quod capsam impellat versus exteriorem partem.*" Again, the English is "And, if the box is of good quality, we should also have a *gamelum*, that impels it towards the outside of its path." The undefined word *gamelum* is at least correctly understood in its technical meaning by means of the Heidelberg drawing, and it is only in this way that we have found the correct translation for the word *castellum* (ύπομόχλιον) as "support point of the lever", which is not defined in any dictionary.

From the pictures in the Heidelberg Military Manuscript and their correspondence with the assertions of Sanutus, we may thus gain an understanding of the types of counterweights that are possible, which deviate strongly from the concepts towards which the seemingly extremely clear words of Aegidius lead us: *vertens se circa huiusmodi virgam.*

Initially, I had imagined that the attachment of the movable counterweight was such that, with the ballast material in a fully enclosed box, the box was rotated so that, when the engine is fully rotated backwards, the box would rest on the top of the lever arm. The box would be attached via a bolt about which it could rotate. When the arm began to rise, the box would spin about the bolt to fall underneath the short end of the arm, thus traversing a semicircle with the bolt as the center point. However, the engineering issues with this idea soon became apparent; first, this mechanism could only be successfully executed with extremely light counterweights, otherwise the bands holding the mechanism together would break. Further, the rotating motion of the box would introduce variations into the system, thereby eliminating any possibility of precise shooting and altering the timeliness of the release of the stone. If one does not wish to accuse Aegidius of error, then his words must be considered in the context of the Heidelberg drawings and correspondence with those of Sanutus. The moving counterweight thus differs from the fixed counterweight in that the bands connecting the weight box to the bolt are lengthened so that the box can be pushed out quite far when the gun is drawn back. This pressure, which raises the box above its natural center of gravity, stems from the longer arm of the lever, which pushes the connecting beam when the arm is pulled back. This, in turn, causes the beam to push the box upwards. When the arm snaps up, the box falls, passing through approximately a quarter circle, into its natural position: hanging vertically beneath the bolt, and this momentum adds itself to that of the heavy weight of the box. However, the precision of the engine is reduced, as this momentum, quite naturally, introduces fluctuations to the amount of energy transferred to the shot. This is why Aegidius says the following of the moving counterweight, "*licet plus trahat ratione motus, non tamen sic uniformiter trahit; ideo plus proicit, non tamen sic recte et uniformiter percutit*." In English, "Though it does impart more power due to the movement, this movement is not uniform; therefore, it does not shoot as rightly for it does not strike uniformly." In Sanutus, this engine is, therefore, simply referred to as the *machina lontanaria*, or long-ranged engine.

As to the fixed counterweight engine, the pictures confuse the issue further, rather than clarifying it. At first, everyone will naturally consider that the fixed counterweight was attached to the short lever arm in the same manner as are the pieces of iron that are attached to the barriers of railroad crossings, i.e. held fast by iron straps. However, this simple method of attachment seldom appears in the pictures of engines, and likely only where, in addition to the counterweights, human hands still apply power by means of traction. In the case of larger engines, the counterweight appears to be attach to a bolt that passes through the arm by means of metal bands from which the weight hangs freely. Thus, this counterweight changes its position as the bolt from which it hangs moves when either the rod is pulled down or snapped up, and, therefore, this counterweight could still, so far, be called moving. However, it differs fundamentally from the previously described type of counterweight, which we have recognized as being mobile, for under all circumstances, this weight always hang vertically beneath the bolt. Thus, the counterweight always acts upon the same point of the rod and only by the power of its own, heavy weight. Aegidius says of this free hanging counterweight, "*Inter ceteras autem machinas haec rectius proicit, eo quod contrapondus semper uniformiter trahat; ideo semper eodem modo impellit*." In English, "In comparison to the other engines, this is more precise, however, as it launches forth, because the counterweight is uniform of travel, and so it always shoots in the same way." So, if one looks only at its functioning, one can call the counterweight fixed, even though it floats freely in the air.

If we accept this explanation, the following distinction results: The counterweight is called fixed if it works only by its weight, but it is called moving if, in addition to its weight, it also acts through its fall. The fixed always hangs directly below the bolt, and the moving is forcibly pushed out of this natural position in order to swing backwards when released.

The only question is whether or not that is what Aegidius wished to express. Sanutus, however, quite clearly knew only a free floating counterweight, not one that was permanently attached to the arm, and the authoritative drawings concur.

3: The Manessian Manuscript of Songs

The Heidelberg Library also has a far older depiction of a trebuchet. In the Manessian Manuscript of Songs (German Palatine Manuscripts No. 848) on folio 255 is a picture included on the title page of the section containing the songs of the poet von Trostberg, despite a lack of relationship to the contents of the poems. This portion of the manuscript belongs to the foundation of the collection, ie it dates from the beginning of the XIV century, but as we are concerned with, in this case, a mere decorative drawing, one must not expect any clarification of technical details from this drawing. The attachment of the sprockets at the top is vague at best; clearly, the artist wished to emphasize the master gunner who is about to strike the trigger pin, about which the rope holding the arm is looped, with a mighty hammer blow. When the hammer falls, then the engine is discharged.

A very similar picture has been provided by Alwin Schultz[119] from Viollet-le-Duc, and he has provided us with a special accounting of this picture as he cannot find its name. Schultz identified in it the second form of artillery from Aegidius, those with moving counterweights, also known as the *biffa*. That is the name given by Aegidius for that particular type of engine, without variation, in all of the authoritative manuscripts, as well as the misappelation *blida*, which Schultz has identified as a lapse in transcription via his justifiable mistrust of "the unreliable incunabula printings." As to the above, A. Schultz says in II 376:

> "Another difficulty is indicated by the Picard architect Villard de Honnecourt, who lived around the middle of the XIII century and gives us a picture of the trebuchet in his sketchbook, as studied by Viollet-le-Duc. However, this machine has a moveable weight box, so it does not correspond to the *trabicium*, but rather to the *biffa* of Aegidius. Who of the two was wrong, the learned cardinal or the practical architect? I find myself unable to decide this question; suppose, however, that the cardinal, in a finished book that he submitted to the critique of experts, was more guilty of error than the architect, who sketched the drawings and made the notes only for his own use."

This crisis of conscience can be resolved in the easiest manner if we simply trace the origins of this image. Schultz borrowed the picture from Viollet-le-Duc, who in turn took the picture from Lassus's book *Album de Villard de Honnecourt*, Paris 1858 p. 204. In this book, however, the picture has no signature at all, and it is not even within the sketchbook, but rather, it is borrowed from elsewhere in Lassus so that the readers get a replacement for a picture that is missing in the manuscript of the sketchbook. Simply to elucidate his readers as to what is actually mentioned, Lassus has inserted two miniature depictions from other manuscripts into his text: first, the above-mentioned image

---

[119] Alwin Schultz, "Das hoefische Leben zur Zeit der Minnesinger." Leipzig, 1889. II 380.

from the Manessian Manuscript of Songs, and, secondly, an image from an unspecified French manuscript of the XIV century.[120] Thus, the picture wrongly attributed to the Picard architect is, at best, on par with that from the Manessian, but in order to authenticate them, their origin would need to be determined beforehand.

Accordingly, Lassus is innocent of the misunderstandings of the latter, for he has clearly stated the facts.

4: Villard de Honnecourt

From the sketches of Villard de Honnecourt comes a plan for the trebuchet with an explanatory note detailing its construction. The following is written beneath the drawing in the Paris manuscript (National Library codex S. G. latin 1104 fol 30):

> "*Se vus voles faire le fort engieng con apiele trebucet prendes ci gard. Ves ent ci les sole si com il siet sor tierre. Wes la devant les II. windas et le corde ploie a coi on ravale le verge. Veir le poes en cele autre pagene.* [The next page is missing from the manuscript.] *Il i a grant fais al ravaler, car li contrpois est mult pezans. Car il i a une huge plainne de tierre, ki II grans toizes a de lonc, et VIIII pies de le, et XII pies de profont. Et al descocier de la fleke penses, et si vus en donez gard. Car ille doit estre atenue a cel estan con la devant.*"

In English, this roughly translates to:

[120] Pg 264: Of the stone throwing trebuchets closest to the text of Villard de Honnecourt, we have two miniature versions presented here from the fourteenth century, one from Germany and the other French.

"We have pictured here the siege engine known as the trebuchet. We see here only the front of the machine as it sat on the ground. The two windlasses at the front draw back the ropes to pull back the engine. See the poem on the next page for more information. [The next page is missing from the manuscript.] It has entirely to do with the projectile, for the control is of great weight. As well, this machine has a huge footprint, being almost 200 feet high, sixty feet long, and twelve feet wide. With all of this considered, it must still be thought of as though from the base."

The transcription into Modern French by Lassus, as well as its accompanying explanations, is deficient, as are those of Viollet-le-Duc.[121] However, it is beyond me to judge whether or not there are engineering details that need to be corrected here. As Villard de Honnecourt is the only technically trained author to describe lever powered artillery, I would like to call particular attention to his work, as it may be of particular interest to reconstructionists that would like to study the words and drawings produced by this clever XIII century architect.

5: Konrad Kyeser

The representations given to us in the military manual "Bellifortis" come from an expert warrior. The primary manuscript is the centerpiece of the Göttingen library (cod. Ms Phil 63) because off the numerous, excellent scale drawings in it, the majority of which are hand drawn by the author Konrad Kyeser. The text, however, is less than praiseworthy, for the author writes poor prose, and his Latin hexameter forces rhyme too much, so that it defies all laws of logic and quantity.

---

[121] Viollet-le-Duc. *Dictionnaire raisonné de le'architecture française.* Paris 1861. V p. 224 ff.

Konrad Kyeser was a Frankish nobleman born to the city of Eichstädt in the year 1366, as his verse under the self-portrait of folio 139 professes:

Annis millenis praeteritis atque trecentis
Et sexaginta senis Mercurii di transactis
Post festum sancti Barth. Apos excoriati
Kyeser Konradus Eystetensis sum mundo natus.

"Three hundred years, as well as the thousand that have passed,
Another sixty and six, on the day of the god Mercury
Just after the Feast of Saint Bartholomew, amid great pain
Kyeser Konradus Eystetensis was born into the world."

According to his statement in the *Praefatio*, Konrad was famous amongst the princes of Europe as the most knowledgeable of warriors. However, he must have fallen out of favor, for the dedication of his manuscript to Kaiser Ruprecht von der Pfalz shows that he was living in exile (in Bohemia) at the time that he concluded the work: *Datum sub castro Mendici in habitatione Exulis a. D. MCCCCV*. "The supplicant is living in exile, dated 1405."

The Göttingen manuscript has two pictures depicting trebuchets contained on folios 30 and 48. The first picture is missing its description, as the space reserved for it on the reverse of folio 29 is empty. However, the following description of the picture on folio 48 can be found on the reverse of folio 47:

Haec est blida grandis, qua castra cuncta vincuntur.
Nam lapides proicit, turres et moenias scindit,
Oppida castella urbes reserat civitates.

"This is the giant *blida*, by which all are vanquished.
By the stones it throws, towers and walls are destroyed.
Fortified towns, cities, and villages are laid open before it."

Thus, the name *blida* is firmly appended to the second engine. However, because Kyeser called it the *grandis*, it remains uncertain whether he would have named the first engine the *blida communis*, or if he would have used something like *Tribok, Manga*, *et cetera*. Yet, that should not bother us much, for the primary consideration is that the unnamed engine in the picture is excellently drawn. The robust construction of the posts carries the arm of the engine, which rotates about a strong bolt, the head of which thickens considerably. An iron sheet held in place by many nails protects the wooden heads of the vertical posts. The arm is pulled down by winding ropes that from the arm to a winch. The drum of the winch sits between two strong posts, and the two exterior sides of the winch have handspikes extending from them, so that the gun teams may rotate the drum. The ropes attached to the tip of the arm connect it to the stone ball in the projectile trough. The box for the counterweight hangs from the short end of the lever arm; however, the box is both empty and not hanging vertically from the pivot bolt. The draughtsman has included these two deviations, which the viewer may easily correct in their mind, in order to demonstrate more clearly the construction of the wooden counterweight box. The ladder resting against the front of the posts was used to fill the box and to lubricate the bolt at the support point of the arm, or when anything else needed to be done on top of the engine. Three wooden poles are hammered into the top side of the arm for similar reasons. The device for pushing the box forward is not visible. There is a mistake in the drawing in the presence of the board beneath the support points of the arm, for this board would inhibit the free movement of the arm. That Kyeser erred here simply out of carelessness is evident from the picture of the other engine.

On the large engines (*blida grandis*), the arm has its path completely clear. The box is suspended immediately below its pivot bolt by iron bands, though it is shown empty here as well. The arm is shown in cross-section on the longer lever arm, but the tip of the arm as shown in this drawing is in error, for now it is shaped like a spoon. This cannot be seriously implied as being the actuality, for this spoon is in place of the sling. There must, instead, be an iron hook or pin here, the position of which is, according to Sanutus, of significant influence on the range of the projectile. Engines that have a spoon instead of a sling are strongly deficient in range, and they are generally only useful for burning projectiles. However, the "Big Blida", as its name indicates, was a powerful, long-range engine, and, therefore, a complicated device was constructed as part of it in order to pull down the arm as part of tensioning it. The arm was powered by particularly heavy counterweights. The teams serving the weapon were protected from the enemy by a wooden wall.

The "Bellifortis" is preserved in a series of manuscripts, but all of them are inferior to the Göttingenmanuscript. Sometimes it is only the merest small extracts with badly drawn pictures that are completely worthless, such as the Heidelberg Codec Palat. Germ. 787. Among the better manuscripts is a copy from the Innsbruck Library (XXIX f. 7), in which a later editor has inserted a sketch of the *blide* and the following description of it on folio 20's reverse:

> "*Nota daz antwerch sol gemacht werden in dem dryangel, und der seyten aine sol haben 48 werchschuch, und halben so vil unten tberch uber der sweller sol auch alzo lang sein bis zu dem nagel, darnach bis zu dem nagel, der an dem kasten hangt, sol sein 8 schuech. - Daz loch in den sweller, dar inn er get in dem antwerch, sol sein unthalb der mittel riss, mitten in dem sweller daz ander loch zu dem mittel ryss. - Die sayl mit den halsen so sy eingezogen synd, sullen nit lenger sein dan pis mitten auff dem*

antwerchnagel; die selben leng der sail man man mit auff daz weytist werffen. Wildu aber neher werffen, so mach daz ain sail an dem swenkel kürzer und daz ander dail in der halsen; alzo magstu verr oder nohent werffen. Der nagel, daran der sweller get, sol in dem sweller sinbel sein und in dem antwerch bey dem haupt geviert. Der hinterist nagel in dem sweller, daran der kasten hangt, sol in dem sweller geviert sein und in dem kasten sinwel."[122]

In rough English, this is,

"Note that the construction of the supports should be in the form of a triangle, and the arm should be of 48 units in total length. The half that is the lower arm of the trebuchet should also be as long, therefore, as 8 units long from the nail about which the arm turns to the nail from which the basket hangs. A hole pierced the top of the support, which then passed the pivot nail through the arm, and then it passed through a hole in the other support. The ropes and chains of the sling should extend to under the middle of the pivot nail and no further to achieve the longest shot. When one wishes to shoot more closely, then one should shorten the sling or adjust the chains, and thus it will be possible to shoot at nearer targets. The nail that passes through the supports should be mobile at the arm and rotating at the supports. Similarly, the foremost nail, that from which the basket hangs, should be fixed at the basket and rotating in the arm."

While there is little to be found in emendations from such unknown writers, the initial account of Konrad Kyeser from the year 1405 is quite valuable as a source.

---

[122] Compare to Alwin Schultz, "Das hoefische Leben zur Zeit der Minnesinger." Leipzig, 1889. II 384.

6: Wurstisen of Basel's Chronicle

About a generation later, a trebuchet was still in successful operation, as the Basel Chronicle of 1445 testifies,[123] "There is also a room with a throwing machine that stood in the churchyard, so that in times of great need during defense it could throw gravestones and the like."

However, of greater importance to us is that the author, Christian Wurstisen, who was the Freyer Professor of Mathematics at the Academy of Basel and died in the year 1588, included in his book a drawing of the above described machine. Its caption reads, "Such a throwing machine was first built by the city of Basel in the year 1424; it was first assembled and tested in front of the Gate of Spalen."

The picture also has the following clarifications.

> "The rear part of the moving beam, which is somewhat thicker and weighted with an unspeakably heavy load, is raised upwards by means of a reel, and, hereby the front of the beam, to which the sling is attached, is brought down to the Earth. The sling is then tethered by a rope to a heavy stone, weighing many centners.[124] When the trigger rope is pulled: the beam swings due the downward movement of the heavy, hanging load, the stone is flung into the air, and it abjectly destroys whatever it stikes."

---

[123] Christian Wurstisen, *Chronicle of Basel*, published in Basel 1765, p. 422.

[124] Translator's Note: The exact value of the centner is unknown in this case, for it was simply a word meaning 100 of the base unit of weight. Contemporary English has the similar word "hundredweight". In modern usage, centner typically refers to 100kg; however, the kilogram was not yet invented at this period. Standardized measurements would have to wait until the Napoleonic era to begin their debut. We may reasonably assume that this stone weighed in the 200-300 pound range.

Furthermore, all of the parts associated with the trebuchet are described alongside it. We see the "hanging box, loaded and filled with the heaviest weights," "the short rope holding back the beam," and even the word "*lapis*" or stone.

The pictorial depictions of the lever powered engines is, therefore, more than sufficient to give us clear insight into the construction of these strange machine, and they have also shown us the differences between the fixed and moving counterweight. Even if we have not always succeeded in providing particular names for the individual forms of engines, this is probably due to the arbitrariness and ignorance of the Medieval authors themselves, for they likely could not distinguish the various forms of engine themselves and even used pleasant names as mere ornamentation without support. This defect in their work can be overcome. However, it is most unfortunate that we cannot gain any form of definitive, tangible clue, either through the drawings or the text, of the weight of the counterweights or of the stone balls, and the design of the sling apparatus, which was absolutely necessary for proper shooting, remains in the dark.

Reconstructions

1: Dufour

As it is not possible to determine either the range or effects of shooting, neither the historian nor the artillerist can be even remotely satisfied with the final results of the investigations thus far. We are not helped by mere mathematical calculations, and the paper constructions of Viollet-le-Duc border on misleading. The only correct way has already been struck upon by the Swiss officer Dufour, and his discoveries thus far are quite commendable, particularly as his limited resources were only sufficient for him to build a small model:[125]

> "I noticed, not without surprise, that the range of the machine was almost doubled by the addition of the sling; that is, the same ball that was thrown 6 meters with the spoon was thrown 11 meters with the sling which was only a little shorter than the length of the long arm of the lever. The long arm was 51 cm and the sling was 43 cm. The short arm was only 17 cm."

There is no doubt, in responding to the observations of the wise officer, that he was not aware of the literary sources. In his model, the arm (total length of 68 cm) is divided into a ratio of 1:3 (17 cm:51 cm), rather than either of those ratios prescribed by the instructions of Marinus Sanutus, either 11:49 or 1:5. That said, the Swiss officer has performed a great service in that he showed his successors the way to achieve this goal.

---

[125] G.H. Dufour, officer of engineers. *Mémoire sur l'Artillerie des anciens et sur celle du moyen-âge.* Paris-Genève 1840, p. 91.

2: Napoleon and Favé

We have previously established (chapter 1, section 3) how Napoleon III, to his great merit, had compiled a history of artillery. However, that is not all. His captivity in Ham later brought back to his mind the thoughts that had occurred to him during his solitude. As the President of the Republic, he promoted in both word and deed the reconstruction of a trebuchet of the period size, a task with which the War Department commissioned Captain Favé. Sadly, the engine has not survived, and we no longer even possess drawings of it. That is likely why today's military writers have taken so little notice of it. At least, however, we have the report that Captain Favé submitted to the Ministry, and it is from this source alone that we know a great deal of important information concerning the performance of the trebuchet. This information should readily correct a whole range of the prevailing opinions and ideas that are expressed today.

The reconstruction in Vincennes had as its basis the information of Marinus Sanutus. The rod had a length of 10.30 meters, with a length of 10 meters from the tip to the pivot bolt of the counterweight and 0.30 meters from the bolt to the end. The counterweight consisted of two portions: 1,500 kilograms had been attached permanently and directly to the rod, and a further 3,000 kilograms were loaded into a box that hung below the arm from an iron bolt. The ropes of the sling measured 5 meters in length, as measured from the tip of the arm to the sling bag in which the ball rested. The length of the sling had been determined by Napoleon himself, and, likewise, he gave particular instructions for the position of the iron hook at the tip of the rod. Both components are of the utmost importance for the timely release of the ball and the range of the shot. Other things, such as the proper choice of wood (oak) for the arm and the correct position of the winches to draw down the arm, had to be determined experimentally in the trial exercises. After all, the results of the demonstration were as follows:

> "It threw a cannonball of 24 kilograms to 175 meters, a bomb of 22 centimeters diameter that had been filled with sand to 145 meters, and bombs of 27 and 32 centimeters to 120 meters. The lateral deviation of the projectiles was quite small: it never exceeded 3 meters."

Unfortunately, these experiments could not be repeated further, for the frame of the engine was too weak and they feared misfortune. Of course, it was even less possible to think of burdening this understrength machine with a counterweight of 8,000 kilograms, as Napoleon had intended. Thus, while this reconstruction did not fully achieve what it was intended to determine, it is yet of the utmost importance for establishing a correct conception of this strange form of artillery, a type of machine in regards to which the layman is quite at a loss to comprehend how to shoot. In addition, this reconstruction had a much greater significance, "For it was impossible to understand properly the Medieval siege as long as one did not know the throwing machines that served both in the attack and in the defense."[126]

I collected what was left of Napoleon's reconstruction with great care, but I could not, unfortunately, find more than what few words are printed in the appendices. The lost drawings, however, could have been replaced, and what is missing in that report could easily be taken from such hand-drawn pictures. However, I have purposefully renounced this course, which many readers will miss, so that no one may be led to believe that this historical investigation had brought to a conclusion the questions of Medieval artillery, for the proceeds of literary research are to be found in words and pictures on paper. Not even close! Just as the

---

[126] See the appendices.

artillery of antiquity was revived only through the reconstructions of Colonel Schramm,[127] so too can only the reconstructor bring the trebuchet again to life. My work strives towards this goal, and it would be my greatest reward if the promoters of Medieval history not only rebuilt the walls of castles, but also brought these most important weapons of war before our very eyes.

[127] Translator's Note: Later Lieutenant General Schramm.

Appendices

1: Procopios

De bello Gothico I 21, 2ff (from Jacobus Haury Lipsiae, 1905.)

21

2. Ούίττιγις δὲ ταῦτα ἀκούσας τειχομαχεῖν τε πολλῇ σπουδῇ ἐβουλεύετο καὶ τὰ ἐς τὴν τοῦ περιβόλου ἐπιβουλὴν ἐξηρτύετο ὧδε.
3. Πύργους ξυλίνους ἐποιήσατο ἴσους τῷ τείχει τῶν πολεμίων, καὶ ἔτυχέ γε τοῦ ἀληθοῦς μέτρου πολλάκις συμμετρησάμενος ταῖς
4. Τῶν λίθων ἐπιβολαῖς. Τούτοις δὲ τοῖς πύργοις τροχοὶ ἐς τὴν βάσιν ἐμβεβλημένοι πρὸς γωνίᾳ ἑκάστῃ ὑπέκειντο, οἳ δή αὐτοὺς κυλινδούμενοι ῥᾷστα περιάξειν ἔμελλον, ὅπη οἱ τειχομαχοῦντες ἀεὶ βούλοιντο, καὶ βόες τοὺς πύργους συνδεδεμένοι εἷλκον.
5. Ἔπειτα δὲ κλίμακας πολλάς τε τὸ πλῆθος καὶ ἄχρι ἐς τὰς ἐπάλξεις ἐξικνουμένας ἡτοίμαζε καὶ μηχανὰς τέσσαρας, α□ κριοὶ κα-
6. λοῦνται. Ἔστι δὲ ἡ μηχανὴ τοιαύτη. κίονες ὀρθοὶ ξύλινοι τέσσαρες ἀντίοι τε καὶ ἶσοι □ἀλλήλοις ἑστᾶσι. Τούτοις δὲ τοῖς κίοσι δοκοὺς ὀκτὼ ἐγχαροντες τέσσαρας μὲν ἄνω, τοσαύτας δὲ πρὸς
7. Ταῖς βάσεσιν ἐναρμόξουσιν. Οἰκίκου τε σχῆμα τετραγώνου ἐργαζόμενοι προκάλυμμα πανταχόθεν ἀντὶ τοίχων τε καὶ

τείχους διφθέρας αύτῷ περιβάλλουσιν, ὅπως ἥ τε μηχανὴ τοῖς ἕλκουσιν ἐλαφρὰ εἴη καὶ οἱ ἔνδον ἐν ἀσφαλεῖ ὦσιν, ώς πρὸς τῶν ἐναντίων

8. Ἥκιστα βάλλεσθαι. Ἐντὸς δὲ αὐτῆς δοκὸν ἑτέραν ἄνωθεν ἐγκαρσίαν ἀρτήσαντες χαλαραῗς ταῖς ἁλύσεσι κατὰ μέσην μάλιστα τὴν μηχανὴν ἔχουσιν. Ἧς δὴ ὀξεῖαν ποιούμενοι τὴν ἄκραν, σιδήρῳ πολλῷ καθάπερ ἀκίδα καλύπτουσι βέλους, ἢ καὶ τετράγωνον,

9. Ὥσπερ ἄκμονα, τὸν σίδηρον ποιοῦσι. Καὶ τροχοῖς μὲν ἡ μηχανὴ τέσσαρσι πρὸς κίονι ἑκάστῳ κειμένιος ἐπῆρται, ἄνδρες δὲ αὐτὴν

10. Οὐχ ἧσσον ἢ κατὰ πεντήκοντα κινοῦσιν ἔνδοθεν. Οἳ ἐπειδὰν αὐτὴν τῷ περιβόλῳ ἐρείσωσι, τὴν δοκόν, ἧς δὴ ἄρτι ἐμνήσθην, μηχανῇ τινι στρέφοντες ὀπίσω ἀνέλκουσιν, αὖθις τε αὐτὴν ξὺν

11. Ῥύμῃ πολλῇ ἐπὶ τὸ τεῖχος ἀφιᾶσιν. Ἡ δὲ συχνὰ ἐμγαλλομένη κατασεῖσαί τε ὅπη προσπίπτοι καὶ διελεῖν ῥᾷστα οἵα τέ ἐστι, καὶ ἀπ’ αὐτοῦ τὴν ἐπωνυμίαν ταύτην ἡ μηχανὴ ἔχει, ἐπεὶ τῆς δοκοῦ ταύτης ἡ ἐμβολὴ προὔχουσα πλήσσειν ὅπου παρατύχοι,

12. Καθάπερ τῶν προβάτων τὰ ἄρρενα, εἴωθε. Τῶν μὲν οὖν τειχοναχούντων οἱ κριοί τοιοίδε εἰσί.

13. Γότθοι δὲ πάμπολύ τι φακέλλων χρῆμα ἔκ τε ξύλων καὶ καλάμων ποιησάμενοι ἐν παρασκευῇ εἶχον, ὅπως δὴ ἐς τὴν ὑάφρον ἐμβαλόντες δμαλόν τε τὸν χῶρον ἐρλάωνται καὶ ταύσῃ διαβαίνειν αἱ μηχαναὶ ἥκιστα εἴργωνται. Οὕτω μὲν δὴ Γότθοι παρασκευασάμενοι τειχομαχεῖν ὥρμηντο.

14. Βελισάριος δὲ μηχανὰς μὲν ἐς τοὺς πύργους ἐτίθετο, ἃς καλοῦσι βαλλίστρας. Τόξου δὲ σχῆμα ἔχουσιν αἱ μηχαναὶ αὖται, ἔνερθέν τε αὐτοῦ κοίλη τις ξυλίνη κεραία προὔχει, αὐτὴ μὲν

15. Χαλαρὰ ἠρτημένη, σιδηρᾷ δὲ εὐθείᾳ τινὶ ἐπικειμένη. Ἐπειδὰυ οὖν τοὺς πολεμίους ἐνθένδε βάλλειν ἐθέλουσιν ἄνθρωποι, βρόχου βραχέος ἐνέρσει τὰ ξύλα ἐς ἄλληλα νεύειν ποιοῦσιν, ἃ δὴ τοῦ τόξου ἄκρα ξυμβαίνει εἶναι, τόν τε ἅπερ ἐν τῇ κοίλῃ κεραίᾳ τίθενται, τῶν ἄλλων βελῶν, ἅπερ ἐκ τῶν τόξων ἀφιᾶσι, μῆκος

16. Μὲν ἔχοντα ἥμισυ μάλιστα, εὗρος δὲ κατὰ τετραπλάσιον. Πτεροῖς μέντοι οὐ τοῖς εἰωθόσιν ἐνέχεται, ἀλλὰ ξύλα λεπτὰ ἐς τῶν πτερῶν τὴν χώραν ἐνείροντες ὅλον ἀπομιμοῦνται τοῦ βέλους τὸ τχῆμα, μεγάλην αὐτῷ λίαν καὶ τοῦ πάχους κατὰ λόγον τὴν

17. Ἀκίδα ἐμβάλλοντες. Σφίγγουσί τε ⟨σθένει⟩ πολλῷ οἱ ἀμφοτέρωθεν μηχαναῖς τισι, καὶ τότε ἡ κοίλη κεραία προιοῦσα ἐκπίπτει[128] μὲν, ξὺν ῥύμῃ δὲ τοσαύτῃ ἐκπίπτει τὸ

βέλος ὥστε ἐξικνεῖται μὲν οὐχ ἧσσον ἢ κατὰ δὺο τῆς τοξείας βολάς, δένδρου δὲ ἢ λίθου

18. Ἐπιτυχὸν τέμνει ῥᾳδίως. Τοιαύτη μὲν ἡ μηχανή ἐστιν ἐπὶ τοῦ ὀνόματος τούτου, ὅτι δὴ βάλλει ὡς μάλιστα, ἐπικληθεῖσα. Ἑτέρας δὲ μηχανὰς ἐπήξαντο ἐν ταῖς τοῦ περιβόλον ἐπάλξεσιν ἐς λιθων

19. Βολὰς ἐπιτηδείας. Σφενδόνῃ δὲ αὗταί εἰσιν ἐμφερεῖς καὶ ὄναγροι ἐπικαλοῦνται. Ἐν δὲ ταῖς πύλαις λύκους ἔξω ἐπετίθεντο, οὓς δὴ

20. Ποιοῦσι τρόπῳ τοιῷδε. Δοκοὺς δύο ἱστᾶσιν ἐκ γῆς ἄχρι καὶ ἐς τὰς ἐπάλξεις ἐξικνουμένας, ξύλα τε εἰργασμένα ἐπ' ἄλληλα θέμενοι τὰ μὲν ὀρθά, τὰ δὲ ἐγκάρσια ἐναρμόζουσιν, ὡς τῶν ἐνέρ-

21. Σεων τὰ. Ἐν μέσῳ εἰς ἀλλήλους τρυπήματα φαίνεσθαι. Ἑκάστης δὲ ἁρμονίας ἐμβολή τις προὔχει, κέντρῳ παχεῖ ἐς τὰ μάλιστα ἐμφερὴς οὖσα. Καὶ τῶν ξύλων τὰ ἐγκάρσια ἐς δοκὸν ἑκατέραν πηξάμενοι, ἄνωθεν ἄχρι ἐς μοῖραν διήκοντα τὴν ἡμίσειαν, ὑπτίας

22. Τὰς δοκοὺς ἐπὶ τῶν πυλῶν ἀνακλίνουσι. Καὶ ἐπειδὰν αὐτῶν ἐγγυτέρω οἱ πολέμιοι ἵκωνται, οἱ δὲ ἄνωθεν ἄκρων δοκῶν

---

[128] Ἐκπίπτει has entered the text here improperly, for the following reason. The "grooved, wooden slat", ie the Diostra, stops as it reaches the rear, and only the "hand" attached to it moves upwards, thereby releasing the string. This process is what the above translation attempts to express.

ἁψάμενοι ὠθοῦσιν, αὗται δὲ ἐς τοὺς ἐπιόντας ἐκ τοῦ αἰφνιδίου ἐμπίπτουσαι τοῖς προέχουσι τῶν ἐμβολῶν, ὅσους ἂν λάβοιεν, εὐπετῶς κτείνουσι. Βελισάριος μὲν οὖν ταῦτα ἐποίεί.

2: Richeri Historiarum libri IV

The Siege of the Fortress of Leon, 938
MG SS II 589, 29 sq.:

Fecit itaque ex vehementissimis lignis compactis machinam instar longilaterae domus duodecim virorum capacem, humani corporis staturae in alto aequalem. Cuius parietes de ingenti lingorum robore, tectum ver de duris ac intextis cratibus exstruxit. Cui etiam intrinsecus rotas quattuor adhibuit, unde machina ab iis qui intrinsecus leterent usque ad arcem impelleretur. At tectum non aeque stratum fuit, verum ab acumine dextra laevaque dependebar, ut iactis lapidisibus facilius lapsum praeberet. Quae exstructa tironibus mox impleta est ac ad arcem rotis mobilibus impulsa. Quam cum a superioribus hostes rupibus opprimere conarentur, a sagittariis undique dispositis contumeliose repulsi sunt. Ad arcem itaque machina deducta muruss ex parte suffossus atque eversus est. Hostes mulittudinem armatorum per hunc hiatum possibile introduci formidantes arma deponunt ac regiam clementiam implorant. Rex ergo amplius tumultuari prohibens intactos paene comprehendit, praeter hos qui in militari tumult sauciati fuere, suosque ad urbis tutelam in arce deposuit.

The Siege of the Fortress of Leon, 989
MG SS III 635, 53 sq.:

Interea rigore hiemali elapso cum aëre mitiori ver rebus arrideret et prata atque campos virescere faceret, reges exercitu collecto urbem praedictam cum octo milibus aggressi sunt. Castra inprimis aggere et fossa muniunt. Inde ex struitur aries frangendis muris.

Cuius machinam ex quattuor mirae grossitudinis et longitudinis trabibus longilatero schemate erexerunt, in cacumine et basi per quattuor latera repagulis transverse annexis; in medio vero solummodo laevum latus et dextrum ligna transmissa habuere. At super trabium erectarum superiores commissura longurios duos straverunt immotosque effecerunt, partem tertiam superioris spatii trabium in medio obtinentes; a quibus longuriis funes implicitos deposuerunt. Funibus quoque trabem cum ferrato capite multae grossitudinis suspenderunt. Cui etiam trabi in medio et extremo funes alligatos adhibuerunt, qui a multitudine tracti et remissi ferratae moli motum darent. Unde et huiusmodi machina quia more ariestis retro tracta, ante cum impetu ruit, aries appelatur, cuiuscunque soliditatis muris frangendis aptissimus. Quam etiam machinam super tres rotas triangulo schemate positam aptaverunt, quo facilius obliquata, quocunque oporteret, verti valeret. At quia urbis situs accedere prohibuit, eo quod ipsa urbs in eminenti montis cacumine eminet, aries fabricatus cessit.

The Siege of Verdun, 984

MG SS III 629, 23 sq.:

Lignorum trabes ex Argonna aggregari iusserunt, ut, si ab hostibus extra machinae muris applicarentur, ipsi quoque interius obtinentibus machinis obstare molinrentur. Crates quoque viminibus et arborum frondibus validas intexuerunt, machinis erectis, si res exposceret, supersternendos. Sudes ferro acuminatos et igne subustos ad hostes quamplures aptaverunt. Missilia varii generis per fabros transfodiendos expediere. Funium millena volumina ad usus diversos convexerunt. Clipeos quoque habendae testudini ordinandos instituerunt. Praeterea centena mortis tormenta non defuere.

Nuntiantur haec Lothario. Qui tantum facinus accidisse acerrime indignatus exercitum dimissum revocavit; et sic cum decem milibus pugnatorum Virdunum petiit atque adversarios repentinus aggressus est. Primo impetu sagittarii contra hostes ordinati sunt. Missaeque sagittae et arcoballistae cum aliis missilibus tam densae in aëre discurrebant, ut a nubibus dilabi terraque exsurgere viderentur. Horum contra impetum testudinem ante se et super capita hostes muro aptavere; in quam relisa missilia ictu frustrato decidebant. Hoc impetu facto Galli circumquaque obsidionem disposuere; fossisque praeruptis obfirmaverunt castra, ne, si ad incautos adversarii prosilirent, accessum facilem invenirent.

Quercus proceras radicitus succisas ad machinam bellicam exstruendam advexerunt. Ex quibus quattuor trabes tricenorum pedum straverunt solo, ita ut duae in longitudinem proiectae et decem pedum intervallo distinctae duabus aliis per transversum eodem intervallo superiacentibus cohaererent. Longitudinis et latitudinis spatium, quod intra commissuras earum tenebatur, decem pedum erat. Quidquid etiam a commissuris extra proiectum erat, simili modo decem pedibus distendebatur. In harum trabium commissuris quattuor sublicas quadragenorum pedum, quadrato quidem schemate sed procero, aequo spatio a se distantes, adhibitis torcleis erexerunt. Transposueruntque bis per quattuor latera festucas decem pedum, in medio scilicet et in summo, quae traductae sublicas sibi fortiter annecterent. A capitibus vero trabium, quibus sublicae nitebantur, quattuor trabes eductae et paene usque ad festucas superiores obliquatae sublicis iungebantur, ut sic ex iis machina extrinsecus firmata non titubaret. Super festucas quoque, quae in medio et in summo machinam connectebant, tigna straverunt. Quae etiam cratibus contexerunt, super quas dimicaturi stantes et eminentiores facti adversarios deorsum iaculis et lapidibus obruerent. Hanc molem exstructam ad stationem hostium deducere cogitabant. Sed quia sagittarios suspectos hebebant, rationem quaerebant, qua hostibus sine suorum laesione appropinquaret. Tandem ratione subtilius perscruntante repertum est eam ad hostes optima arte detrudi posse.

Dictabant enim quattuor stipites multae grossitudinis terrae solidae mandandos, decem pedibus in terra defossis, octo vero a terra erectis; qui etiam transpositis per quattuor latera repagulis vehementissimis solidarentur. Repagulis quoque transmissis funes inserendos; sed funium capita ab hostibus abducta, superiora quidem machinae, inferiora vero bobus annecterentur; at inferiora longius superioribus protenderentur. Superiora vero breviore ductu machinam implicitam haberent, ita ut inter hostes et boves machina staret. Unde et fieret, ut quanto boves ab hostibus trahendo discederent, tanto machina hostibus attracta propinquaret. Quo commento, cylindris suppositis, quibus facilius motum acciperet, machina hostibus nullo laeso appulsa est.

Adversarii quoque similem quidem machinam exstruunt sed altitudine et robore inferiorem. Utraque ergo exstructa a parte utraque ascensum est; conflictumque ab utrisque promptissime, nec tamen ullo modo cedunt. Rex cum propior muris adesset, fundae iaculo in labroo superiore sauciactus est. Cuius inuria sui accensi vehementius bello incubuere. Et quia hostes machina et armis fortes nullantenus cedebant, rex uncinos ferreos adhiberi praecepit/ Qui funibus alligatis cum hostium machinae iniecti essent lignisque transversis admorsi, funes alii demittebant, alii demissos excipiebant, quibus adversariorum machina inclinata atque paene demersa est. Unde alii delabentes per lignorum commissuras descendebant, alii vero saltu sese ad terram demittebant, nonnulli quoque turpi formidine tacti latibulis vitam sibi defendebant. Hostes mortis periculum urgere videntes adversariis cedunt vvitamque supplices petunt; iussi quoque arma deponunt et reddunt. Statimque a rege decretum exivit, hostes sine aliqua ultionis iniuria comprehendendos ac illaesos sibi adducendos. Comprehensi itaque inermes ac indemnes praeter ictus, quos in militari tumultu acceperant, ante regem admissi sunt; qui regis pedibus advoluti vitam petebant, nam regiae maiestatis rei atque convicti de vita diffidebant.

3: Marinus Sanutus, dicus Torsellus

Liber Secretorum Fidelium Crucis Super Terrae Sanctae Recuperatione et Conservatione

(Bongars, Gesta Dei per Francos. Hanoviae 1611. Tom II p79).

Lib. II pars IV. cap 22:

De industria faciendi ar,a, et potissime de construendis machinis et ballistis, quae a longe machinent et ballistent; ac de industria et cautela perficiendi totum quod dignoscitur ad praedictas.

Et cum generaliter et partialiter specificatum sit superius et narratum, quae gens est in hoc sancto negotio opportuna; et quidquid est in praedicto navigio exigendum; et de armis aliquid dictum fuerit similiter, quae sunt necessaria in praedicto (licet non tantum ad plenum quantum mihi videtur fore dicendum): idcirco aliquid tangam, quam potero breviter de praedictis, cum aliquorum ingeniatorum consilio sapientum; nihilominus quidquid dixero cum emendatione sollertium praedicti exercitus enarrabo, et incipiam isto modo.

Primum quod arma defensibilia levia decet esse, ut in iis homines bene valeant se iuvare, et etiam quod defensibilia sint in tantum, in quantum fieri poterunt supradicta. Secundum quod arma quae deputata fuerint ad laedendum talia similiter fore debent, quibus uti bene et habiliter valeant pugnatores. Et licet in praedicto negotio duo sint armorum offendibilium genera opportuna, scilicet ad feriendum cum talio sive puncta, ut superius est expressum, tamen maius inferunt periculum inimicis magisque nocent etiam antedictis, quae cum punctis fuerint ad feriendum proprie deputata, quam illa quae ad abscidendum fiunt absque punctis, quibus duobus sapientes dicti exercitus uti praecipient bellatores, quae pro gente armatae praedictae sibi magis utilia videbuntur.

Ceterum prae ceteris est memoriae commendandum, quod ex longinquo offendere suos hostes tutius est offensoribus, quam eos offendere de propinquo. Et ideo utile comprobabtur, quod omnes maneries tam machinarum quam ballistarum grossarum, quamque etiam aliarum fiant lontanariae atque tales quae in tantum a longe trahant, in quantum ad trahendum longius fieri poterunt supradictae. Circa quod exsequendum multum decet ingeniatores et sapientes exercitus antedicti acuere mentem suam; quoniam si sagittamen tam lapidum machinarum quam telorum longius trahitur quam sagittamen hoostium sagittetur, revera dici potest, quod illa pars, cuius longius trahitur sagittamen, ab altera praerogativam obtinet valde magnam. Nam si Christianorum sagittamen pervenire poterit ad exercitum Paganorum, quorum sagittamen pervenire non poterit ad exercitum Christianum, porro dici potest, quod ex hoc Christiani victoriam reportarent, vel terram et plateam obtinerent continuo super hostes. Et si quis argueret hoc modo: Infideles trahent se anterius et taliter exercebunt, quod sagittamen suum gentem fidelem exercitus sauciabit; huic argumentationi potest taliter responderi, quod ex hoc semper praerogativa aliqua remanet Christianis, quoniam multo maiores erunt ictus, quos sagittamen machinarum inferet ac ballistarum Fidelium Jesu Christi, quam sagittamen Infidelium praedictorum, qui non erunt a Christiano exercitu tam longinqui. Ex quo faciendum est, ut superius est expressum, totum et quidquid fieri potest pro habendis bonis ingeniatoribus ac bono lignamine et perfecto, praesertim ad faciendas perticas atque genas capsarum machinarum, atque ballistarum arcus pro hac praerogativa penitus adsequenda. Et ad hoc ut, quod superius est narratum, ingeniatores praefati causam habeant melius faciendi, aliquod praeambulum inchoabo: et dicam prius de machina communi, ad hoc ut inter machinam communem et machinam lontanariam quae sit differentia cognoscatur.

Ad communem machinam faciendam debent coxae machinae antedictae tanto in soliis fore amplae, quanto alta est praefata machina in castello; ac debet praefata machina desubtus esse aperta in soliis inter duas coxas tertia parte minus: hoc est, si praedicta machina altitudine XXIV pedum extenditur in castello, latitudinem[129] in soliis XVI pedum debet praedicta machina possidere. Dividunt magistri perticam machinae supradictae a fuso capsae usque ad summitatem supremam per quintam et per sextam, et ponitur fusum praedicti castelli inter quintum et sextum; videlicet quod si praedicta pertica est longa longitudine XXX pedum a fuso praedictae capsae usque ad summitatem, quintum illud est VI pedes, et illud sextum superius nominatum V cernitur fore pedes. Qua de re ponitur fusum dicti castelli a longe V pedibus et domidio a fuso capsae superius nominatae.

De machina lontanaria construenda

Debet poni praedictum fusum castelli solum ad V pedes perticae, si erit pertica longitudine XXX pedum; scilicet ad sextum perticae, mensurando a fuso capsae usque ad summitatem perticae. Et debet poni in hunc modum videlicet, quod lineatur pertica per medium, et a latere dictae lineae versus latus mannettae poni debet fusum capsae, tangendo ipsam lineam medii, et ab alio latere tangendo ipsam eandem lineam medii fusum castelli. Debentque stringi latera tibiarum versus fusum machinae supradictae, super quod recolligetur mantum pedibus duobus, aut plus aut minus, secundum quod machina foret maior sive minor, ad hoc ut fusum magis desubtus veniat, ut praedicta pertica tanto magis veniat poderata. Et debet fieri maior capsa et longior, quae fieri potest a Magistris, quia quanto onus bassius est, tanto ipsa malius supinatur; et quanto ipsum maius, tanto expellit amplius ac etiam magis longe et maius pondus; propter quod tanto debet fieri fortior machina supradicta capsa, pertica atque fuso. Ac debet esse in medio bene lumbata[130] dicta pertica et quasi a parte anteriori abscidens. Ac capsa bonum debet habere gamelum,

[129] Schneider used the word *latitudinem* here. Other manuscripts use the *altitudinem*, which is likely incorrect.

[130] In some manuscripts, *lumbata* is rendered as *lumbuta*.

quod capsam impellat versus exteriorem partem. Et quanto machina maior est, tanto eicit maius onus trahitque altius atque longius antedictum. Et quanto lapis altius trahitur atque longius, tanto impetuosiorem ictum infert penitus et maiorem.

Et si quis vellet construere machinam lontanariam in navigio, potest facere solia super latus, ac facere perticam ita magnam, quod ipsa usque ad superfundum navigii perveniret, et facere quod canale super fundum dicti navigii resideret, et capsa veniret quasi usque ad canalem. Quae quidem machina tota totumque navigium fortissime debent fieri, quoniam ipsa proiceret talem lapidem et tam longe, quemadmodum faceret machina tam magne, ut exigeret talis pertica in terra.

Est praeterea quoque sciendum, quod proicere machinarum recte et longum, et in conferendo iis pondus in lapidibus totum constat, ut requirit machinae magnitudo ac quantitas contrarii ponderis dictae capsae; et in faciendo lapides antedictos rotundos; ac etiam constat in ferro capitis perticae, quod tenet saccam casolae, in faciendo ipsum retortum, secundum quod homines volunt in altum proicere, sive longum.

Pro quibus omnibus magistri et ingeniatores praedictae armatae acuent mentem suam utentes machinis supradictis.

De ballistis lontanriis faciendis

Ad faciendum ballistas, tam de ligno lontanarias, quam de cornu, boni magistri bonumque lignamen in talibus exiguntur: tamen quae perfectiores exsistunt, inveniuntur de cornu, quae confinguntur mediante colla de cornibus atque nervis. Quae quidem ballistae de cornu valent melius in contrata sicca, quam in humida; et ballistae magis a longe tempore frigido quam in calido, ut plurimum est expertum. Arcus vero ballistarum de ligno fiunt de quodam ligno, quod Nassus vulgariter appellatur; et melius quod valeat invenire in insula Corsica invenitur, quamvis in multis aliis partibus reperiatur de bono; quod vero lignum oportet abscidi de nemore eo tempore, ut dictum est de alio lignamine amputando. Si autem arcus ballistarum de ligno in longitudine protenduntur et modicum sint plicati, maiorem ascensum suscipiunt et expellunt ulterius tela sua. Verum semper intellegi debent haec talia mensurate. Est etuam utile causa de longe ballistandi, quod sint cordae ballistarum subtiles, in tantum quod possint tensionis et extensioni ballistae violentuam tolerare; unde oportet eas esse de bono canabi congrue laborato. Restat praeterea longinquum trahere ballistarum in sagittamine supradicto. Unde oportunum est, quod fiant ferra telorum ac hastae similiter praedictorum, tales quae convenient una simul et conveniant cum ballistis, nec non oportet quod hastae dictorum telorum optime impennentur, quoniam ipsae pennae multum iuvant ad directe et longe propositum sagittandi. De manubriis vero dictarum ballistarum, quae teneria nuncupantur, nucibus et clavibus praedictarum modicam faciam mentionem; quoniam omnia quae dicta sunt ad perficiendum praedicta, bona et perfecta procul dubio esse debent, tam arcus ballistarum quam alia quae pertinent ad praedictas, ponendo bonum lignamen in opus et miserum comburendo. Expedit etiam dari tendentibus ballistas valida crochorum bonorum auxilium et largoirum, praesertim quod a parte posterior sint ampla crocha praefata et quod praedictas ballistas tendentes utantur praedctis crochis tam tendendo quam etiam ballistando: eo quod consuetudo magnam vim confert hominibus ad tendendum, quia usus in naturam convertitur secundum consuetedinem apporbatam.

Ceterum illas ballistas tam corneas quam ligneas oportet per ballistarios custodiri praecipue a sole, pluvia et a vento, nec non a rore; et quod ipsae ballistae coopertae continuo teneantur, nisi in tantum in quantum ad operandas ballistas dicti ballistarii egerent obsequio praedictarum, et quod in navigio quilibet ballistator sacco[131] operta et loco basso locum sibi habeat

---

[131] Schneider asserts that this should read *sacco.* Some manuscripts have the

deputatum, ubi quilibet ballistam suam, dum commode fiere posset, suspensam teneat, ut est mos.

Est praeterea quoque sciendum, quod validiores ballistae tenduntur cum duobus pedibus quam cum uno, et securius est pro ballista; et idcirco in loco ubi ballistarii firmiter commorentur ad indisias inferendas, tam in navigio quam in terra, in aliqua certa parte debent uti continuo ballistis a duobus pedibus et de aliis, ut de armis in octavo capitulo est narratum. Potest praeterea fieri, quod haec eaedem ballistae tela possent trahere quae muschettae vulgariter appellantur: sed rectae ballistaae, quibus istae muschettae proprie deputantur, sunt ballistae, quae ballistae a pectoribus nuncupantur; de quibus ominbus periti exercitus facient fieri, et praecipient iis uti, quibus ballistandi exercitium committetur,[132] praecipue illis, quae pro Christianorum armate magis utiles videbuntur. Similiter et de aliis ballistis grossis facient illud idem quod in praedicto octavo capitulo est narratum.

Propter quod, sanctissime Pater mi, bene Capitaneus Sanctae matris Ecclesiae debet studere superdictis aedificiis construendis, tam machinis quam ballistis, cum eo toto quod ad suum officium indiget exsequendum; et specialiter pro faciendo eas lontanarias, ut est dictum: quia quando in illa parte fuerint, ubi dicta aedificia fuerint oportuna ad dictum officium peragendum, multum ab hostibus timebuntur, qui eorum terrore vel metu, iis plateam vel campum concedere compellentur.

---

word *succo*.

[132] Schneider renders this as *exercitium committetur*. Some copies of the manuscript assert that the phrase should be *exercitum committentur*.

4: Louis-Napoleon Bonaparte

Études sur le passé et l'avenir de l'Artillerie

II p. 38 n. 2:

Pour ne laisser aucun doute sur la puissance et le mode d'action des trébuchets, il en a été construit un de grandes dimensions, en se conformant, autant que possible, aux dispositions de la fig. 1, planche III. Ce trébuchet a été mis en jeu dans le polygone de l'école d'Artillerie de Vincennes, et les résultats des expériences ont été consignés dans un rapport adressé au Ministre de la guerre par le capitaine Favé; nous en extrairons les passages suivantes:

Monsieur le Ministre,

"Par votre lettre en date du 1er février 1850, vous m'avez chargé de faire établir, d'après les dessins et les renseignements fournis par le Président de la République, une machine à lancer des pierres, pareille à celles qui ont servi à cet usage pendant le moyen âge. Je viens vous rendre compte de l'exécution de vos ordres.

On a employé dans les sièges, au moyen âge, deux sortes de machines de projection: les grosses arbalètes de divers mécanismes, lançant leur traits horizontalement, comme le font nos canons, et les machines qui lançaient des pierres ou d'autres projectiles sous des angels élevés, comme nos mortiers. Ces machines n'étaient plus les mêmes que dans l'antiquité, et c'est à tort que la plupart des auteurs modernes leur donnent les noms de *balistes* et de *catapultes*, ou parlent d'artillerie névro-balistique: car, les machines des Romains avaient pour moteur la force de torsion des câbles de nerfs, et celles du moyen âge n'en faisaient plus usage. Les machines à tir courbe se composaient d'une flèche tournant autour d'un axe horizontal soutenu sur deux supports; à l'un des bouts de la flèche était suspendu un contre-poids; à l'autre était attachée une fronde par laquelle était lancé le projectile. Le jeu de cette fronde est la partie essentielle de la machine, celle qui, jusqu'à présent, n'avait pas été comprise: le Président de la République en a retrouvé la disposition et le mécanisme. Un des bouts de la fronde est fixé à un anneau placé près du bout de la flèche dont l'extremité se prolonge par un crochet légèrement courbé; l'autre bout de la fronde forme une boucle qui entre dans ce crochet. Cette partie de la flèche étant en bas, la fronde est placée horizontalement dans un auget, le projectile est mis dans la poche de la fronde dont la boucle entre dans le crochet qui termine la flèche. Le contre-poids se trouve alors en haut et la flèche est maintenue dans cette position par un déclic; si on le fait ouvrir, le contre-poids tombe et la flèche tourne autour de son axe, entraînant la fronde: en vertu de la force centrifuge exercée par le projectile, la direction de la fronde se rapproche de celle de la flèche; à un certain moment la boucle glisse sur le crochet et la fronde s'échappe, laissant le projectile continuer librement sa trajectoire pour aller tomber du côté d'où il est parti. Le projectile a fait alors une révolution complète autour de la machine. La portée et même la direction dépendent du moment où le projectile est laissé libre: il faut, pour que la machine produise tout son effet utile, qu' à cet instant, le projectile ait acquis son maximum de vitesse, et qu' il s'échappe sous un angle voisin de 45°. Pour que l'angle de départ soit favorable, il faut un certain rapport entre les longueurs des deux parties de la flèche séparées pas l'axe, la longueur de la fronde, le contre-poids, la courbure du crochet et le poids du projectile. Une longue expérience de ces machines avait sans dout transmis aux *engineurs* du moyen âge la tradition de ces divers éléments, mais elle n'est pas parvenue jusqu'à nous. M. le Président de la République a trouvé dans un ouvrage de Marino Sanuto, écrivain du XIV siècle, que, pour une flèche de 30 piedes, il fallait en prende 5 d'un côté et 25 de l'autre. On est partu de ces données, et, pour la machine à construire, l'on a adopté 10^{m},30 pour longueur de la flèche, afin d'avoir 0^{m},30 au delà du point de suspension du contre-poids. Ce contre-poids a été composé de deux parties, l'une fixée invariablement à la flèche par des frettes en fer, l'autre contenue dans une caisse suspendue à un axe traversant la flèche. Le crochet de l'autre extrémité, destiné à recevoir la boucle de la fronde, été disposé de manière qu'on pût varier son inclinaison."

Les détails de la construction présentèrent des difficultés qu'il serait trop long de rapporter, on dira seulement qu' on se rapprocha le plus possible des dispositions représentées planche III fig. 1.

"La machine fut d'abord montée dans le chantier de l'entrepreneur de charpente pour s'assurer qu' elle serait en état de fonctionner. On reconnût bientôt qu' un seul câble ne pouvait suffire pour abaisser la flèche, et qu' il en fallait deux: le premier agissant par l'intermédiaire d'une poulie de renvoi placée à une dizaine de mètres en arrière de la machine, le second s'enroulant directement sur le treuil pour remplacer le premier, lorsque celui-ci ne pouvait plus servir à abaisser la flèche. On avait à craindre que le mouvement des câbles nécessaires pour élever le contre-poids et abaisser la flèche ne brisât quelque partie de la machine, on trouva heureusement le moyen de s'en débarrasser en les passant en arrière de l'axe de suspension avant de lâcher le déclic et de faire jouer la machine. Le chantier n'était pas assez grand pour qu'on hasardât de lancer un projectile, et l'on dut faire partir la machine à vide; mais alors, le mouvement de la flèche fut si viollent qu'elle alla choquer plusieurs fois successivement la caisse du contre-poids; cette caisse se retourna et des poids en tombèrent, mais sans causer un grand dommage. On rembourra les bords de la caisse et l'on fixa mieux, dedans, les contre-poids. On vit, du reste, par les expériences suivamtes que la machine a d'autant moins à souffirer qu' elle lance un poids plus lourd; elle ne se fatigue jamais tant qu' en jouant à vide.

La machine, paraissant en état de fonctionner, fut transportée et montée dans le polygone de Vincennes. On n'avait aucun renseignement certain sur la longueur à donner à la fronde; on se décida, d'après l'avis de M. le Président de la République et quelques essais faits en petit, à adopter la longueur de 5 mètres comptés de l'un des bouts au fond de la poche. On mit dans la fronde une bombe de 32 centimètres, et on fit partir la machine: la bombe fut lancée en arrière, à 70 mètres environ. La même chose arriva pour une bombe de 27 centimètres. On recommença les jours suivants en augmentant l'inclinaison du crochet pour retarder le départ du projectile qui retomba encore en arrière, mais moins loin. On avait placé au bout libre de la fronde un anneau en fer qu' on introduisait dans le crochet, afin de nepas user la corde: alors le projectile fut lancé en avant. Ainsi, une différence dans la direction opposée à celle qu' il doit avoir. On a eu occasion d'observer dequis, que, lorsque la corde est mouillée, cette circonstance suffit pour modifier l'angle de départ du projectile."

Le rapport entre ensuite dans des détails relatifs à un accident survenu pendant la manoeuvre. La flèche qui était en sapin ayant été brisée fut remplacée par une flèche en chêne, et on rendit plus facile et plus sûre l'opération nécessaire pour passer d'un câble à l'autre, sus le treuil, en abaissant la flèche.

"Le contre-poids fut porté de 3,000 à 4,500 kilogrammes, savoir: 1,500 kilogrammes en lingots de plomb, fixés invariablement à la flèche, et 3,000 kilogrammes dans la caisse suspendue à un arbre en fer passé dans la flèche. Dans les expériences qui suivirent, on lança de boulet de 24 à la distance de 175 mètres, une bombe de 22 centimètres remplie de terre à 145 mètres et les bombes de 27 et 32 centrimètres remplies de terre à 120 mètres. Les montants en charpente qui portaient l'axe de la flèche manquaient un peu de force, et les arcs-boutants n'étaient pas assez inclinés; l'ébranlement de la machine après le départ du projectile faisait craindre pour la solidité, et on n'a pas osé augmenter le contre-poids pour le porter à 8000 kilogrammes comme M. le Président de la République l'avait demandé. Le grand ébranlement éprouvé par la machine à chaque coup, a empêché de répéter les expériences assez pour arriver au maximum d'effet; mais on a pu reconnaître:

1. Que l'ébranlement de la machine diminue quand le tir se rapproche de la verticale.
2. Que le projectile échappe d'autant plus promptement, toutes choses égales d'ailleurs, à la fronde, qu' il est plus lourd.
3. Qu' en augmentant la longueur de la fronde, on retarde au contraire le départ, qui a lieu sous un angle moins élevé.

La rectitude du tir de cette machine est remarquable: elle n'a jamais eu trois mètres de déviation latérale.

Ces machines n'ont pas servi seulement à lancer des pierres, on les a employées à projeter des marmites rondes, percées de trous, remplies de feu grégeois, des tonneaux remplis de compositions incendiaires, ou de matières putréfiées, des morceaux de fer rougis au feu; enfin, on a lancé, par leur moyen, des quartiers de chevaux morts et même des hommes vivants. Lorsque la machine devait lancer des projectiles incendiaires, on mettait à la fronde une poche de fer, afin qu' elle ne fût pas brûlée.

Tous les différents effets rapportés par les chroniqueurs sont actuellement si faciles à comprendre et même à reproduire, qu' il a paru inutile de faire pour cela des expériences spéciales. Le mode d'action de la machine explique ses différents emplois.

Les résultats obtenus avec le trébuchet construit dans le polygone de Vincennes, sont comparables aux effets produits, pendant le moyen âge, dan la plupart de sièges; ils sont inférieurs à ceux qui sont indiqués par les chroniqueurs dans quelques circonstances particulières, où l'on a lancé des projectiles énormes; mais il n'y a nul doute qu' en s'exerçant à cette sorte de construction, et en y employant des bois de très-forte dimension, on parviendrait à réaliser ces effets.

Le trébuchet est une machine si différente de tout ce qui est en usage actuellemen, que les personnes qui le voient tout monté et prêt à lancer, ne savent pas dire de quel côté ira le projectile; sa construction présentait donc une question d'archéologie intéressante par elle-même; elle avait, en outre une véritable importance, car il était impossible d'arriver à comprendre les sièges du moyen âge sans connaître les machines de jet dont se servaient l'attaque et la défense."

P. 46 n. 1:

Le trébuchet établie dans le polygone d'artillerie de Vincennes avait un contre-poids de 4,500 kg. Le poid des autres matériaux qui entraient dans la construction ne peut être évalué à moins de 7,000 kg, et on fut obligé de placer sur la base un poids dépassant 6,000 kg, qui était soulevé, dans le mouvement de la machine, d'un decimètre au moins. Ainsi le poids total de ce trébuchet dépassait 17,500 kg.

C'est par une sorte d'abstraction, et pour faire mieux comprendre la partie caractéristiqu de la machine, que les dessins du moyen âge représentent souvent l'axe de la verge soutenu sur deux minces colonnes. Les bâtis en charpente, destiné à soutenir le poids porté par cet axe et la réaction occasionnée par le jeu de la machine, devait avoir une grande quantité de bois; la faute commise dans la construction du trébuchet à Vincennes a précisément consisté à n'en pas mettre assez.

P. 48:

Nous avons voule, par des calculs, nous persuader de la possibilité de construire de semblables machines, et nous avons trouvé qu'un trébuchet à fronde lancerait environ à soixante-dix mètres, distance plus que suffisante pour l'emploi des anciennes machines dans les sièges, une pierre de mille quatre cents kg. Ce contre-poids, quoique immense, peut être représenté par six cent cinquante-six boulets en pierre de vingt-cinq kg, et tiendrait dans une caisse cubique de un mètre soixante-sept centimètres de côté. Le grand levier de ce trébuchet aurait seize mètres cinquante centimètres, le petit trois mètres trente centimètres.

Cette machine serait monstrueuse, absurde même, mais possible, On peut donc supposer qu'elle ait existé; mais il faut bien se garder de conclure de là, comme Daru (*Histoire de Venise*. Paris 1826, tome II livre VII p. 103) et le général Bardin, que les Orientaux et les Venétiens étaient fort avancés dans l'art de la balistique. Selons nous, au contraire, cette exagération est une preuve évidente de l'enfance de l'art: car en général, on peut avancer que, plus une machine est grossière, plus ses dimensions sont susceptibles de développement. L'énorme poids des projectiles dont il a été question ne saurait, d'ailleur, être une raison de croire à l'emploi des machines à câbles tordus pendant le moyen âge, car les Romains ne lançaient jamais, avec les balistes ou catapultes, que des poids qui n'excédaient pas six à sept cents livres.

Quant à la question de faire brèche, il est clair que si l'on entend par là l'opération qui consiste, comme aujourd'hui, à couper le mur par sa base, ni les machines des Romains, ni celles du moyen âge n'étaient capables de produire ce résultat; mais, les trébuchets lancants leurs pro jectiles sous un angle élevé, il arrivait quelquefois qu'ils pussent écrêter le haut de la muraille, en détruire les défenses, et même finir par le renverser, lors qu'elle n'avaint pas une grande épaisseur.

5: Aegidii Romani *De Regimine Principum* libri tres

For producing this version of the text, the following manuscripts have been used:

A. Ms. lat. Folio 97 of the Pergamen Manuscript from the Military Library of Berlin (XIV century)
B. Codex msc. Phil. 12 (H. J. IV 3). Pergamen Manuscript from the Military Library of Bamberg (XIII/XIV century)

These two manuscripts complement and improve one another, and when the two of them fail the newer copies offer no real aid. For 1. III p. III cap 18, the few discrepancies between A and B are clearly delineated; the miniscule yield will justify the fact that only in cases of extreme variance are the differences noticeable.

Following the text, the parallel passages from Aristotle and Vegetius are presented.

Prologus in librum 'De Regimine Principum' editus a fratre Egidio Romano ordinis fratrum Eremitarum S. Augustini incipit feliciter.

Ex regia ac sanctissima prosapia oriundo domino suo speciali domino Philippo prime genito et heredi praeclarissimi viri domini Philippi, dei gratia illustrissimi regis Francorum, suus devotus frater Egidius Romanus ordinis fratrum Eremitaruum S. Augustini cum recommandatione se ipsum et ad omnia famulatum.

Liber I

Pars I.

1. Quis sit modus procedendi in "Regimine Principum."
2. Quis sit ordo dicendorum.
3. Quanta sit utilitas in dicendis.

4. Quot sunt modi vivendi, et quomodo in iis felicitas habet esse.
5. Quod maxime expedit regiae maiestati suum finem et suam felicitatem cognoscere.
6. Quod non decet regiam maiestatem suam felicitatem ponere in voluptatibus.
7. Quod non decet regiam maiestatem suam felicitatem ponere in divitiis.
8. Quod non decet regiam maiestatem suam felicitatem ponere in honoribus.
9. Quod non decet regiam maiestatem suam felicitatem ponere in gloria et in fama.
10. Quod non decet regiam maiestatem suam felicitatem ponere in civili potentia.
11. Quod non decet regiam maiestatem suam felicitatem ponere in robore corporali vel pulchritudine vel in aliis bonis corporis.
12. Quod in actu prudentiae est ponenda felicitas.
13. Quantum sit praemium regis bene regentis populum sibi commissum.

Pars II.

1. Quomodo dividuntur potentiae animae, et in quibus potentiis habent esse virtutes.
2. Quomodo distinguuntur virtutes, et quomodo se habent in intellectu et appetitu.
3. Quot sunt virtutes morales, et quomodo earum numerus est sumendus.
4. Quod bonarum dispositionum quaedam sunt virtutes, quaedam supra virtutem, quaedam ancillantes sunt virtutibus et praeparationes ad virtutem.
5. Quod virtutum quaedam sunt principales et cardinales, quadem vero annexae.
6. Quomodo diversitate notificari potest, quid est prudentia.
7. Quod decet reges et principes esse prudentes.

8. Quot et quae oporteat habere regem, si debeat esse prudens.
9. Quomodo reges et principes possunt se ipsos prudentes facere.
10. Quot sunt modi iustitiae, et circa quae iustitia habet esse, et quomodo ab aliis virtutibus est distincta.
11. Quod absque iustitia nequeunt regna subsistere.
12. Quod maxime decet reges esse iustos et in suo regno iustitiam observare.
13. Quid est fortitudo et circa quae habet esse, et quomodo possumus nos ipsos facere fortes.
14. Quot sint species fortitudinis, et secundum quam fortitudinem decet reges et principes esse fortes.
15. Quid sit temperantia et circa quae habet esse, et quae sint species eius et quomodo possumus nos ipsos facere temperatos.
16. Quod exprobrabilius est esse intemperatum quam timidum, et quod maxime decet reges et principes esse temperatos.
17. Quid est liberalitas et circa quae habet esse, et quomodo possumus nos ipsos facere liberales.
18. Quod impossibile est quodammodo reges et principes esse prodiigos, et quod maxime detestabile est eos avaros esse, et quam potissime decet eos esse liberales.
19. Quid est magnificentia et circa quae habet esse, et quomodo possumus nos ipsos magnificos facere.
20. Quod maxime detestabile est reges et principes esse parvificos, et quod decet eos magnificos esse.
21. Quae sunt proprietates magnifici, et quod proprietates illas reges et principes habere debent.
22. Quid est magnanimaitas et circa quae habet esse, et quomodo possumus nos ipsos magnanimos facere.
23. Quae sunt proprietates magnanimi, et quod decet reges et principes esse magnanimos.
24. Quod decet reges et principes esse amatores honorum, et qualis est virtus illa, quae dicitur honoris amativa.

25. Quod humilitas dici potest honoris amativa, et quod omnis magnanimus est humilis.
26. Quid est humilitas et circa quae habet esse, et quod decet reges et principes esse humiles.
27. Quid est mansuetudo et circa quae habet esse, et quod decet reges et principes esse mansuetos.
28. Quid est amicabilitas et circa quae habet esse, et quod decet reges et principes esse amicabiles.
29. Quid est veracitas et circa quae habet esse, et quod decet reges et principes esse veraces.
30. Quid est iucunditas et circa quae habet esse, et quod decet reges et principes esse iucundos.
31. Quod maxime decet reges et principes omnes virtutes habere, quia, si una careant, nullam habent.
32. Quod diversi sunt gradus bonorum et alorum, et in quo gradu reges et principes esse decet.
33. Quot sunt gradus virtutum, et cuiusmodi virtutes habere decet reges et principes.
34. Quomodo bonarum dispositionum quaedam sunt virtutes, quaedam supra virtutes, quaedam annexae virtutibus, quaedam disponentes ad virtutem.

Pars III.

1. Quot sunt passiones animae, et quomodo accipiendus est earum numerus.
2. Quae praedictarum passionum sunt priores et quae posteriores, et quem ordinem habent ad invicem.
3. Quomodo decet reges et principes se habere ad odium et amorem.
4. Quomodo et quae debeat reges et principes desiderare et abominari.
5. Quomodo reges et principes se habere debeant circa spem et desperationem.
6. Quomodo decet reges et principes se habere circa audadiam et timorem.

7. Quomodo differt ira ab odio, et quomodo reges et principes se habere debeant ad iram et eius oppositum.
8. Quomodo reges et principes se habere debeant circa delectationes et tristiatias.
9. Quod harum passionum quadam sunt magis principales, quaedam minus.
10. Quomodo passiones aliae ad passiones praehabitas reducuntur.
11. Quae praedictarum passionum sunt laudabiles et quae vituperabiles, et quomodo reges et principes ad illas debeant se habere.

Pars IV.

1. Qui sunt mores iuvenum laudabiles, et quomodo reges et principes ad mores illos debeant se habere.
2. Qui mores iuvenum sunt vituperabiles, et quomodo reges et principes ad huiusmodi mores debeant se habere.
3. Qui mores senum sunt vituperabiles, et quomodo reges et principes vitare debeant dictos mores.
4. Qui mores senum sunt laudabiles; et qui sunt mores eorum, qui sunt in statu, et qualiter reges et principes ad huiusmodi mores debeant se habere.
5. Qui sunt mores nobilim, et quomodo reges et principes habere se deneamt ad illos mores.
6. Qui sunt mores divitum, et qualiter reges et principes se debeant habere ad illos mores.
7. Qui sunt mores potentium, et quomodo ad illos mores reges et principes debeant se habere.

Liber II

Pars I.

1. Quod naturale est homini vivere in societate, et quod decet hoc reges et principes diligenter advertere.
2. Quomodo se habeat communitas domus ad communitates alias, et quomodo huiusmodi communitas sit necessaria in humana vita.

3. Quod communitas domus est aliquo modo communitas prima, et quod est communitas naturalis, et quod reges et principes et universaliter omnes cives hoc ignorare non debent.
4. Qualis sit communitas domus, et quod oportet domum ex pluribus constare personis.
5. Quod oportet in domo saltem duas communitates esse, et quod oportet eam constare saltem ex tribus generibus personarum.
6. Quod in domo perfecta oportet tres communitates esse, et quattuor genera personarum et tria regimina.
7. Quod homo est animal naturaliter coniugale, et quod nolentes nubere non vivunt ut homines, sed ut bestiae, vel sunt dii.
8. Quod omnes cives et maxime reges et principes debent suis coniugibus inseparabiliter adhaerere.
9. Quod omnes cives et maxime reges et principes una sola uxore debent esse contenti.
10. Quod coniuges omnium civium et maxime regum et principum uno viro debent esse contentae.
11. Quod decet omnes cives et maxime reges et principes non ducere coniuges nimia consanguinitate sibi coniunctas.
12. Quomodo reges et principes et universaliter omnes cives deceat uxores accipere ornatas exterioribus bonis.
13. Quod decet omnes cives et maxime reges et principes quaerere in suis coniugibus non solum bona exteriora sed etiam interiora tam corporis quam animae.
14. Quod omnes cives et maxime reges et principes non decet suas uxores regere eodem regimine, quo regendi sunt filii.
15. Quod omnes cives et maxime reges et principes non decet suas coniuges regere eodem modo, quo regendi sunt servi.
16. Quod detestabile est omnibus civibus et maxime regibus et principibus in aetate nimis iuvenili uti copula coniugali.

17. Quod tempore frigidi, quo flant venti boreales, magis est dandum operam procreationi filiorum quam tempore calido, quo flant venti australes.
18. Quod in mulieribus quaedam sunt laudabilia, quaedam vituperabilia.
19. Quo regimine omnes cives et maxime reges et principes debeant suas coniuges regere.
20. Qualiter omnes cives et maxime reges et principes ad suas coniuges debeant se habere.
21. Qualiter feminae coniugatae circa ornatum corporis debeant se habere.
22. Quod non decet reges et principes et universaliter omnes cives erga suas coniuges nimis esse zelotypos.
23. Quale sit consilium mulierum, et quod earum consilio non est utendum simpliciter sed in casu.
24. Quod non decet reges et principes et universaliter omnes cives propriis coniugibus suis aperire secreta.

Pars II.

1. Quod decet omnes parentes circa proprios filios esse sollicitatos.
2. Quod maxime decet reges et principes sollicitari circa regimen filiorum.
3. Quod regimen paternale sumit originem ex amore, et quod non eodem regimine debent regi filii, quo regendi sunt servi.
4. Quod amor, qui debet esse inter parentem et filium, sufficienter inducat, quod patres debent filios regere, et filios decet parentibus oboedire.
5. Quod decet omnes cives et maxime reges et principes sic sollicitari circa regimen filiorum, ut ab ipsa infantia instruantur in fide.
6. Quod decet omnes cives et maxime reges et principes sic sollicitari erga proprios filios, ut ab ipsa infantia bonis moribus imbuantur.

7. Quod filii nobilium et maxime principum et regum ab infantia sunt tradendi litteralibus disciplinis.
8. Quas scientias debeant addiscere filii nobilium et maxime regum et principum.
9. Qualis debeat esse magister, qui filiis nobilium et maxime regum et principum est praeponendus.
10. Qualiter circa loquelam, visum et auditum instruendi sunt iuvenes.
11. Quot modis peccatur circa cibum, et qualiter iuvenes se habere debeant circa ipsum.
12. Qualiter sunt pueri instruendi, ut se habeant circa potum vel circa venerea et circa coniugia contrahenda.
13. Qualiter pueri sive iuvenes se habere debeant in ludis, in gestibus et in vestitu.
14. Quod in aetate iuvenili cavenda sit maxime prava societas.
15. Qualis cura gerenda sit de pueris a principio nativitatis usque ad VII annos.
16. Qualis cura habenda sit de pueris a septimo anno usque ad quartum decimum.
17. Qualis cura habenda sit de filiis ab anno XIV et deinceps.
18. Quomodo omnes iuvenes aequaliter exercitandi sunt ad corporalia exercitia et labores.
19. Quod filiae civium et maxime nobilium et regum et principum a discursu et evagatione sunt cohibendae.
20. Quod universaliter omnes cives et multo magis nobiles et reges et principes debent sollicitari circa filias, ne velint vivere otiose.
21. Quod decet reges et principes et universaliter omnes cives sollicitari erga filias, ut siint modo debito taciturnae.

Pars III.

1. Quod ad gubernationem domus spectat non solum determinare de servis, sed etiam de his, qui supplent indigentiam corporalem.

2. Quomodo distinguenda sunt organa gubernationis domus, et quomodo ad invicem operantur.
3. Qualia aedificia decet habere reges et principes et universaliter omnes cives quantum ad operis industriam et aëris temperamentum.
4. Qualia aedificia debent esse quantum ad salubritatem aquarum et quantum ad ordinem universi.
5. Quod possessio est quodammodo homini naturalis, et quod abrenuntiantes possessionibus quodammodo non vivunt ut homines, sed ut hominibus meliores.
6. Quod utile est in vita politica quemlibet propriis gaudere possessionibus.
7. Quomodo est utendum exterioribus rebus, et quis modus vivendi sit licitus.
8. Quod cives et multo magis reges et principes non debent infinitas possessiones appetere.
9. Quot sunt species commutationum, et quae fuit necessitas invenire denarios.
10. Quot sunt species pecuniativae, et quae illarum est laudabilis et quae vituperabilis.
11. Quod usura est simpliciter detestabilis, et quod decet reges et principes eam prohibere.
12. Quod diversi sunt modi lucrandi pecuniam, et quod aliqui istorum modorum sunt regibus et principibus congruentes.
13. Quod aliqui sunt naturaliter servi, et quod expedit aliquibus, aliis esse subiectos.
14. Quod praeter servitutem naturalem, quae est quasi servitus simpliciter, est dare servitutem legalem et positivam.
15. Quod praeter servitutem et ministrationem naturalem et legalem est dare ministrationem conductam et dilectivam.
16. Quomodo in domibus regum et principum sunt ministris officia committenda/
17. Quomodo a regibus et principibus providenda sunt indumenta ministris.

18. Quid est curialitas, et quod decet ministros regum et principum esse curiales.
19. Quomodo reges et principes erga suos subditos debeant se habere.
20. Quod in mensis regum et principum et virorum nobilium tam recumbentes quam etiam ministrantes non decet in eloquiis abundare.

Liber III

Pars I.

1. Quod communitas civitatis est aliquo modo principalissima, et est alicuius boni gratia constituta.
2. Quot et quae bona homines consequunteur ex constitutione communitatis politicae, quae civitas nuncupatur.
3. Quod homo est naturaliter animal civile, non obstante, quod contingit aliquos non civiliter vivere.
4. Quibus rationibus probari potest, civitatem esse quid naturale, et hominem naturaliter esse animal politicum et civile.
5. Quod praeter communitatem civitats utile fuit in vita humana esse communitatem regni.
6. Quod diversi sunt modi generationis civitatis et regnis.
7. Quomodo Socrates et Plato dixerunt civitatem ordinandam esse, et quid senserunt de civili regimine.
8. Quod non oportet civitatem maximam unitatetm et conformitatem habere, ut Socrates et Plato statuerunt.
9. Quod non expedit civitati omnia sic esse communia, ut Socrates ordinavit, et quod reges et principes hoc decet cognoscere.
10. Quae mala sequuntur, si in civitate uxores et filii ponantur esse communes.
11. Quomodo expediat civitati possessiones esse proprias et quomodo communes.
12. Quod reges et principes non debent sic disponere civitatem, quod mulieres ordinentur ad opera bellica, ut Socrates statubat.

13. Quod reges et principes non sic debent disponere civitatem, ut semper iidem in iisdem magistratibus praeponantur.
14. Quod non sic ordinanda est civitas, ut Socrates statuebat.
15. Quomodo positio Socratis circa regimen civitatis trahi possit ad bonum intellectum.
16. Quomodo philosophus Felleas[133] statuit civitatem ordinandam esse.
17. Quod non oportet possessiones esse aequatas, ut Felleas statuebat.
18. Quod principalis intentio legislatoris debet esse circa repressionem concupiscentiarum, et non circa aequalitatem possessionum, ut Felleas ordinavit.
19. Qualis fuit politia Ypodonni,[134] et quid Ypodonius statuit circa regimen civitatis.
20. Quae et quot sunt reprehensibilia in his, quae statuit Ypodonius circa gubernationem civium.

Pars II.

1. Quomodo regenda est civitas tempore pacis, et quae et quot consideranda sunt in tali regimine.
2. Quot sunt modi principatuum, et qui illorum sunt boni et qui mali.
3. Quod melius est civitatem et regnum regi uno quam pluribus, et quod regnum est optimus principatus.
4. Quibus rationibus ostendi potest, quod appareat melius esse civitatem vel provinciam regi pluribus quam uno, et quomodo solvi possunt taiones illae.
5. Quod melius est regimen regni et principatus ire per hereditatem et successionem filiorum quam per electionem aliquam.
6. Quae sunt, in quibus rex alios debet excedere, et quomodo rex differat a tyranno.

---

[133] Aristole: *Politics*. II 1266a 39: Φαλέας δ Χαλκηδόνιος.

[134] Aristole: *Politics*. II 1267b 22: Ἱππόδαμος… Μιλήσιος.

7. Quod tyrranides est pessimus principatus, et quod summe debent cavere reges et principes, ne eorum dominium in tyrannidem convertatur.
8. Quod est officium regis, et qualiter rex se habere debeat in regimine civitatis et regni.
9. Quae sunt illa, quae debet operar verus rex, quae simulat facere se tyrannus.
10. Quae et quot sunt cautelae, quibus tyrannus nititur se in suo dominio praeservare.
11. Quot sunt illa, ad quae reducuntur cautelae tyrannicae, et quod reges cavere debent, ne efficiantur tyranni; quia opera regia sunt optima, tyannica vero sunt pessima.
12. Quod detestabile est regiam maiestatem declinare ad tyrannidem, quia, quidquid corruptionis est in aliis perversis principatibus, totum in tyrannidem congregatur.
13. Quod summe expedit regibus recte gubernare populum et cavere, ne tyrannizent, quia multis de causis contingit subditos insidiari tyrannis.
14. Quod maxime rex cavere debet, ne efficiatur tyrannus, eo quod pluribus modis corrumpatur tyrannides quam regius principatus.
15. Quae sunt, quae salvant dominum regium, et quot oporteat regem facere, ut se in suo principatu praeservet.
16. Quae sunt consiliabilia, et circa quae oportet consilia adhibere.
17. Quid est consilium, et qualiter consilia sunt fienda.
18. Quales consiliarios assumere deceat regiam maiestatem.
19. Quot oportet scire consiliarios, et circa quot sunt consilia adhibenda.
20. Quod quantum possibile est, sunt omnia legibus determinanda, et quam pauciora sunt arbitrio iudicum commttenda.
21. Qualiter est in iudicio procendendum, et quod sermones passionales sunt coram iudice prohibendi.

22. Quae et quot oporteat habere iudices, ut contingat eos debite iudicare.
23. Quae et quot oporteat considerare iudices, ut indulgeant humanis et ut sint clementes potius quam crudeles.
24. Quod diversa sunt genera legum et diversi sunt modi iustitiae, et quod in ius naturale cetera talia reducuntur.
25. Quomodo ius gentium et ius animalium a iure naturali habet esse distinctum.
26. Qualis debeat esse lex humana, et quod condere tales leges sit utile regno et civitati.
27. Quod non cuiuslibet est leges ferre, et quod, ut leges vim obligandi habeant, oportet eas promulgatas esse.
28. Quot et quae opera debent continere leges, quae a regibus et principibus sunt condendae.
29. Qualiter melius regitur civitas aut regnum: utrum melius regatur optimo rege, aut optima lege.
30. Quod praeter legem humanam et naturalem oportuit dare evangelicam legem et divinam.
31. Quod, quantum possibile est, sunt leges patriae observandae, et quod cavendum est assuescere innovare aut immutare leges.
32. Quid est civitas et quid est regnum, et qualem oportet esse populum exsistentem in regno et civitate.
33. Quod tunc est optima civitas et optimum regnum et optimus populus, quando est ex multis personis mediis constitutus.
34. Quod expedit populo cum magna reverentia regibus oboedire, et cum summa diligentia leges regias observare.
35. Qualiter se debent habere cives et universaliter habitarores regni, ne reges provocentur ad iracundiam contra ipsos.
36. Quomodo reges et principes debeant se habere, ut amentur a populo, et quomodo, ut timeantur; et quod licet utrumque sit necessarium, amari tamen debent plus appetere quam timeri.

Pars III

1. Quid est militia, et ad quid est instituta, et quod omnis operatio bellica sub militia continetur.
2. Quae sunt regiones illae, in quibus sunt meliores bellatores; et ex quibus artibus eligendi sunt homines bellicosi.
3. In qua aetate assuescendi sunt iuvenes ad opera bellica, et ex quibus signis cognoscere possumus homines bellicosos.
4. Quae et quot habere debent homines bellicosi, ut bene pugnent et ut eos strenue bellare contingat.
5. Qui sunt meliores bellatores: an urbani et nobiles, vel agricolae et rurales.
6. Quod in opere bellico nimium valet exercitatio armorum, et quod ad incedendum gradatim et passim et ad cursum et saltum exercitandi sunt bellatores.
7. Quod non sufficit ad incedenum serie et gradatim et ad cursum et saltum exercitare bellantes, sed sunt plura alia, ad quae exercitandi sunt homines bellicosi.
8. Quod utile est in exercitu facere fossas et constuere castra, et qualiter construenda sunt castra, et quae sunt attendenda in constructione castrorum.
9. Quae et quot sunt consideranda in bello, si debeat pugna publica committi.
10. Quod utile est in bello ferre vexilla et constituere duces praepositos, et quales esse debeant, qui in exercitu vexilla portant, et qui equitibus et peditibus praeponuntur.
11. Quibus cautelis debet uti dux belli, ne suus exercitus laedatur in via.
12. Qualiter ordinandae sunt acies, si debeamus contra hostes vel contra adversarios dimicare.
13. Quod deridendi sunt in bello omnes percutientes caesim, et quod eligibilius est percutere punctim.
14. Quot et quae sunt illa, quae hostes potentiores reddunt; et quot modis et qualiter debemus hostes invadere.
15. Quomodo homines bellatores stare debeant, si velint hostes percutere, et quomodo debeant eos circumdare; et

quomodo debeant declinare a pugna, si non sit bonum pugnam committere.

16. Quot sunt genera bellorum; et quot modis devincendae sunt menitiones et urbanitates, et quo tempore melius est obsidere civitates et castra.
17. Quomodo se debent munire obsidentes, et quomodo per cunculos impugnari possunt munitiones obsessae.
18. Quae et quot sunt genera machinarum eicientium lapides, per quae impugnari valent munitiones obsessae et devinci possunt civitates et castra.
19. Quomodo per aedificia lignea impulsa ad muros civitatis vel castri impugnari possunt munitiones obsessae.
20. Qualiter aedificanda sunt castra et civitates, ne per pugnam ab obsidentibus faciliter devincantur.
21. Quomodo muniendae sunt civitates et castra et universaliter omnes munitiones, ut ab obsidentibus difficilius capiantur.
22. Quomodo resistendum est impugnationi factae per cuniculos, et qualiter machinis lapidariis et aliis aedificiis obsessi debeant obviare.
23. Qualiter constituenda est navis, et qualiter committendum est navale bellum; et ad quid singula bella ordinantur.

Incipit tertia pars tertii libri

Cap. I. Quid est militia et ad quid est instituta, et quod omnis operatio bellica sub militia continetur.

Peractis duabis partibus huius tertii libri, quibus ostensum est, quid senserunt antiqui philosophi de regimine civitatis et regni, et determinatum est qualiter regenda sit civitas atque regnum tempore pacis, reliquum est tractare de opere bellico, ut sciant reges et principes, qualiter committenda sint bella; nam, ut plurimum, in certamine bellorum industria, ut patet per Vegetium in libro de re militari, plus confert ad obtinendam victoriam quam faciat multitudo vel etiam fortitudo bellantium.[135] Opus autem

---

[135] Vegetius I 1 (p6,5): *Etenim in certamine bellorum exercitata paucitas ad victoriam pomptior est, rudis et indocta multitudo exposit semper ad caedem.*

bellicum, ut patebit in prosequendo, continetur sub militari; quare si de opere bellico tractare volumus, videndum est, quid sit militia et ad quid sit instituta. Sciendum igitur militarem esse quandam prudentiam sive qundam speciem prudentiae. Possumus autem, quantum ad praesens spectat, distinguere quinque species prudentiae, videlicet prudentiam singularem, oeconomicam, regnativam, politicam sive civilem, et militarem Dicitur enim aliquis habere singularem vel particularem prudentiam, quando se ipsum scit regere et gubernare; et haec est minor prudentia quam oeconomica et regnativa, nam minus est scire regere se ipsum quam scire regere familiam et civitatem et regnum.

Secunda species prudentiae debet esse oeconomica. Nam prudens ex hoc aliquis dicitur, ut patet ex sexto ethicorum, quia scit bene consiliari et scit bene dirigere ad bonum finem;[136] ubi ergo reperitur alia ratio boni, ibi reperitur et alia species predentiae. Quare cum bonum domesticum et bonum totius familiae sit aliud a bono alicuius singularis personae, sicut bonumt commune est aliud a bono aliquo singulari, oeconomicam, sive prudentiam, per quam quis scit regere domum et familiam, oportet esse aliam a prudentia, qua quis novit se ipsum regere. Tertia species prudentiae dicitur esse regnativa vel legum positiva. Nam sicut persona aliqua singularis est pars domus, ita domus est pars civitatis et regni; et sicut bonum domesticum est aliud a bono alicuius singularis personae, sic bonum totius civitatis et regni est aliud a bono domestico. Prudentia ergo regnativa et legum positiva, i.e. prudentia, quae requiritur in rege et principante, cuius est leges ferre et regere regnum et civitatem, est alia aprudentia oeconomica, quae requiritur in patre familiae, cuius est gubernare domum. Immo quanto bonum civitatis et regni excedit bonum domesticum et bonum alicuius singularis personae, tanto prudentia, quae requiritur in rege, debet excedere prudentiam

---

[136] Aristotle. *Ethics* VI 1140 29: τοὺς περὶ τὶ φρονίμους λέγομεν, ὅταν πρὸς τέλος τι εὖ λογίσωνται.

patris familiae vel prudentiam alicuius singularis hominis; propter quod bene dictum est, quod ait Vegetius in primo libro de re militari, quod "*neque quemquam magis decet vel meliora scira vel plura quam principem, cuius doctrina omnibus subiectis prodesse potest.*"[137] Inde est igitur quod in erudiendo reges et principes hunc totalem librum divisimus in tres libros, quia in primo libro docuimus regem esse prudentem, prout rex aut princeps est quaedam persona in se, et prout habet se ipsum regere. In secundo vero docuimus ipsum, ut est pater familiae, et ut habet dispensare bona domestica. In tertia vero eruditur rex aut princeps, ut est caput regni aut principatus, et ut habet ferre leges et gubernare cives. Omnes autem has tres prudentias decet habere regem, videlicet: particularem, oeconomicam et regnativam. Quarta species prudentiae dicitur esse politica sive civilis. Nam sicut in principante requiritur excellens prudentia, quae sciat alios dirigere, sic in quolibet cive requiritur prudentia aliquis, quae noscat adimplere leges et mandata principantis. Non enim sic obsequitur civis principi aut regi sicut martellus fabro, quia martello nulla est cognito, sed solum agitatur a fabro; sed in cive requiritur prudentia, per quam habeat bonam opinionem de his, quae imperantur a rege. Differt autem haec prudentia a prudentia particulari, quam collocavimus in prima specie; nam aliud est, quod homo sciat se regere, ut est aliquid in se, et aliud, ut est subiectus principanti. Nam etsi quis solitariam vitam duceret, adhuc oporteret ipsum habere aliqualem prudentiam, qua sciret se regere et gubernare; non tamen esset in ipso prudentia civilis nec oeconomica nec regnativa, quia nec esset civitas nec pars civitatis. Quinta species prudentiae dicitur esse militaris. Nam regimen regi et civitatis, si sit rectum et ordinatum, assimilatur his, quae videmus in uno et eodem homine. Sicut ergo quilibet homo habet duas virtutes animae: unam, per quam sequitur bonum et fugit malum, et aliam, per quam aggreditur et resistit prohibentibus, sic quaelibet civitas et regnum indiget duplici virtute

---

[137] Vegetius 4,4: *neque quemquam magis decet vel meliora scire vel plura quam principem, cuius doctrina omnibus potest prodesse subiectis.*

et duplici prudentia, videlicet legum positiva et militari, ut per legum positivam tota civitas et totum regnum prosequatur proficua et fugiat nociva, per militarem vero et per operationem bellicam aggrediatur et superet impedientia et prohibentia/ Militaris ergo est quaedam species prudentiae, per quam superantur hostes et prohibentes bonum commune et civile.

Ex hoc autem apparet, ad quid sit militia instituta. Nam sicut leges, ut supra ostendebatur, principaliter respiciunt commun bonum, sic et militia est principaliter instituta ad defensionem communis boni vel civitatis aut regni. Quare cum commune bonum directe videatur impediri per impugnationem hostium, ex consequenti vero ex seditione civium et ex oppressione debilium personarum, dicere possumus, quod, sicut ad fortem principaliter spectat bene se habere in opere bellico, ex consequenti vero spectat bene se habere in aliis tarribilibus, sic ad milites principaliter spectat bene se habere in opere bellico et per actiones bellicas opprimere impedimentum hostium, ex consequentis vero spectat ad ipsos secundum iussionem regiam et secundum mandata principantis impedire omnes seditiones civium et omnes oppressiones eorum, qui sunt in regno, per quas potest turbari tranquillitas civium et commune bonum. Hanc autem prudentiam, videlicet militarem, maxime decet habere regem. Nam licet exsecutio bellorum et removere impedimenta communis boni spectat ad milites et ad eos, quibus rex aut princeps voluerit committere talia, scire tamen, quomodo committenda sint bella, et qualite caute removeria possint impedientia commune bonum, maxime spectat ad principantem. Ex hoc autem patere potest, quales sint ad militiam admittendi; nam militia videtur esse quaedam prudentia operis bellici ordinata ad commune bonum; videntur enim se habere milites in opere bellico sicut magistri et doctores in scientiis aliis. Quare sicut nullus efficiendus est magister in aliis scientuus, nisi constet ipsum esse doctum in arte illa, sic nullus assumendus est ad dignitatem illam militarem, nisi constet ipsum diligere bonum regni et commune, et nisi habeatur spes, quod sit bonus in opere bellico, et quod velit secundum iussionem principantis impedire seditiones civium, pugnare pro iustitia, et pro viribus removere, quaecunque impedire possunt commune bonum. Ex hoc patere potest omnem operam bellicam contineri sub militari. Nam licet bellare contingat homines pedites vel etiam equestres non exsistentes milites, debent tamen milites esse magistri bellorum et ordinatores aliorum in bello. Ideo sub militari dicitur operatio bellica contineri. Ex hoc etiam patet, quod cum milites esse debeant magistri bellorum, licet exsecutio belli spectet ad fortitudinem, militia tamen continetur sub prudentia.

Cap. II. Quae sunt regiones illae, in quibus sunt meliores bellatores; et ex quibus artibus eligendi sunt homines bellicosi

Videtur, quantum ad praesens spectat, in opere bellico duo necessaria esse, scilicet: strenuitas bellandi et prudentia erga bella; quare si scire volumus, in quibus regionibus sunt meliores bellatores, oportet attendere circa praedicta duo. In partibus igitur nimis propinquis soli non sunt eligendi bellatores, quia in iis deficit strenuitas et animositas circa bellum, ut ait philosophus VII politicorum;[138] ratio autem huius assignatur a Vegetio primo libro de re militari capitulo secundo, ubi dicit quod "*nationes quae vicinae sunt soli, nimïo calore siccati amplius quidem sapiunt, sed modicum abundant in sanguine, ac propterea non habent pugnandi constantiam neque fiduciam, quia naturaliter metuunt vulnera.*"[139] Nam cum naturaliter habeant modicum sanguinis, naturaliter timent sanguinis amissionem. Non ergo sunt prompti ad bella nec ad percussiones. Rursus in partibus nimis septentrionalibus et nimis a sole remotis non sunt eligendi

---

[138] Aristotle. *Politics.* IV 1327 23: τὰ μὲν γὰρ ἐν τοῖς ψυχροῖς τόποις ἔθνη... θυμοῦ μέν ἐστι πλήρη, διανοίας δὲ ἐνδεέστερα καὶ τέχνης.

[139] Vegetius, I 2 (p. 6,15) Omnes nationes quae vicinae sunt soli, nimio calore siccatas, amplius quidem sapere, sed minus habere sanguinis dicunt, ac propterea constantiam ac fiduciam comminus non habere pugnandi, quia metuunt vulnera qui exiguum sanguinem se habere noverunt.

bellantes, quia, etsi illis est sanguinis copia, ut vulnera non metuant, tamen propter sanguinis abundantiam et impetum sunt quasi furibundi et imprudentes.[140] Ideo non omnino sunt utiles operibus bellicis, quia consilium et prudentia in dimicatione non est modicum utilis. Experimento enim videmus, ut plane vult hoc philosophus VII. politicorum,[141] quod gentes nimis propinquae soli abundant sagacitate et industria, sed deficiunt strenuitate et animositate; gentes vero a sole remotae e contrario prudentia deficiunt et animositate superabundant. Quare, si tam animositas quam industria necessaria est in bellis, ex neutris partibus eligendi sunt bellatores, sed ex regione media, nec omnino a sole remota nec omnino soli propinqua, eligendi sunt bellantes, ut tam animositate quam prudentia participent.[142] Advertendum tamen, cetera talia documenta accipienda esse ut in pluribus; nam in omnibus partibus sunt aliqui industres et aliqui animosi, ut plurimum tamen soli propinqui animositate deficiunt, remoti vero prudentia. Advertendum etiam, quod, licet in bellis tam animositas quam prudentia sit necessaria, magis tamen est animositas utilis. Ideo etsi gentes omnino propinquae soli et omnino remotae non sunt penitus utiles actibus bellicis, magis tamen inter medicas regiones eligendi sunt ad opera bellica remotiores a sole quam propinquiores, ut magis animositate participent.

Viso ex quibus partibus meliores sunt bellatores, videre restat, ex quibus artibus eligendi sunt bellatores. Enumeranda igitur sunt ea, quae requiruntur in hominibus bellicosis, ut sciamus, quales homines sunt eligendi ad bellum, et ex quibus artibus sunt

---

[140] Vegetius, I 2 (p/ 6, 20): Contra septentrionales populi, remoti a solis ardoribus, inconsultiores quidem, sed tamen largo sanguine redundantes, sunt ad bella promptissimi.

[141] Aristotle. *Politics*. 1327 27: τὰ δὲ περὶ τὴν' Ασίαν διανοητικὰ μὲν καὶ τεχνικὰ τὴν ψυχήν, ἄθυμα δέ.

[142] Vegetius, I 2 (p. 7, 1): Turones igitur de temperatioribus legendi sunt plagis, quibus et copis sanguinis suppetat ad vulnerum mortisque contemptum et non possit deesse prudentia, quae et modestiam servat in castris et non parum prodest in dimicatione consiliis.

assumendi bellantes. Sciendum ergo, quod, cum bellantes debeant habere membra apta et assueta ad percutiendum, non debeant horrere effusionem sanguinis, debeant esse animosi ad invadendum et potentes ad tolerandum labore, dicere possumus, quod fabri ferrarii et carpentarii sunt utiles a opera bellica, quia ex arte sua habent bracchia apta et assueta ad percutiendum; sic etiam utiles sunt macellarii, quia non horrent effusionem sanguinis, cum assueti sunt ad occisionem animalium et ad effundendum sanguinem.[143] Venatores etiam aprorum admittendi sunt ad huiusmodi opera, quia non sine magna audacia contingit aliquos invadere apros, sunt ergo tales animosi et strenui ad bellandum, immo forte non minus peroculosum est bellare cum apro quam pugnare cum hoste; ideo non timentes aprorum pericula, signum est eos non timere hostium bella. Rursus venatores cervorum non sunt repudiandi ab actibus bellicis, eo quod tales assueti sunt ad labores nimios. Ex his ergo artibus propter ea, quae diximus, eligendi sunt homines bellatores. Barbitonsores autem et suotres, si consideretur ars propria, ad pugnandum sunt inutiles.[144] Nam numquam bene vibrabit clavam aut ensem, qui debet habere manum levem et non assuetus est retinere in manibus nisi rasorium aut acum. Quae enim est proportio acus ad lanceam et rasorii ad clavam? Sic etiam apothecarri, aucupes et piscatores non sunt eligendi ad huiusmodi opera, eo quod non habeant artem conformem operibus bellicosis. Poteset ergo contingere, quod in qualibet arte sint aliqui bellicosi et audaces, aliqui vero timidi et pusillanimes; sed quantum est ex genere artis, et prout ars ipsa reddit hominem aptum vel inertem ad opus bellicum, aliqua genera artium diximus esse utilia ad actiones bellicas et aliqua inutilia.

---

[143] Vegetius, I 7 (p. 11, 4): fabros ferrarios, carpentarios, macellarios et cervorum aprorumque venatores convenit sociare militiae.

[144] Vegetius, I 7 (p. 11, 1): Piscatores, aucupes, dulciarios, linteones omnesque, qui aliquid tractasse videbuntur ad gynaecea pertinens, longe arbitror pellendos a castris.

Cap. III. In qua aetate assuescendi sunt iuvenes ad opera bellica, et ex quibus signis cognoscere possumus homines bellicosos.

Diximus supra philosophum velle in VIII. politicorum,[145] iuvenes a XIIII anno ultra assuefaciendos esse ad labores fortes, ut ad labores militares et belisosos; quod concordat cum Vegetio de re militari dicente, quod a tempore pubertatis assuescendi sunt iuvenes ad militares labores;[146] immo quia, quae a iuventutes inchoamus, nimis diligimus et delectamur in illis, si vult legislator cives bellatores facere et reddere ipsos aptos ad pugnandum, potius debet praevenire tempus quam praetermittere. Nam ut ait Vegetius: "*Melius est, ut iuvenis exercitatus causetur aetatem nondum advenissepugnandi, quam doleat praeteriisse.*"[147] Est etiam ratio specialis, quare oporteat iuvenes ab ipsa iuventute assuescere ad artem bellandi, quia non parva nec levis ars esse videtur habere armorum industriam. Nam sive quitem sive peditem oportet esse bellantem, qui fortuitu videtur pervenire ad palmam, si careat industira bellandi; tam enim in pedestri quam in equestri pugna sunt multae adhibendae cautelae. Fatuum est quidem non prius, sed tunc velle addiscere bellare, quando imminet pugnandi necessitas, ubi vita periculis mortis exponitur. Ut ergo bellatores habeant spatium ad discendum signula, quae requiruntur ad bellum, ab ipsa pubertate assuescendi sunt ad opera bellica. Quare si legislator, ut rex aut princeps, debeat committere bellum, viros exercitatos et bellatores strenuos debet assumere.

---

[145] Aristotle. *Politics*. IV 1336 37: δύο δ' εἰσὶν ἡλικίαι πρὸς ἅς ἀναγκαῖον διῃρῆσθαι τὴν παιδείαν, μετὰ τὴν ἀπὸ τῶν ἑπτὰ μέχρις ἥβης, καὶ πάλιν μετὰ τὴν ἀφ' ἥβης μεχρὶ τῶν ἑνὸς καὶ εἴκοσιν ἐτῶν. V 1339 4: ὅταν δ' ἀφ' ἥβης ἔτη τρία πρὸς τοῖς ἄλλοις μαθήμασι γένωνται, τότε ἁρμόττει καὶ τοῖς πόνοις καὶ ταῖς ἀναγκοφαγίαις καταλαμβάνειν τὴν ἐχομένην ἡλικίαν.

[146] Vegetius, I 4 (p. 8, 10): incipientem pubertatem ad dilectum cogendam.

[147] Vegetius, I 4 (p. 9, 2): Melius enim est, ut exercitatus iuvenis causetur aetatem nondum advenisse pugnandi, quam doleat praeterisse.

Viso in qua aetate assuescendi sunt, qui debent effici bellatores ad actiones bellicosas, videre restat, ex quibus signis cognosci habent homines bellicosi. Sciednum ergo viros audaces et cordatos utiliores esse ad bellum quam timidos. Rursus homines fortes et duro corpore, qui potentiores sunt viribus, sunt magis eligendi ad opus bellicum. Amplius, cum videamus aliqua animalia bellicos, aliqua vero timida, homines similiores bellicosis animalibus utiliores videntur esse ad bellum. Tribus ergo generibus signorum cognoscere possumus bellicosos viros. Primo quidem per signa, secundum quae arguitur animositas et audacia. Secundo vero per signa, secundum quae ostenditur virilitas et fortitudo corporis. Tertio autem per signa, secundum quae conformamur animalibus bellicosis. Sunt autem signa, per quae ostenditur animositas et strenuitas cordis: vigilantia oculorum et erectio cervicis. Ideo dicit Vegetius quod "*adulescens Martio operi deputandus debet esse vigilantibus oculis et erecta cervice.*"[148] Signa vero, per quae ostenditur fortitudo corporis et vires membrorum, sunt: durities carnis, compactio nervorum, musculorum et lacertorum. Nam secundum philosophum VIII politicorum opus bellicosum et industria mentis omnino requirunt modum contrarium. Nam ut scribitur in II de anima.[149] Molles carne aptos mente dicimus, sed e contrario duri carne, habentes compactos nervos et lacertos, sunt virosi, et fortiores corpore sunt aptiores ad pugnam. Signa vero conformantia nos animalibus bellicosis sunt: magnitudo extremitatum et latitudo pectoris. Videmus enim leones, animalium fortissimos, habere magna bracchia et latum pectus. Quando ergo in homine videmus, quod sit vigilans oculis, erectus cervice; durus in carne, compactus in nervis et musculis, habens longa bracchia et latum pectus,

---

[148] Vegetius, I 6 (p. 10, 13): Sit ergo adulescens Martio operi deputandus vigilantibus oculis, erecta cervice, lato pectore, umeris musculosis, valentibus brachiis, digitis longioribus, ventre modicus, exilior clunibus, suris et pedibus non superflua carne distentis sed nervorum duritia collectis.

[149] Aristotle. *On the Soul.* II 421 25: οἱ μὲν γὰρ σκληρόσαρκοι ἀφυεῖς τὴν διάνοιαν, οἱ δὲ μαλακόσαρκοι εὐφυεῖς.

debemus arguere, ipsum esse bellicosum et aptum ad pugnam. Tales ergo quaerendi sunt bellatores, quia ut plurimum contingit eos esse aptos ad actiones bellicas.

Cap. IV. Quae et quot habere debent homines bellicosi, ut bene pugnent et ut eos strenue bellare contingat.

Quantum ad praesens spectat, enumerare possumus octo, quae habere debent homines bellatores, secundum quae, quantum ad praesens spectat, investigare poterimus, quos aut quales bellatores debet rex aut princeps eligere. Primo enim oportet, pugnativos homines posse sustinere magnitudinem poderis. Secundo, posse sufferre quasi assiduos membrorum motus et magnos labores. Tertio, posse tolerare parcitatem victus. Quarto, non curare de incimmiditate iacendi et standi. Quinto, respectu iustitiae et boni communis quasi non apprtiari corporalem vitam. Sexto, non horrere sanguinis effusionem. Septimo, habere aptitudinem et industriam ad protegendum se et feriendum alios. Octavo, verecundari et erubescere eligere turpem fugam.

Est enim prim necessarium bellantibus, posse sistinere ponderis magnitudinem. Nam inermes, a quacunque parte feriantur, occumbunt; quare, nisi quis possit sustinere armorum pondera, inutilis est ad bellum. Secundo bellantibus expedit, posse sufferre quasi assiduos membrorum motus. Nam si quis in bello non continue se ducat, adversarius non fallitur in percutiendo, quare semper exponitur ad sustinendum fortiores ictus; expertum enim est, quod homine continue se ducente et movente, vix aut numquam ad plenum aliqua percussio potest impum attingere, sed vulnera semper subterfugit. Nam sicut, si signum se moveret et non staret fixum, non sic de facili percuteretur ab arcu, sic homo se circumvolvens, non sic de facili vulneratur ab hoste. Continuus ergo membrorum motus est necessarius ad vitandum plagas, sic etiam est necessarius ad incutiendum eos; propter quod tales debent esse homines pugnativi, ut diu tolerare possint assiduum membrorum motum. Tertio homines pugnativos decet, non curare de parcitate victus. Nam grave est ultra armorum pondera et eorum, quae requiruntur ad defensionem exercitus, deferre in abundantia victualium copiam; immo etsi absque gravamine adesset pugnantibus ciborum utilitas, adhuc esset iis necessaria ciborum abstinentia et non gravare se ex nimio cibo, ut melius possent tolerare pugnandi laborem. Quarto decet eos non curare de incommoditate iacendi et standi. Nam expedit aliquando pugnantibus die noctuque in armis esse, propter quod nec in stando nec in iacendo est iis commodum aut requies. Quinto decet ipsos propter iustitam et commune bonum quasi non appretiari corporalem vitam. Nam cum tota operatio bellica exposita sit periculis mortis, numquam quis est fortis animo et bonus bellator, nisi aliquo modo sit impavidus circa pericula mortis. Spectat enim ad fortem et ad bonum bellatorem, ut innuit philosophus III ethicorum,[150] non curare in bello bene mori; tunc enim quis dicitur bene mori in bello, quando bellans iuste, ut pro defensione patriae vel pro aliquo alio magno bono, iuste et audacter exponit se mortis periculis. Dum autem quis, ultra quam debeat, diligit corporalem vitam, de facili eligit turpem fugam. Sexto pugnantes non debent horre sanguinis effusionem. Nam si quis cor molle habens, muliebris exsistens, horreat effundere sanguinem, non audebit hostibus plagas infligere, et per consequens bene bellare non poterit. Septimo decet eos habere aptitudinem et industriam ad protegendum se et ad feriendum alios. Nam ut dicitur I. ethicorum: "*finis militaris est victoria.*"[151] Sed cum omnis operatio bellica contineatur sub militari, ut supra ostendebatur et ut habetur a philosopho circa principium ethicorum, omnis actionis bellicae dicetur vicotira esse finis; quare, cum maxime contingat bellantes vincere, si bene sciant se protegere et alios ferire, industria protegendi se et feriendi valde est expediens bellatoribus. Qualiter

---

[150] Aristotle. *Nicomachean Ethics*. III 1115 32: κυρίως εἠ λέγοιτ' ἂν ἀνδρεῖος ὁ περὶ τὸν καλὸν θάνατον ἀδεής.

[151] Aristotle. *Nichomachean Ethics*. I 1094 9: στρατηγικῆς δὲ νίκη (τὸ τέλος).

autem talis industria habeatur, et qualiter sit feriendum hostem, et quae adminiculentur ad ista, infra patebit. Octavo decet bellatores verecundari et erubescere turpem fugam.[152] Nam ut dicitur III ethicorum: "*Apud illos sunt viri fortissimi, apud quos honorantur fortes.*"[153] Inter cetera autem, quae reddunt hominem bellicosum, est diligere honorari ex pugna et erubexcere turpem fugam. Advertendum autem, quod, cum dicimus bellatores non horrere effusionem sanguinis, non debere multum appretiari corporalem vitam et cetera alia, quae diffusius enumeravimus, intellegendum est: si habeant iustum bellum. Nam pro defensione iustitiae et pro communi bono exponenda est periculo corporalis vita, non est cavenda sanguinis effusio, et cetera alia sunt fienda, per quae iustitia et commune bonum defendi potest. Ex his autem plane patet, quales bellatores et quos viros pugnativos rex aut princeps eligere debeat. Nam illi sunt eligendi, in quibus plura reperiuntur de his quae requiruntur ad pugnam.

Cap. V. Qui sunt meliores bellatores: an urbani et nobiles, vel agricolae et rurales.

Enumeratis his, quae habere debent bellatores viri, restat inquirere, qui sunt meliores bellantes: an urbani et nobiles, vel agricolae et rurales. Videtur autem, si considerentur praedicta, rurales meliores esse. Huius autem opinionis visus est esse Vegetius dicens: "*Numquam credo potuisse dubitari aptiorem armis rusticam plebem.*"[154] Ad hoc etiam videntur facere, quae superius diximus. Dicebatur enim, viros pugnativos tales esse debere, qui possent sustinere magnitudinem ponderis, continuum laborem membrorum, parcitatem victus, incommoditatem iacendi

---

[152] Aristotle. *Nichomachean Ethics.* III 1116 19: τοῖς μὲν γὰρ αἰσχρὸν τὸ φζύγειν καὶ ὁ θάνασος τῆς τοιαύτης σωτηρίας αἱρετώτερος.

[153] Aristotle. *Nichomachean Ethics.*III 1116 20: καὶ διὰ τοῦτο ἀνδρειότατοι δοκοῦσιν εἶναι παρ' οἷς οἱ δειλοὶ ἄτιμοι καὶ οἱ ἀνδρεῖοι ἔντρμοι.

[154] Vegetius I 3 (p. 7, 7): numquam credo potiusse dubitari aptiorem armis rusticam plebem.

et standi, non timere mortem, non horrere effusionem sanguinis et cetera alia, quae tetigimus in capitulo praecedenti. Constat autem ruralem populem maxime habere praedicta. Sunt enim rustici assueti ad magnitudinem ponderum; non enim in bellis gravabit eos armorum sarcina, qui assidue tempore pacis assueti sunt ad maiora pondera. Nec etiam eos fatigabit cursus vel ductio bracchiorum, vel aliorum membrorum motus, qui ad hos et ad maiores labores sunt continue assueti. Rursus eos non affliget pacitas victus, quibus potus aquae satisfaciebat in siti et grossus panis sufficiebat ad esum. Amplius rurales non affliguntur incommoditate iacendi vel standi, qui solis ardorem non timent, umbras non curant balneorum solatia nesciunt. In solida terra iacentes suavius dormiunt, quam urbani et nobiles requiescant in fulcris. Hos etiam probabile est non multum timere mortem. Nam tanto quis mortem magis timere videtur, quanto magis delicate vixit, et quanto plurium solatiorum est expertus in vita. Hi etiam non videntur horrere effusionem sanguinis; nam inter ceteras gentes ruralium genus videtur esse crudelius. Ad hoc igitur intendentibus videtur censendum esse, meliores bellatores esse rurales. Sunt autem alia, per quae videtur ostendi, urbanos et nobiles meliores esse pugnantes. Nam inter cetera, per quae quis redditur bonus pugnativus, est, ut dicebatur, velle honorari ex pugna et erubescere turpem fugam. Hoc est enim, ut ait philosophus III ethicorum, quod Hectorem fecit audacem.[155] Dicebat enim Hector: "*Si ex pugna fugiam Polimidas mihi redargutiones ponat*". Sic etiam et Diomedes hoc modo effectus fuit strenuus, quia dicebat: "*Si in bello terga vertam, Hector, cum contionabitur in Troianis, dicet: a me devictus est Diomedes*". Quare cum velle honorari et erubescere de aliquo turpi facto magis conveniat nobilibus quam rusticis, hi meliores et esse videntur ad pugnam, eo quod verecundentur fugere. Rursus in bello multum

---

[155] Aristotle. *Nichomacean Ethics*. III 1116 21: τοιούτους δὲ καὶ Ὅμηρος ποιεῖ, οἶον τὸν Διομήδην καὶ τὸν Ἕκτορα. Πουλυάμας μοι πρῶτος ἐλεγχείην ἀναθήσει καὶ Διομήδης, Ἕκτωρ γάρ ποτε φήσει ἐνὶ Τρώεσὸ ἀγορεύων Τυδείδης ὑπ' ἐμεῖο.

valet industria et prudentia; nam sagacitas et versutia aliquando plus facit ad obtinendam vicotriam, quam populi fortitudo. Quare, cum communiter nobiles homines industriores sunt rusticis, sequitur, hos esse meliores pugnantes. Videntur enim haec duo maxima esse ad obtinendam victoriam, videlicet: erubescentia fugiendi et sagacitas bellandi. Ut ergo sciatu, quid sit de quaesito tenendum, oportet advertere, quod secundum diversitatem pugnandi diversi eligendi sunt bellatores. Potest enim esse pugna pedestris et equestris. In pedestri itaque certamine magis eligendi sunt rurales quam nobiles, eo quod maxime ibi valet assuefactio ad portationem ponderum et tolerantiam laborum. In equestri vero magis eligendi sunt nobiles, eo quod equorum fortitudo supplet defectum, quem patiuntur nobiles in non posse tantos sustinere labores, quantos consueverunt sustinere rurales/ In huiusmodi enim pugna nimium valet bellandi sagacitas, sociata erubescentiae fugiendi. Sciendum tamen, quod, ut nobiles ex omni parte efficiantur strenui bellatores, assuefaciendi sunt ad portandum armorum pondera et ad sustinendum laborem et motum bracchiorum et aliorum membrorum corporis, ut requirit operatio bellica. Quae autem et quot sunt illa, ad quae debeant exercitari bellantes, in sequenti capitulo ostendetur.

Cap. VI. Quod in opere bellico nimium valet exercitatio armorum, et quod ad incedendum gradatim et passim et ad sursum et saltum exercitandi sunt bellatores.

Recitat Vegetius in libro de re militari[156] "*execitationem armorum et industriam bellandi fuisse ea, quae terrarum orbem Romanon populo subiecerunt. Nam quid potuisset paucitas*

---

[156] Vegetius, I 1 (p. 5, 13): Nulla enim alia re videmus populum Romanum orbem subegisse terraruym nisi armorum exercitio, disciplina castrorum usuque militiae. Quid enim adversus Gallorum multitudinem paucitas Romana valuisset? Quid adversus Germanorum proceritatem brevitas potuisset audere? Hispanos quidem non tantum numero sed et viribus corporum nostris praestitisse manifestum est; Afrorum dolis atque divitiis semper impares fuimus; Graecorum artibus prudentiaque nos vinci nemo dubitavit.

Romanorum adversus mulititudinem Hispaniorum, contra dolos Afrorum et prudentiam Graecorum, nisi plus illis exercitati fuissent in armis et magis habuissent bellandi industriam." Non enim est inconvenisens, virum prudentem et sagacem in uno propter particularium inexperientiam esse imprudentem in alio; unde multotiens contingit, quod prudentes in rebus aliis, propter inexercitium armorum non sunt indistres in rebus bellicis. In quolibet enim negotio praebet audaciam exercitium, ut non metuat illud facere. Nam scundum Vegetium[157] "*nemo facere metuit quod se bene didicisse confidit*". Inde est, quod tantum valet armorum exercitium, quod *in bellorum certamine paucitas exercitata sit prompta ad victoriam, et multitudo rudis et indocta semper sit exposita ad fugam et ad caedem.*[158] Viso armorum exercitium esse perutile ad opera bellica, restat ostendere, quomodo exercitandi sunt bellantes ad incedendum gradatim et passim et ad cursum et ad saltum. Nam ista, ut in prosequendo patebit, necessaria sunt in bellis, et inexercitatio circa ipsa bellantibus est nociva. Primo enim milites et pedites et universaliter bellantes assuefaciendi sunt ad gradum et passum bellicum, ut gradatim pergant, ita ut quilibet se in suo ordine teneat.[159] Nam si acies sive peditum sive equitum non ordinate incedat, duo mala inde consequuntur. Nam non servato debito ordine, in una parte erit acies quasi sparsa et pervia ultra quam debeat; in alia vero arta et stricta plus quam oporteat. Primo ergo, ex eo quod in aliqua parte pervia est, citius ab hostibus perforabitur et dividetur, et per consequens debellabitur. Secundo in parte illa, in qua nimis arta est, impedietur ad percutiendum. Nam cum bellator a suo consortio nimis comprimitur, sua impediuntur bracchia, ne possit hostibus plagas infligere. Haec enim duo sunt in acie necessaria, ut scilicet non possit de facili perforari ab hostibus, et non impediatur ad percutiendum, quod non servato debito gradu et

---

[157] Vegetius, I 1 (p. 6, 4): nemo facere metuit quod se bene didicisse confodot.
[158] Vegetius, I 1 (p. 6, 5): in certamine bellorum exercitata paucitas ad victoriam promptior est, rudis et indocta multitudo exposita semper ad caedem.
[159] Vegetius, I 9 (p. 13, 13): Primis ergo mediationum auspiciis tirones militarem edocendi sunt gradum.

debito ordine in incessu fieri non potest. Tam ergo pedites quam equites bellatores, antequam bella exerceant, sunt multotiens simul congregandi et exercitandi, ut onerati armis ordinate incedant, ac si deberent pugnam committere; et cum viderit magister bellorum aliquem non tenere ordinem debitum in acie, ipsum increpet et corrigat, vel si nimis delinquat, ipsum omnino repellat ab acie tamquam inutilem bellatorem. Secundo exercitandi sunt bellatores tam pedites quam equites ad cursum, ut sint habiles in praecurrendo. Videtur enim hoc valere ad tria. Primo ad explorandum inimicorum facta. Nam bonum est, in exercitu aliquos agiliores praecurrere, qui de facili non possint ab ipsis hostibus comprehendi, explorantes condiciones et facta hostium. Secundo hoc est utile ad obtinendum meliorum locum. Nam etiam locus multum facit ad pugnam. Ideo si bellatores exercitati sunt ad cursum, facilius obtinebunt aptiorem locum ad pugnandum. Est etiam hoc utile ad persequendum hostes fugientes. Nam de difficili quis potest evadere manus agilium et praecurrentium. Tertio exercitandi sunt bellatores ad saltum, ut sciant saltim vel per saltum incedere. Quod etiam ad tria est utile. Primo ad removendum impedimenta, secundo ad terrendum adversarios, tertio ad infligendum maiores plaga. Contingit enim aliquando invenire fossas et alia impedimenta in via, quae sine saltu transiri non possunt; quare utile est ad removenda impediment, ut per saltum foveas et alia impedimenta pertranseant; et pedites et etiam milites, si contingat eos pedestres esse, si volunt boni bellatores exsistere, sic ab ipsa iuventute exercitandi sunt ad saliendum, ut possint per saltum foveas et alia impedimenta transire. Terrentur etiam ex hoc adversarii, quando sic vident hostes per saltum incedere. Rursus ipse saltus ratione motus facit, ut plaga amplior infligatur.

Cap. VII. Quod non suffcit ad incedendum serie et gradatim et ad cursum et saltum exercitare bellantes, sed sunt plura alia, ad quae exercitandi sunt homines bellicosi.

Possumus autem praeter tria praedicta, ad quae exercitandos diximus bellantes, enumerare octo alia, ad quae exercitari debent homines bellicosi. Primo enim exercitandi sunt ad portandum pondera; secundo ad invadendum et percutiendum cum clava; tertio ad emittendum tela sive iacula et ad percutiendum cum lancea; quarto ad iaciendum sagittas; quinto ad proiciendum lapides cum fundis; sexto ad percutiendum cum plumbatis; septimo ad ascendendum equos; octavo ad scienndum artem natandi. Esset etiam ulterius dicendum, quomodo exercitandi sunt bellatores ad percutiendum cum gladiis et ensibus, sed de hoc speciale capitulum faciemus. Primo enim sunt bellatores exercitandi ad portandum pondera, ut plus ponderis portare assuescant etiam, quam sit armorum sarcina.[160] Nam consuetudo est quasi natura quaedam, cum ergo quis assuetus est ad portandum maius pondus, videtur sibi quasi quod levis incedat, si oneretur minori pondere. Rursus non solum arma, sed etiam plura alia sunt ferenda in bello. Ideo etiam ad maiora pondera non est inutile assuescere bellatores. Secundo exercitandi sunt bellantes ad invadendum et percutiendum cum clava.[161] Recitat enim Vegetius, quod antiquitus apud Romanos in campo aliquo multi pali infigebantur, et iuvenes, quos volebant facere optimos bellatores, exercitabant ad palos illos; ita ut quilibet haberet scutum dupli ponderis, quam sit scutum, quod portatur in bello, et clavam ligneam etiam dupli ponderis, et quilibet illorum iuvenum sic oneratus contra aliquem illorum palorum quasi contra adversarium incedebat, et nunc percutiebat palum in summitate, nunc in imo, nunc in medio; et contra palum illum sic impetuose se gerebat percutiendo ipsum et cooperiendo se et alia faciendo, quae requiruntur ad bellum, ac si contra hostem dimicaret. Et cum diu, mane et sero, iuvenes sic exercitati essent, cum postea veniebant ad bellum, non gravabantur in percutiendo cum clava,

---

[160] Vegetius, I 19 (p. 21, 5): Pondus quoque baiulare usque ad LX libras et iter facere gradu militari frequentissime cogendi sunt iuniores.

[161] Vegetius, I 11 (p. 15, 8): Antiqui, sicut invenitur in libris hoc genere exercuere tirones. -- (p. 15, 14): Palorum enim usus non solum militibus sed etiam gladiatoribus plurmum prodest.

vel in sustinendo quoscunque labores bellicos. Tertio exercitandi sunt bellatores ad emittendum tela et iacula et ad percutiendum cum lancea, quod etiam ad defixum palum fieri habet.[162] Fiebat enim antiquitus, cum iuvenes exercitati erant ad percutiendum palos infixos cum clava, quod exercitabantur ad percutiendum cum telo, vel cum iaculo, sive cum lancea. Stabant enim a remotis et assuedaciebant bracchia, ut possent palum illum percutere, vel saltem prope illum proicere. Est autem attendendum, quod in prociendo telum aut lanceam primo vibrandum est telum ipsum et postea fortiter impellendum; vibrato enim telo propter maiorem motum, quem afficit in aëre, longius pergit et amplius vulnus infligit. Quarto exercitandi sunt bellantes ad iaciendum sagittas, vel cum arcubus, vel cum ballistis.[163] Nam quia contingit, quod ipsos hostes non possumus immediate attingere, utile est eos sagittis impugnare; immo dato, quod pugnantes se cum hostibus possint coniugere, antequam coniungantur, proficuum est eos arcubus et ballistis terrere. Legitur enim de Africano Scipione quod cum pro populo Romano certare deberet, "*non aliter contra hostes se obtinere credebat, nisi in omnibus aciebus electos sagittarios miscuisset.*"[164] Quinto sunt bellatores exercitandi ad iaciendum lapides cum fundis. Hic enim modus bellandi in quibusdam marinis insulis fuit inventus, in quibus pueri, ut Vegetius recitat,[165] adeo industrs erant, ut "*matres nullum cibum iis exhiberent, quem non primo cum funda percuterent.*" Est enim hoc exercitium utile, "quia fundam portare nullus est labor. Interdum tamen evenit, ut in

---

[162] Vegetius, I 14 (p. 17, 21): Tiro, qui cum clava exercetur ad palum, hostilia quoque ponderis gravioris, quam vera futura sunt iacula, adversum illum palum tamquam adversum hominem iactare compellitur.

[163] Vegetius, I 15 (p. 18, 8): Sed prope tertia vel quarta pars iuniorum... arcubus ligneis sagittisque lusoriis illos ipsos exercenda est semper ad palos.

[164] Vegetius, I 15 (p. 18, 21): Africanus quidem Scipio, cum adversum Numantions, qui exercitus populi Romani sub iugum miserant, esset acie aliter se superiorem futurum esse non credidit, nisi in omnibus centuriis lectos sagittarios miscuisset.

[165] Vegetius, I 16 (p. 19, 6): Fundarum usum primi Balearium insularum habitarores et invenisse et ita perite exercuisse dicuntur, ut matres parvos filios nullum cibum contingere sinerent, nisi quem ex funda destinato lapide percussissent.

lapidosis locis habeatur conflictus, et ut mons sit aliquis defendendus."[166] In impugnatione tamen castrorum et civitatum non inutile est lapides cum fundis eicere. Sexto exercitandi sunt bellantes ad percutiendum cum plumbatis,[167] Nam pila plumbea vel ferrea cum catena aliqua coniuncta manubrio ligneo vehementem ictum reddit. Nam propter vehementiorem motum aëris vehementius percutit pila cum catena hastae infixa, quam si ipsi hastae vel ipsi manubrio esset coniuncta. Ad omne enim genus percussionum exercitandi sunt bellantes et contra alios et alios hostes aliter et aliter percutiendo dimicent. Septimo bellatores exercitandi sunt ad ascensiones equorum. Nam ut Vegetius recitat,[168] fiebant antiquitus equi lignei, ad quos ascendentes iuvenes in hieme exercitabantur sub tecto, aestate vero in campo. Et primo equos illos ascendebant inermes, deinde armatis, et adeo ad hoc assuefiebant, ut a sinistris et a dextris et undique equos illos ascenderent; immo quod plus erat, evaginatis gladiis conscendebant in illos. In tantum ergo circa hoc exercitabantur in pace, quod in tumultu proelii sine de facili ascendebant equos. Octavo assuescendi sunt bellatores, ut etiam natare sciant.[169] Nam non semper pontes sunt prompti, et multotiesn ignoratur aquae profunditas, propter quod ex ignorantia natandi contingit multos periclitatos esse. Inde est, quod apud

---

[166] Vegetius, I 16 (p. 19, 16): quia fundam portare nullus est labor. Et interdum evenit, ut in lapidosis locis conflictus habeatur, ut mons sit aliquis defendendus aut collis.

[167] Vegetius, I 17 (p. 19, 21): Plumbatarum quoque exercitatio, quos mattiobarbulos vocant, est tradenda iunioribus.

[168] Vegetius, I 18 (p. 20, 17): Equi lignei hieme sub tecto, aestate ponebantur in campo; supra hos iuniores primo inermes, dum consuetudo proficeret, deinde armati cogebantur ascendere. Tantaque cura erat, ut non solum a dextris sed etiam gladios vel contos tenentes. Hoc item adsidua meditatione faciebant, scilicet ut in tumultu proelii sine mora ascenderent qui tam studiose exercebantur in pace.

[169] Vegetius, I 10 (p. 14, 18): Non enim semper pontibus flumina transeuntur. -- (p. 14, 23): Ideoque Romani veteres... campum Martium vicinum Tiberi delegerunt, in quo iuventus post exercitium armorum sudorem pulveremque dilueret ac lassitudinem cursus natandi labore deponeret. Non solum sutem pedites sed et equites ipsosque equos vel lixas... ad natandum exercere percommodum est.

Romanos antiquitus erat consuetudo, quod iuvenes futuri bellatores, postquam per magnam partem diei exercitati essent ad arms, si tempus erat natationis congruum, ducebantur ad fluvium, ut artem natandi addiscerent; immo non solum pedites, sed equites etiam ipsos equos ad natandum exercebantur. Advertendum autem, quod in praedictorum exercitiorum quaedam utrisque; quod quomodo sit, non magna consideration eget et sollertem mentem latere non potest: nam ascendere equos est proprium peditibus. Alia vero sunt aliquo modo applicabilia ad utrosque.

Cap. VIII. Quod utile est in exercitu faceree fossas et construere castra, et qualiter construenda sunt castra, et quae sunt attendenda in constructione castrorum.

Negotia bellica inter ceterea periculosiora esse videntur, ideo in iis est magna diligentia adhilenda; in talibus igitur non potest quis superabundare cautelis. In pugna enim est omnino eligendum, maiorem diligentiam habuisse, quam bella commissa requirerent, quam circa ipsa in aliquo neglexisse. Nam recitat Vegetius[170] Catonem dixisse: "*quod in aliis rebus, si quid erratum est, potest postmodum corrigi; delicta vero proeliorum emendationem non recipiunt, sed statim poena errorum consequitur, quia imperite et imprudenter pugnantes vel confestim pereunt, vel in fugam conversi adeo efficiuntur timidi, quod contra suos victores vix aut numquam audent bella committere*". Quare si in bellis omnino est superabundandum cautelis, non est praetermittendum, quidquid in aliquo casu potest exercitui esse proficuum, ne debelletur ab hostibus. Contingit autem pluries diurno et nocturno tempore, quod exercitu absque fossis et castris exsistente et non credente hostes esse propinquos,

---

[170] Vegetius, I 13 (p. 17, 16): in aliis rebus, sicut ait Cato, si quid erratum est, potest postmodum corrigi; proeliorum delicta emendationem non recipiunt, cum poena statim sequatur errorem: nam aut confestim pereunt qui ignave imperiteque pugnaverint aut in fugam versi victoribus ultra pares esse non audent.

supervenientibus hostibus fuit exercitus debellatus.[171] Igitur postquam exercitus suam dietam compleverit et alicubi vult pernoctare vel ulteriorem moram contrahere, si ad locum illum in aliquo casu vel in aliquo eventu hostes supervenire possunt, statim circa exercitum fiendae sunt fossae, erigendae sunt munitione aliquae quasi ad modum castrorum; quia "*nihil neque tam salutare neque tam necessarium invenitur in bello, sicut si debite factae sunt munitiones et recte constituta sunt castra*".[172] Viso utile esse exercitum facere fossas et construere castra, restat ostendere, qualiter huiusmodi munitones et castra sunt construenda. Nam si hostes sunt absentes, facile est fossas circa exercitum fodere, munitiones erigere et castra construere; sed si adversarii praesentes adsint, difficilius est castra munire.[173] Sunt enim in tali casu duo necessaria, videlicet: hostibus resistere et castra construere. In tali ergo eventu, secundum sapientum sententiam, est exercitus dividendus ita, quod omnes equites et una pars peditum debet ordinari in acie ad pellendum impetum hostium; reliqua vero pars peditum, quae possit sufficere ad talem constructionem castrorum, debet celeriter castra construere. Oporter autem super construendis castris et faciendis fossis aliquos magistros praestitui, qui neglegentes sollicitent et unicuique iniungant, quid ipsum oprteat agere.[174] Ostenso utile esse castra construere, et qualiter etiam praesentibus hostibus construenda sunt castra, reliquum est declarare, quae sunt attendenda in construçtione castrorum. In faciendis enim fossis et

---

[171] Vegetius, I 21 (p. 25, 7): Sic diurno vel nocturno superventu equitum barbarorum multo exercitus scimus frequenter adflictos.

[172] Vegetius, I 21 (p. 25, 1): nihil enim neque tam salutare neque tam necessarium invenitur in bello; quippe si recte constituta sunt castra, ita intra vallum securi milites dies noctesque peragunt, etiam si hostis obsideat, quasi muratam civitatem videantur secum ubique portare.

[173] Vegetius, I 25 (p. 26, 23): Sed facile est abdentibus adversariis castra munire; verum, si hostis incumbat, tunc omnes equites et media pars peditum ad propulsandum impetum ordinantur in acie, reliqui post ipsos ductis fossis muniunt castra.

[174] Vegetius, I 25 (p. 27, 5): Post hoc a centurionibus fossa inspicitur ac mensuratur et vindicatur in eos, qui neglegentius fuerint operati.

in construendis castris, intra quorum spatium est exercitus collocandus, tria sunt consideranda, videlicet: situs, forma et munitionis modus. Circa situm, quantum ad praesens spectat, sunt quattuor attendenda: primo, ut sit ibi copia aquae et aliorum, quae sunt execitui necessaria;[175] secundo non debet ibi esse vicinus mons alius vel locus aliquis, a quo possit exercitus impugnari;[176] tertio circa situm considerandum est spatium ut pro numero bellatorum. Accipiendum est spatium, circa quod sint munitiones erigendae, ut non plus accipiatur de spatio quam requirat huiusmodi multitudo, nec etiam accipiat tam modicum, ut ultra quam debeat exercitum constringi et constipari.[177] Quarto, si oporteat in loco illo exercitum moram contrahere et adsit possibilitas, est eligenda circa situm salubritas aëris; nam in exercitu non solum sunt cavenda vulnera hostium, sed, ut offerat se facultas, cavendae sunt pestes morborum.[178] Declarato ergo, quae sunt attendenda circa situm castrorum, declarandum est, qualis debeat esse forma eorum; videtur autem velle Vegetius munitiones et fossas fiendas circa exercitum debere habere formam quadrilateram oblongam.[179] Attamen, quia figura circularis est capacissima, eligibilius est facere muntiones secundum circularem formam, vel secundum formam multorum angulorum, quia, si multum timetur de impetu hostium, oportet foveas facere multorum aangulorum, eo quod illa forma est magis defensioni apta, ut infra patebit. Talis itaque forma est melior in constructione castrorum, nisi loci situs impediat; nam contingit aliquando, situm

---

[175] Vegetius, I 22(p. 25, 15): ut lignorum et pabuli et aquae suppetat copia.

[176] Vegetius, I 22 (p. 25, 17): cavendum etiam, ne mons sit vicinus aut collis altior, qui ab adversariis captus possit officere.

[177] Vegetius, I 22 (p. 25, 20): Pro numero autem militum vel impedimentorum munienda sunt castra, ne maior multitudo constipetur in parvis neque paucitas in latioribus ultra quam oportet cogatur extendi.

[178] Vegetius, I 22 (p. 25, 16): si diutius commorandum sit, loci salubritas eligatur.

[179] Vegetius, I 23 (p. 25, 23): Interdum autem quadrate, interdum trigona, interdum semirotunda, prout loci qualitas aut necessitas postulaverit, castra facienda sunt. Compare to III 8 (p. 82, 22): pulchriora creduntur, quibus ultra latitudinis spatium tertia pars longitudinis additur.

illum non pati talem formam. In tali igitur casu construenda sunt castra semicicularia, triangluaria, quadrata, vel secundum aliquam aliam formam, quam requiit dispositio et aptitudo situs. Porta autem principalis ex illa parte fienda est quae respicit hostes, vel circa quam profecturus est exercitus.[180] Sunt etiam in castris ponenda insignia ad terrendum hostes, et etiam ad hoc, ut, si continget aliquos de exercitu elongari a castris, visis insigniis melius sciant ad castra redire. His itaque pertractatis superest videre, quis munitionis modus attendendus sit in constructione castrorum. Nam si exercitus diu ibi morari intendat, erigendae sunt fortiores munitiones et fiendae ampliores fossae; sed si solum ibi pernoctare cupit aut ibidem per modicum tempus exsistere, non oportet tantas munitiones expetere. Modum autem et quantitatem fossarum tradit Vegetius dicens: quod si non immineat magna vis hostium, fossa debet esse lata pedum IX, alta VII;[181] sed si adversariorum vis acrior imminet, convenit fossam ampliorem et altiorem facere, ita ut sit lata pedum XII et alta IX.[182] Est tamen advertendum, quod, si fossa sit alta pedes IX, propter terram erectam supra fossam crescit quasi pedes IV, ita quod tota fossa erit alta quasi pedes XIII. Debet enim fossa esse inantes ex parte hostium, et terra proicienda est ad partem intra, ubi est exercitus collocandus. In terra autem illa figendi sunt stipites et ligna et munitiones aliae, quas secum exercitus portare debet.[183] Sic ergo castris constitutis, sic fossis factis poterit exercitus morari securus.

---

[180] Vegetius, I 23 (p. 26, 2): Porta autem, quae appellatur praetoria, aut orientem spectare debet aut illum locum, qui ad hostes respicit, aut si iter agitur, illam partem debet adtendere, ad quam est profecturus exercitus.

[181] Vegetius, I 24 (p. 26, 13) tumultuaria fossa fit lata pedes IX et alta pedes VII.

[182] Vegetius, I 24 (p. 26, 14): Sed ubi vis acrior imminet hostium, tunc legitima fossa ambitum convenit munire castrorum, ita ut XII pedes lata sit et alta sub linea, sicut appellant, pedes IX. Supra autem saepibus hinc inde factis, quae de fossa levata fuerit, terra congeritur et crescit in altum IIII pedes; sic fit, ut sit XIII alta.

[183] Vegetius, I 24 (p. 26, 20): supra quam sudes de lignis fortissimis, quas milites portare consueverunt, praefiguntur.

Cap. IX. Quae et quot sunt consideranda in bello, si debeat pugna publica committi.

Ut patet per praehabita, circa negotia bellica est cautela maxima adhibenda. Nam quia bellorum casus irremediabiles sunt, diligenter videnda sunt, quaecunque circa bella consideranda exsistunt, priusquam pugna publica committatur; melius enim est, pugnam non committere, quam absque debita provisione fortunae casui se exponere. Videmus autem in bello duo exsistere, videlicet: viros pugnantes et auxilia alia, quae requiruntur ad pugnam. Ex parte autem virorum pugnantium, quantum ad praesens spectat, sex sunt attendenda, sic etiam ex parte auxiliorum et adminiculantium sex alia enumerari possunt, quae sunt etiam attendenda. In universo igitur rex aut princeps aut dux exercitus, qui debet esse vigilans, sobrius, prudens et industris,[184] duodecim considerare debet, scilicet: sex ex parte virorum, et sex ex parte adminisumlantium, priusquam eligat publican pugnam committere. Sunt enim sex ex parte hominum bellatorum, quae faciunt ad obtinendam victoriam. Primum enim numerus bellantium. Nam ubi plures sunt bellantes, ceteris aliis paribus, secundum quae huiusmodi sunt, victoriam obtinere debent; nam ut dicitur II. politicorum:[185] "*Quantitas in compugnatione est utilis, sicut maius pondus magis trahit*". Secundo ex parte bellatorum inassueta ad percutiendum et membra inexercitata ad bellandum, deficiunt in sustinendo pugnam. Est enim consuetudo quasi altera natura, ut quilibet virilius et expeditius et sine maiori labore et poena faciat opera consueta. Tertio attendenda est tolerantia erga necessitates corporis; nam exsistentes in exercitu oportet multa incommoda tolerare. Quare, si sint ibi aliqui molles et muliebres, renuentes incommoditates aliquas sustinere, devicti propter

---

[184] Vegetius, III 9 (p. 89, 9): Dux... vigilans, sobrius, prudens.

[185] Aristotle. *Politics.* II 1261 25: τὸ μὲν γὰρ τῷ πόσῳ χρήσιμον, κἂν ᾖ τὸ αὐτὸ τῷ εἴδει βοηθείας γὰρ χάριν ἡ συμμαχία πέφυκεν, ὥσπερ ἂν εἰ σтХϑμὸς πλεῖον ἑλκύση.

incommoditates, quas sustinent, bellare recusant et exercitum fugiunt. Quarto consideranda est fortitudo et durities corporis. Multum enim interest inter duritiem ferri et mollitiem panni serici, et inter suavitatem ludi et asperitatem pugnae. Considerato enim bello in universali omnes volunt esse boni bellatores, sed postquam veniunt ad experientiam particularium gestorum et gustant, quant sit durities ferri, et quantum affligunt vulnera hostium, ut plurimum est durus carne et robustus corpore, si propter talia non retrahitur a bellando. Nam etsi contingat, molles carne etiam, postquam gustaverint bella, appetere pugnam, hoc est ut raro, nam habentes carnes molles, ut supra tangebatur, sunt aptiores ad intellegendum, sed ut plurimum sunt inepti ad pugnandum; nam tales difficilius sustinent armorum pondus, vehementius dolent ex illatione vulnerum. Quinto consideranda est in bellantibus versutia et industria ad bellandum Nam quanto cautiores sunt bellatores, tanto citius victoriam obtinent. Sexto attendenda est virilitas et audacia mentis, quia audaciores et magis cordati ut plurimum in pugna victoriam obtinent. Rex ergo aut princeps vel dux exercitus, priusquam publice dimicet, ex parte hominum bellatorum sex considerare debet. Primo, ex qua parte sunt plures bellatores; secundo, qui sunt magis exercitati, tertio, qui sunt fortiores in sustinendo necessitates et incommoda; quarto, qui sunt robustiores et duriores in corpore; quinto, qui sunt industriores et sagaciores in mente; sexto, qui sunt audaciores et viriliores corde.[186] Et tunc dux sobrius et vigilans, prout viderit suum exercitum in his conditionibus abundare aut deficere, poterit accelerare pugnam vel differre, vel bellare publice et aperte, vel per insidias et latenter.

Enumeratis sex condicionibus, quae considerandae sunt, priusquam committatur bellum publicum ex parte hominum bellatorum, reliquum est sex enumerare alia, quae sumuntur ex

---

[186] Vegeitus, III 9 (p. 86, 19): utrum maiorem numerum pugnatorum ipse an hostes habeant, utrum ipsius an adversariorum homines magis armatis sint et muniti, qui magis exercitati, qui sint in necessitatibus fortiores.

parte adminiculantium et eorum, qui auxiliantur ad bellum. In bello quidem auxiliantur equi, arma, victualia, loca pugnandi, tempus, et auxilium praestolatum. Debet ergo dux exercitus considerare: primo, ex qua parte sunt plures equi et meliores; secundo, ex qua parte sunt meliores sagittarii, plures armati et habentes meliora arma; tertio, ubi plus victualia abundant, nam aliquando absque vulnere et absque bello adversarii cedunt deficitentes in victualibus et ob modicitatem non valentes moram contrahere; quarto considerandum est impugnationis locus, qui sunt in altiori situ vel meliori ad pugnandum; quinto circa pugnam attendendum est tempus, utrum tempore, quo committenda est pugna, sol sit oppositus faciebus eorum vel hostium, et utrum sit aliquis ventus flans et elevans pulverem contra ipsos vel contra adversarios; nam habentes solem et ventum sive pulverum contra se, offenduntur in oculis, ut dimicare non possint; sexto est attendendum, qui plures auxiliatores exspectant. Nam si hostes plura exspectant auxilia, vel non est bellandum, vel acceleranda est pugna; si autem ipsi plures auxiliatores exspectant, est compugnatio differenda. His igitur omnibus diligenter inspectis prudens dux exercitus sufficienter advertere potest, utrum debeat publicam pugnam committere; nam prout viderit se in pluribus condicionibus praefatis abundare vel dificere, sic se habere poterit erga bellum. Forte nuquam continget, omnes conditiones praedictas concurrere ex una parte, ubi tamen plures et meliores condiciones concurrunt, est pars potior ad bellandum.

Cap. X. Quod utile est in bello ferre vexilla et constituere duces praeositos; et quales esse debeant, qui in exercitu vexilla portant et qui equitibus et peditibus praeponuntur.

Semper virtus unita et ordinata fortior est se ipsa dispersa et confusa. Contingit autem aliquando commisso bello ordines et acies turbari et confundi. Ne igitur hoc possit accidere, observabatur antiquitus, ut dividerentur exercitus in turmas et acies, et singulis singula vexilla constituebant, ita ut in quolibet vexillo per litteras vel per evidentia signa apte ostenderetur, cuius aciei vel cuius turmae esset vesillum illud, ut, si contingeret aliquem bellatorem deviare a propria acie, de facili rediret ad illam.[187] Utile ergo fuit in bellis insignia et vexilla deferre, ne confunderetur exercitus. Rursus expediebat constituere duces, centuriones, decanos et alios praepositos belli. Nam totus exercitus se habet ad similitudinem unius corporis, quare sicut omnia membra corporis se invicem iuvant, sic omnes bellatores et omnes partes exercitus se invicem defendunt. Quare sicut confunduntur membrorum opera, nisi dirigantur per ipsum caput, in quo viget sensus et cognitio, sic confunduntur bellatores in exercitu, si careant centurione aut duce, qui debet esse eorum caput et eorum directivum. Inde est, quod antiquitus, ne accideret confusio in bello, constituebatur dux aliquis, qui toti exercitui erat praepositus. Sub hoc autem duce erant centuriones, et sub centurione vero erant decani. Dicitur autem decanus a X sicut centurio a centum;[188] habebat enim centurio sub se decem decanos, itaque praeerat centum bellatoribus et decem decanis, quorum quilibet decanorum sub se decem viros pugnativos habebat. In galea enim centurionis scriptae erant litterae aliquae vel signum aliquod evidens, quod respicientes decani agnoscebant centurionem proprium et sciebant, quem sequi aliquod erat impressum, per quod decem bellatores viri, quibus ipse erat praepositus, decanum proprium agnoscebant. Hoc itaque modo vel etiam alio tam in aciebus equitum quam etiam peditum constituendi sunt duces et praepositi et ferentes vexilla, ut quilibet sciat, quid debeat agere. Est enim tantus terror in bello propter armorum strepitum et percussiones illatas, quod verba et montiones non sufficiunt ad dirigendum

---

[187] Vegetius, II 13 (p. 46, 9): antiqui quia sciebant in acie commisso bello celeriter ordines aciesque turbari atque confundi, ne hoc posset accidere, cohortes in centurias diviserunt et singulis centuriis singula vexilla constituerunt, ita ut, ex qua cohorte vel quota esst centuria, in illo vexillo litteris esset adscriptum, quod intuentes vel legentes milites in quantovis tumultu a contubernalibus suis aberrare non possent.

[188] Vegetius, II 8 (p. 43, 9): erant autem centuriones, qui singulas centurias curabant... erant decani, denis militibus praepositi. II 14 (p. 47, 12).

bellatores, sed oportet dare evidentia signa, ut quilibet ex solo intuitu sciat se tenere ordinate in acie et cognoscat, quid sit acturus. Ex hoc autem patere potest, quales debeant esse potantes insignia et vexilla; nam vexillo confracto, totus exercitus est confusus. Cum magna igitur diligentia est vexillifer eligendus, ut sit fortis corpore, animo constans, fidelis principi et expertus in armis, et <habeat> alia singula, quae requiruntur ad probum et strenuum bellatorem. Contigit enim etiam nostris temporibus totum populum cuiusdam civitatis devictum esse a bellatoribus paucis, eo quod vexillifer fraudem committens velavit vexillum et abscondit ipsum,[189] quare confundebantur bellatores, quasi non habentes caput et ignorantes, ad quid deberent attendere; propter quod, si in debellatione vita multorum hominum periculis mortis exponitur, cum magna diligentia vexillifer est quaerendus. Ex dictis etiam patere potest, qualis esse debeat, qui in exercitu est peditibus et equitibus praeponendus. Nam sicut caput est praestentius membris aliis, debet esse magis strenuus aliis et magis expertus in his, quae requiruntur ad pugnam. Quare cum pedites, si debeant

---

[189] This passage refers to Henry of Essex, whose crimes and eventual fate were long on the lips of Europe. Compare with *Jocelini de Brakelonda Cronica*, by Thomas Arnold in the Memorials of St. Edmund's Abbey vol I (London, 1890) p. 273: insurrecit in eum (Henricum de Esexia) Robertus de Monteforti, ipsius consanguineus, nec genere nec viribus impar, in conspectu principum terrae damnans et accusans eum de proditione regis. Asseruit nempe eum in expeditione belli apud Walliam in difficili transitu de Coleshelle (in year 1157) vexillum domini regis fraudulenter abiecisse et mortem eius sublimi voce proclamasse et in praesidium eius venientes in fugam convertisse. In rei veritate praedictus Henricus de Esexia inclitum regem Henricum secundum Walensium fraudibus interceptum diem clausisse credidit extremum; quod revera factum fuisset, nisi Rogerus comes Clarensis, clarus genere et militari clarior exercitio, cum suis Clarensibus maturius occurrisset et domini regis vexillum elevasset ad corroborationem et animationem totius exercitus. Henrico quidem resistente praedicto Roberto in contione et obiecta penitus infitiante, evoluto brevis temporis spatio ad corporale duellum perventum est (in year 1163). -- p. 274: Quid multa? Victus uccbuit (Henricus). Cumque mortuus crederetur, ad magnam petitionem magnatum Angliae, eiusdem Henrici consanguineorum, concessum est monachis eiusdem loci, ut darent eius corpus sepulturae. Postea tamen convaluit et resumpto sanitatis beneficio sub regulari habitu superioris aevi labe, detersit, et longam dissolutae aetatis hebdomadam uno saltem sabbato curans venustare studia virtutum in frugem felicitatis excoluit.

boni bellatores exsistere, debeant esse fortes viribus, proceri statura, scientes eicere hastas et tela, scire etiam debent gladium vibrare ad percutiendum, rotare scutum ad protegendum se,[190] debent esse vigilantes, agiles, sobrii, habentes armorum experientiam: oportet omnia haec peramplius et perfectius reperiri in eo, qui est supra pugnatores pedites praeponendus. Debet ergo, qui in pugna peditibus praeponitur, esse fortis viribus, procer statura, sciens eicere hastas et iacula, sciens dimicare gladio ad percutiendum, rotare scutum ad se protegendum, vigilans, agilis, sobrius, habere omnem armorum experientiam, ut sciat erudire pugnantes sibi commissos, et cogat eos ad bene bellandum et ad arma tergendum. Nam ipse armorum nito terrorem incutit hostibus, ut portans huiusmodi arma credatur bonus esse bellator.[191] Ipsa enim rubigo ermorum arguit inertiam bellandi in eo qui portat illa. Si ergo talis debet esse, qui praeponitur peditibus bellatoribus, multo magis debet esse armorum expertus et procer corpore et fortis viribus, qui est equitibus praeponendus, quia in bello equestri maior conflictus efficitur quam in pedestri pugna. Oportet igitur praepositum et ducem militaris belli esse habilem corpore, ut possit etiam armatus agiliter equum conscendere, scire fortiter equitare cum lancea parcutere, iacula eicere, cum scuto se protegere, cum clava et ense dimicare, habere omne armorum exercitium, ut possit suos commilitones de pugna erudire, ut fortiter pugnent, arma tergant et alia faciant, quae requiruntur ad bellum.

---

[190] Vegetius, II 14 (p. 47, 15): (decurio) sicut centurio eligendus est magnis viribus, procera statura, qui hastas vel missilia perite iaculetur et fortiter, qui dimicare gladio et scutum rotare doctissime noverit.
[191] Vegetius, II 14 (p. 48, 9): Plurimum enim terroris hostibus armorum splendor importat.

Cap. XI. Quibus cautelis debet uti dux belli, ne suus exercitus laedatur in via.

Mors est quid terribilissimum et finis omnium terribilium, ut dicitur III ethicorum.[192] Ubi igitur quaeritur mors populi et ubi hostes insidiantur morti civium, est omnis cautela adhibenda, ut exercitus servetur illaesus, et ut vita civium conservetur. Non ergo sufficit considerare ea, quae sunt consideranda in pugna publica committenda, nisi sciantur cautelae ad removendum impedimenta viarum, ne exercitus per insidias hostium periclitetur in via. Possumus autem, quantem ad praesens spectat, octo cautelas enumerare, quas debet dux belli retinere memoriter, ut salvetur vita pugnatorum, qui sunt sub ipso. Prima est, ut itinera regionum, per quae exercitus proficisci debet et intervalla locorum et qualitates virorum et compendia et deverticula et montes et flumina exsistentia in itinere illo debet habere conscripta, immo itinera illa et passus et flumina, dux exercitus habere etiam depicta, ut quasi oculorum aspectu prospiceret, qualiter exercitus deberet pergere, ut tutius posset suum exercitum ducere.[193] Sic enim marinarii faciunt, qui videntes maris pericula, ne eorum naves patiantur naufragium, descripserunt maris mappam, ubi portus marini, ubi discrimina maris et cetera talia proportionabiliter sunt descripta, quae marinarii intuentes statim percipiunt, qualiter debeant pergere, et in quo loco exsistunt, et a quibus debeant sibi cavere; quare, cum propter insidias hostium exercitus totus quasi vel etiam pluribus periculis exponatur in via quam nautae in mari, nullo modo debet exercitus pergere per viam aliquam, in qua pati

---

[192] Aristotle. *Nichomachean Ethics.* III 1114 26: φοβερώτατον δ' ὁ ϑάνατος πέρας γάρ, καὶ οὐδὲν ἔτι τῷ τεϑνεῶτι δοκεῖ οὔτ' ἀγαϑὸν οὔτε κακὸν εἶναι.

[193] Vegetius, III 6 (p. 75, 11): Primum itineraria omnium regionum, in quibus bellum geritur, plenissime debet habere perscripta, ita ut locorum intervalla non solum passuum numero sed etiam viarum qualitate perdiscat, compendia, deverticula, montes, flumina ad fidem descripta consideret, usque eo, ut sollertiores duces itineraria provinciarum, in quibus necessitas gerebatur, non tantum adnotata sed etiam picta habuisse firmentur, ut non solum consilio mentis verum aspectu oculorum viam profecturus eliget.

possit insidias, nisi qualitates viarum, montes et flumina et cetera reperta in illo itinere habet dux conscripta et etiam depicta. Secunda cautela est, ut simul cum hoc quod habet vias et qualitates viarum conscriptas et depictas, ducat dux belli conductores aliquos bene scientes vias illas, qui pluries peragraverunt et experti sunt illas.[194] Nam <per> videre aliqua conscripta et depicta non sunt ita nota, sicut per se ipsa sensibiliter videremus ipsa; nam potior est cognitio rei, per quam cognoscitur in se ipsa, quam per quam cognoscitur in pictura vel in suo simili. Ne tamen conductores moliantur fraudes aliquas, debet dux circa eos bonas apponere custodias, ne possint fugere; debet etiam iis minari mortem, si in aliquo fraudulenter se habeant, et promittere dona, si se fideliter gesserint. Tertia est, secum habere sapientes plures fideles principi, exercitatos in bellis, de quorum consilio agat, quidquid viderit esse fiendum.[195] Nam ubi currit tantum periculum, nullus debet inniti proprio capiti nec credere sibi soli. Quarta cautela est, ut itinera ignorentur, per quae debet exercitus proficisci.[196] Nam consilium ducis, quanto minus publicum est, tanto, quae sunt in consiliis deliberata, minus impediuntur et citius fini debito mancipantur. Postquam igitur deliberatum est, per quas vias debet exercitus pergere, et vias illas dux habet conscriptas et depictas, et habentur ductores aliqui fideles, quanto hoc minus est publicum et magis celatum ab hostibus, tanto exercitus magis secure proficiscitur. Quinta est, in quolibet agmine et in qualibet acie habere aliquos equites fidelissimos et strenuissimos, habentes equos veloces et fortes, qui ante et a tergo et a dextra et a laeva praecurrunt illustrantes et

---

[194] Vegetius, III 6 (p. 75, 19): Ad hoc a prudentioribus et honoratis ac locorum gnaris separatim debet universa perquirere et veritatem colligere de pluribus; praeterea viarum duces idoneos scientesque praecipere eosque custodiae mancipare addita poenae ostentatione vel praemii.

[195] Vegetius, III 6 (p. 76, 4): Providendum quoque, ut sapientes exercitatique quaerantur, ne duorum aut trium error discrimen pariat universis; interdum autem imperita rusticitas plura promittit et credit se scire quae nescit.

[196] Vegetius, III 6 (p. 76, 8): Sed cautelae caput est, ut, ad quae loca vel quibus itineribus sit profecturus exercitus, ignoretur; tutissimum namque in expeditionibus creditur facienda nesciri.

disco operientes insidias, ne hostes aliqui latitantes ex aliqua parte molestent exercitum.[197] Nam etsi nullis esset notum ducis consilium, eo tamen ipso, quod per aliquas vias incipit exercitus iter arripere, coniecturari quis potest, per quas partes debeat proficisci; et quia probabile est, semper in talibus aliquos exploratores adesse, cogitare debet dux belli, quod et hoc posset ad aures hostium pervenire. Itaque cum pericula provisa minus noceant, per velocissimos equites sunt detegendae insidiae, ne exercitus circa aliquam partem ex improviso patiatur molestias. Sexta est, ut semper ex illa parte exercitus probiores milites et magis bellicosi pedites apponantur, ex qua creditur maius periculum imminere; quodsi ex omni parte de periculo dubitatur, undique sunt remedia adhibenda.[198] Septima est, ne exercitus dispersim vadat, nam interrupta acie facilius debellatur.[199] In qualibet enim hora sic exercitus se debet habere, ut, si etiam tunc hostes praesentes adessent, iis non possent efficere nocumentum. Unde etiam proverbialiter dicitur, quod 'qui est munitus, non est derisus'. Semper ergo dux belli, cui commissa est tantorum vita, debet esse attentus et vigilans, ne hostes eum invadere possint quasi neglegentem et dormientem. Debet etiam dux exercitus, centuriones, decani et alii, qui operibus bellicis praeponuntur, semper monere milites et pedites, ut sint parati ad arma, ut, si contingeret aliqua invasio subita, possent invadentibbus resistere. Sic enim dicendo, dato quod accideret aliquis repentinus insultus, esset quasi provisus et minus praestaret nocumentum.[200] Octava cautela est, considerare

---

[197] Vegetius, III 6 (p. 76, 18): Dux cum agmine exercitus profecturus fidelissimos argutissimosque cum equis probatissimis mittat, qui loca, per quae iter faciendum est, in progressu et a tergo, dextra laevaque perlustrent, ne aliquas adversarii moliantur insidias.

[198] Vegetius, III 6 (p. 77, 9): Illud tamen praecipue servandum est, ut ea pars, ad quam hostis venturus creditur, oppositis lectissimis equitibus et levi armatura necnon etiam peditibus sagittariis muniatur; quodsi undique circumfunduntur inimici, undique debent praeparata esse subsidia.

[199] Vegetius, III 6 (p. 78, 15): Illudque vitandum, ne per neglegentiam aliis festinantibus, aliis tardius incedentibus interrumpatur acies aut certe tenuetur; continuo enim hostes inter pellata pervadunt.

exercitum, in quibus sit copiosior, utrum magis abundet peditibus vel equitibus. Nam equites melius se defendunt in campis, pedites vero in locis silverstribus et montuosis.[201] Itaque prout viderit dux belli se abundare in equitibus vel peditibus, eligere poterit vias campestres et ammplas, vel montanas, silvestres et nemorosas et alias, prout noverit expedire.

Cap. XII. Qualiter ordinandae sunt acies, si debeamus contra hostes vel contra adversarios dimicare.

Postquam diximus, sub quo continetur operatio bellica, et ex quibus regionibus sunt meliores pugnantes, et ex quibus artibus sunt meliores bellicosi, declaravimus etiam, qualiter in exercitu construendae sunt munitiones et castra, et quae sunt consideranda, si debeat publica pugna committi, et ex quibus cautelis abundare decet bellorum ducem, ne suus exercitus laedatur in via, quantum ad campestre bellum nihil, ut videtur, ulterius dicere restat, nisi ut doceamus ordinare acies et percutere adversarios et invadere hostes. Prius tamen dicemus de irdine acieruml si enim ordo servetur in acie, non modicum valet ad pugnam. Nam, ut ait Vegetius: Nisi bellantes sint ordinati et occupent debitum spatium,[202] bene pugnare non poterunt. Nam si nimis sunt constricti, impediuntur, ne alios percutere possint; si vero nimis rari et interlucentes aditum praestant hostibus, facilius devincantur. Servare autem debitum ordinaem in acie, ut equites et pedites suam aciem servent, non sine magno exercitio fieri potest. Qui igitur in tempore aliquo vult bellare, per diuturna tempora debet exercitare pugnatores ad servandum debitum

---

[200] Vegetius, III 6 (p. 77, 16): in necessitate subita conterrent, provisa non solent esse formidini.

[201] Vegetius, III 6 (p. 78, 12): Nam in campis patentibus equites magis solent impugnare quam pedites; at vero in locis silvestribus vel montuosis sive palustribus pedestres magis formidandae sunt copiae.

[202] Vegetius, I 26 (p. 27, 13): Nam et constipati perdunt spatia pugnandi et sibi invicem impedimento sunt, et rariores atque interlucentes aditum parrumpendi hostibus praestant.

ordinem in acie et ad faciendum ea, quae requiruntur in bello. Modus autem, per quem pugnatores huiusmodi ordinem servare discant, est, ut frequenter tam equites quam pedites ducantur ad campos. Et ille, qui est exercitatus in bellis et qui debet equitibus vel peditibus esse praepositus, primo debet equites et pedites linealiter disponere, ita ut seriatim maneant et aequaliter a se invicem distent secundum distantiam, quam requirit acies equestris vel pedestris;[203] postea praecipere debet, ut duplicent aciem, ita quod medietas aciei statim separet se a medietate alia et seriatim ordinet se ante aliam vel post ipsam;[204] quo facto statim debet praecipere dux belli, ut aciem quadratam faciant,[205] et deinde, ut constituant trigonum,[206] quod faciliter fit. Nam acie quadruplata et secata diametro et partibus quadratis coniunctis simul faciunt trigonum, vel ut sit ad unum dicere, quod non omnes hos modos geometricos capiunt, ductis pugnatoribus ad campos sive equitibus sive peditibus imperare debet dux belli, quod pugnatores ordinent se secundum formam quadrangularem et postea secundum triangularem, et deinde secundum rotundam, et sic deinceps debet assuefacere bellantes, ut sciant construere aciem secundum quamcunque formam.[207] His visis sciendum, quadrangularem formam aciei inter ceteras formas esse magis inutilem,[208] ideo secundum hanc formam numquam est formanda acies simpliciter sed in casu, ut si situs loci talem formam requirat; in huiusmodi casu construenda est forma praedicta. Formae autem acierum secundum se ad bellandum utiles sunt: pyramidalis et rotunda et forficularis. Nam pugnantes vel solum volunt se

---

[203] Vegetius, I 26 (p. 27, 19) in aciem dirigendi, ita ut primo simplex et extenta sit acies, ne quos sinus ne quas habeat curvaturas, ut aequali legitimoque spatio miles distet a milite.

[204] Vegetius, I 26 (p. 27, 22): ut subito duplicent aciem, ita ut in ipso impetu is, ad quem respondere solent, ordo servetur.

[205] Vegetius, I 26 (p. 28, 1): ut quadratam aciem repente constituant.

[206] Vegetius, I 26 (p. 28, 1): quo facto in trigonum, quem cuneum vocant, acies ipsa mutanda est.

[207] Vegetius, I 26 (p. 28, 4): ut instruant orbes.

[208] Vegetius, III 20 (p. 106, 6): Una depugnatio est fronte longa quadro exercitu sed hoc genus depugnationis periti armorum non optimum iuducant.

defendere vel sustinere ictus, vel volunt alios invadere. Si ergo bellantes non sentiunt se tantae potentiae, ut alios debellare possint, sed sufficit iis, ut se defendant, tunc est construenda acies secundum rotundam formam, et pugnantes debent se magis constringere et constipare, ut acies non possit ab hostibus transscindi. Circa aciem autem in summitate et exteriori parte constituendae sunt homines gravioris armaturae et meliu armati, qui absque minori gravamine possint ictus suscipere.[209] Si vero pugnantes credunt se esse tantae potentiae, ut possint adversarios incidere, tunc vel secundum eorum proportionem hostes sunt pauci, vel multi. Si hostes sunt valde pauci, construenda est acies secundum formam forficularem,[210] ut acies sit aperta ad modum ferri equi et quasi forficis, ut adverarios quasi in medio capiat et concludat. Si vero hostes sunt multi, construenda est acies secundum formam, quam appellant cuneum, id est secundum formam pyramidalem et acutam, ut possit hostes scindere et dividere, nam divisis hostibus facilius debellantur.[211] Acies ergo constructa in forma rotunda utilis ad sustinendum, in forma vero forficulari est utilis ad circumdandum et concludendum, com hostes sunt pauci; sed in forma acuta et pyramidali utilis est ad scindendum et dividendum, cum hostes sunt plures. Sciendum est ergo, quod numerus acierum construendus est secundum multitudinem pugnatorum; prout quis plures aut pauciores acies construere. Sciendum etiam, quod semper in cornu aciei et in locis, ubi maius periculum est, ne acies confundatur, apponendi sunt probiores pugnatores, qui possint virilius dimicare.[212] Est etiam advertendum, quod in qualibet acie

---

[209] Vegetius, III 19 (p. 105, 1): unum remedium est, ut alam cornumuque replices et rotundes, quatenus conversi tui sociorum terga defendant; sed in angulo ipsius extremitatis fortissimi conlocentur, quia ibi impetus amplior fieri consuevit.

[210] Vegetius, III 19 (p. 105, 10): ordinatio ponitur quam foricem vocant. Nam ex lectissimis militibus in V litteram ordo componitur.

[211] Vegetius, III 19 (p. 105, 6): Cuneus dicitur multitudo peditum, quae iuncta cum acie primo angustior deinde latior procedit et adversariorum ordines rumpit, qua a pluribus in unum locum tela mittuntur. Quam rem milites nominant caput porcinum.

praeter numerum pugnatorum constituentuim aciem reservandi sunt aliqui strenui bellatores extra ipsam aciem, qui possint ad illam partem succurrere, ubi viderint magis aciem deficere. Haec igitur tria observanda sunt in constitutione acierum: primo, ut acies bene ordinetur secundum formam rotundam, acutam et forficularem, ut requirit bellum committendum; secundo, ut probiores bellatores in illis partibus aciei apponantur, in quibus magis potest confundi et perforari acies; tertio, ut extra quamlibet aciem reserventur aliqui milites strenui et audaces, qui possint succurrere ad illam partem, erga quam viderint aciem titubare et deficere.

Cap. XIII. Quod deridendi sunt in bello omnes percutientes caesim, et quod eligibilius est percutere punctim.

Ostenso qualiter sunt acies ordinandae et constituendae, reliquum est ostendere, qualiter pugnantes percutere debeant, utrum eligibilius sit percutere caesim vel punctim. Possumus autem quinque viis ostendere, quod deridendi sunt percutientes caesim, et quod eligibilius est percutere punctim. Prima sumitur ex prohibitione armorum, secunda ex resistentia ossium, tertia ex providentia vulnerum, quarta ex fatigatione membrorum, quinta ex detectione percutientium. Prima via sic patet: nam quanto ensis aut gladius plus capit de armis, tanto propter armorum resistentiam difficilius itur in carnem. Inde est, quod bellorum experti dicunt pugnantes semper debere habere loricas amplas, ita ut anuli loricarum se restringant; quia, quanto illi anuli magis sunt compacti, tanto oportet plures ex iis frangere, ut vulnera noceant.[213] Sic percutientes caesim oportet de armis plus incidere quam percutientes punctim. Ut ergo vulnus perveniat citius ad carnem, magis eligibile est percutere punctim quam caesim. Modica autem

---

[212] Vegetius, III 17 (p. 101, 21): ad victoriam plurimum confert, ut lectissimi de peditibus et equitibus... habeat dux post aciem praeparatos, alios circa cornua alios circa medium, ut, sicubi hostis vehementes insistit, ne rumpatur acies provolent subito.

[213] Vegetius, I 12 (p. 16, 11): cum et armis vitalia defendantur et ossibus.

armorum incisio sufficit ad laedendum carnem percuutiendo punctim, quae non sufficeret, si percuteretur caesim. Secunda via ad investigandum hoc idem sumittur ex resistentia ossium: nam etsi quis quasi inermis exsisteret in percussione caesim, priusquam perveniretur ad cor vel ad membra vitalia, oporteret magnam plagam facere et multa ossa insiderel sed percutiendo punctim, duae inciae sufficiunt ad hoc, quod fiat plaga mortalis et sit letale vulnus.[214] Considerare quidem debemus, quod, quidquid est hosti nocivum, secundum quod huiusmodi est nobis proficuum. Ideo in exercitu, ubi quaeritur mors adversariurum, percutiendum est punctim, quia sic feriendo citius onfligitur plaga mortifera. Tertia via sumitur ex providentia vulnerum. Nam quanto hostis magis vulnera providet, magis potest se protegere et citius potest illa vitare; quia iacula provisa minus laedunt. In percutiendo autem caesim, quia oportet fieri magnum bracchiorum motum, priusquam infligatur plaga, adverserius ex longinquo potest providere vulnus, ideo potest magis sibi cavere et cooperire se ab ictibus.[215] Ideo ait Vegetius, quod punctim percutere '*adversarium sauciat, antequam videat*'. Unde hoce genere percutiendi potissime usi sunt Romani; *deridebant* enim Romani milites omnes percutientes caesim, et ipsi volebant percutere punctim. Quarta via sumitur ex fatigatione membrorum. Inter cetera enim in bellis est hoc potissime attendendum, ut pugnantes absque nimia sui fatigatione possint adversarios laedere; nam si bellantes nimis se fatigent, non valentes laborem illum tolerare, de facili dimittunt aciem et convertuntur in fugam. Quare, cum percutiendo caesim propter magnum bracchiorum motum insurgat ibi magnus labor, punctim vero feriendo fatigatio modica sufficiat, eligibilius est percutere punctim quam caesim. Caesa enim percussio, quovis impetu veniat, raro occidit, sed puncta modico impetu inflicta, facit letale vulnus. Quinta via sumitur ex detectione percutientis. Nam bonus

---

[214] Vegetius, I 12 (p. 16, 13): at contra puncta duas uncias adacta motalis est.

[215] Vegetius, I 12 (p. 16, 15): dum caesa infertur, bracchium dextrum latusque nudatur; puncta autem tecto corpore infertur et adversarium sauciat, antequam videat.

bellator, si potest, sic debet adversarium laedere, ut tamen ipse non laedatur. Omnis ergo ille modus percutiendi est magis eligendus, secundum quod feriens minus discooperiture et detegitur, quia sic feriendo minor laesio potest ei accidere; quare cum percutiendo punctim et tecto coprore possit minus adversarius laedere, melius est percutere punctim quam caesim; percutiendo enim caesim oportet elevare bracchium datur hosti materia, ut possit nos facilius laedere. Name levius infertur laesio et nocumentum corpore nudato quam tecto.

Cap. XIV. Quot et quae sunt illa, quae hostes potentiore reddunt. Et quot modis et qualiter debemus hostes invadere.

Ut dicebatur superius, quod hosti est proficuum, nobis est nocivum, et converso;[216] quaecunque igitur reddunt hostes fortiores ad resistendum bellantiubus, quia illa sunt iis proficua, eorum opposita sunt iis nociva, et reddunt eos debiliores, ne possint impugnantibus resistere. Quantum autem ad praesens spectat, possumus septem enumerare, per quae hostes sunt fortiores contra impugnantes. Primum est, si sunt in acie debite ordinati. Nam cum virtus unita, ut supra tangebatur, fortior sit se ipsa dispersa, si hostes sunt bene uniti et debite in acie ordinati, si invadantur, difficilius devincuntur. Secundum, quod reddit hostes fortiores as resistendum, est locus; nam in uno loco hostes facilius se tuentur quam in alio. Nam in transitu fluriorum, inter praecipitia montium et inter difficultates viarum, si contingat hostes in tali situ reperiri, difficilius se defendere poterunt, quia oportet eos sparsim incedere. Quare sicut locus ineptus defensioni, si in eo hostes inveniantur, reddit eos debiles ad bellandum, sic locus aptus facit eos potentiores ad resistendum. Tertium est ipsum tempus. Nam eorum percutit et in quo solares radii opponuntur eorum oculis, difficilius possunt hostes resistere; tempore vero, in quo haec modo opposito se habent, hostes habiliores sunt ad pugnandum.[217]

---

[216] Vegetius, III 26 (p. 120, 12): condicio talis est, ut quod tibi prodest adversarium noceat; quod illum adiuvat tibi semper officiat.

Quartum, quod reddit hostes magis animosis et magis promptos ad renitendum, est provisio; quia, quando provisi sunt et praesciunt pugnatorum adventum, magis se muniunt et minus terrentur ex eorum occursu. Quintum autem est debita et moderata quietatio. Nam quando hostes sunt lassati laboribus, vigiliis et incommoditatibus aliis, si tunc invadantur, facilius devincuntur, quam si debite quievissent; debita ergo quies hostes potentiores reddit. Sextum quidem est amor et concordia ipsorum. Nam si hostes divisi corporaliter devincuntur facilius, multo magis divis amino et voluntate debellantur celerius, quis maior est divisio animorum quam corporum. Et converso: si hostes non sunt sparsi sed sunt totaliter coniuncti, potentiores sunt ad bellandum, et multo magis, si se diligant et sint coniuncti animo et voluntate, quia de se ipsis magis confidunt, erunt viriliores et promptiores ad pugnandum; omnis enim amor est quaedam vis unitiva, et plus amor unti amantium corda quam loci unitas exsistentium corpora, Quare, si unitas loci et congregatio bellantium eos potentiores facit, amor et unitas cordium eos viriliores reddit. Septium, quod facit hostes potentiores ad renitendum, est latentia propriarum condicionum exsistentium circa ipsos. Nam quanto condiciones hostium melius sciuntur, tanto facilior eligitur via, qualiter debeant impugnari; quanto vero eorum negotia sunt magis latenita, magis ignoratur impugnationis modus. Enumeratis itaque, quae reddunt hostes potentiores ad renitendum, de facili patere potest, quomodo et qualiter bellantes suos hostes invadere debeant; nam cum septem modis enumeratis hostes fortiores exsistant, cum modo opposito se habent, sund invadendi et bellandi. Primo igitur dux belli per insidias vel per aliquem alium modum debet diligenter advertere, quando hostes sunt dispersi, et tunc debet eos invadere, quia non habebunt resistendi potentiam. Secundo debet diligenter explorare eorum itinera, ut ad transitus fluviorum, ad praecipitia mantium, ad angustias silvarum, ad difficultares

---

[217] Vegetius, III 14 (p. 96, 20): Nam sol ante faciem eripit visum; ventus contrarius tua inflectit et comprimit, hostium adiuvat tela; pulvis a fronte congestus oculos implet et claudit.

paludum et viarum se hostibus opponat, quia sic facilius devincentur.[218] Tertio debet adspicere ad tempus, ut quando sol reverberatur ad oculos hostium, pulvis et ventus repercutiuntur ad eorum vultus, tunc debet eos invadere, quia oculis ipsorum disgregatis a sole et offensis per ventum et pulverem non bene videre poterunt, qualiter debeant dimicare, propter quod oportebit eos fugam eligere. Quarto dux exercitus sic se temperare debet, ut tali hora faciat suos commilitone cibum capere et requiescere et eorum equos pausare, ut possint invadere hostes ex improvisio, ut eos invadant, quando cibum capiunt, vel quando discalciati, distractis equis, non suspicantes eorum adventum.[219] Quinto debet diligenter explorare, quando hostes fecerunt magnam dietam, sunt fatigitati,[220] habent lassatos equos; tunc enim, si eos invadere poterint, de facili terga vertent. Sexto secundum Vegetium debet dux belli inter suos hostes et inimicos vel per se vel per alios mittere dissensiones,[221] iurgua commovere eos ad lites vel ad inimicitias, ut de se invicem non confidant; hoc enim facto, si eos invadat non habentes fiduciam de se invicem, de facili convertentur in fugam. Sed haec cautela, licet ponat eam Vegetius, non multum est appretianda, quia videtur repugnare bonis moribus.[222] Septimo debet diligenter explorare condiciones

---

[218] Vegetius, III 10 (p. 91, 6): Ad transitus fluviorum, ad praecippitia montium, ad silvarum angustias, ad paludum aut viarum difficultates superventus nullo sciente disponat.

[219] Vegetius, III 10 (p. 91, 9): ita iter suum temperet, ut cibum capientes aut dormientes aut vacantes certe, securos inermes discalciatos, destratis equis, nihil suspicantes ipse paratus invadat.

[220] Vegetius, III 10 (p. 91, 16): si excurrant adversarii, longo itinere fatigatos adgrediatur.

[221] Vegetius, III 10 (p. 92, 2): Inter hostes discordiarum serere causas sapientis est ducis.

[222] This prescription of the high-minded philosopher must not be used to prove the "knightly" or chivalric nature of the warfare of that era, and it is precisely the pupil to whom these warnings were directed that demonstrably failed to obey them in his wars against King Edward I of England. This is reported in an *Anonymous Memoir of the Wars Against England*, "*Philippe ne se contenta pas d' acquérir des alliés, il voulut enlever au roid' Angleterra les siens.*" The opposition sought to outdo him, "*pourchaça de novelles alliances et de coronpre par force de deniers et par mariages de ceus du royaume.*" However, at the

hostium, qualiter se gerant, qualiter se habeant, quis est dux eorum, de quo dux ille magis confidit, quos mores habeat.[223] Nam exploratis condicionibus singulis facilius invenitur via, qualiter possit hostes invadere et debellare.

Cap. XV. Quomodo homines bellatores stare debant, si velint hostes percutere, et quomodo debeant eos circumdare, et quomodo debeant declinare a pugna, si non sit bonum pugnam committere.

Diximus in quodam capitulo praecedenti percutiendum esse punctim non caesim, in quo docuimus milites et etiam pedites. In hoc capitulo specialem doctrinam volumus dare peditibus, qualiter debeant stare, cum volunt hostes percutere. Percussionis autem hostium duplex est modus: unus a remotis, ut cum iaciendo iacula vel missibilia adversarios feriunt; alius autem, cum adeo appropinquantur, quod manu ad manum se percutiunt. Aliter autem debent stare bellatores viri, cum a remotis iacula iaciunt, et aliter, cum ex propinquo se feriunt. Nam iaciendo iacula a remotis debent habere pedes sinistros ante et dextros retro. Nam cor, quod est in animali principium motus, principalius influit in partem dextram; itaque pars dextra in animalibus fortior est in movendo et aptior est ad motum. Et quia semper mobile innititur alicui immobili, ut si movetur manus innititur bracchio stanti, et si movetur bracchium, innititur corpori quiescenti, et si movetur unus pes innititur alteri pedi non moto, oportet, cum movetur pars dextra, quod innitatur parti sinistrae quiescenti. Cum igitur pes sinister anteponitur et latus dextrum elongatur, optime disponitur homo ad iaciendum iacula et missilia, quia tunc quiescit in sinistra,

---

conclusion of peace, Edward abandoned the traitors, and they, thereby, fell to the wrath of the French king, "*Si y doivent les autres prendre exemple.*" Compare with E. Boutaric's *Documents inédits relatifs à l'histoire de France sous Philippe le Bel (Notices et Extraits des manuscrits* XX, 2 p. 121).

[223] Vegetius, III 9 (p. 87, 19): Ad rem pertinent, qualis ipse adversarius vel eius comites optimatesque sint, nosse, utrum temerarii an cauti, audaces an timidi, scientes artem bellicam vel ex usu an temere pugnantes.

et movetur dextra, vibrans ipsum iaculum, quo vibrato vehementius movet aërem et fortius ferit. Licet enim tam secundum partem dextram quam sinistram possumus quiescere et moveri, dextra tamen est aptior ad movendum quam sinistra, et sinistra ad quiescendum. Ideo percutientes a remotis debemus quiescere super sinistrum pedem antemissum et elongare nos cum dextro, ut possimus vehementius impellere et vibrare iaculum. Sed quando manu ad manum pugnatur gladio, debemus e contrario nos habere, ita quod pedem dextrum teneamu ante et sinistrum post. Nam quia latus dextrum aptius est ad motum, si illud sit hosti propinquius, ratione motus poterit melius ictus effugere; vehementius enim percutitur quod stat, quam quod movetur. Rursus si dextrum latus sit hosti propinquius, melius poterit ipsum percutere. Debent enim bellatores, cum ad manum pugnant, tenere pedem sinistrum immobiliter, et cum volunt ictus fugere, cum eodem pede debent se retrahere; sic itaque tenendo pedem sinistrum immobilem et cum dextro se movendo, poterunt fortius hostes percutere et eorum ictus facilius fugere.

Viso, quomodo debeant stare bellantes, si debeant hostes percutere, videre restat, quomodo sunt hostes includendi et circumdandi. Sciendum ergo, quod raro aut numquam sic circumdandi sunt hostes in pugna publica, quod non pateat iis aliquis aditus fugiendi, quia tunc desperantes, quasi necessitate compulsi efficiuntur audaces; videntes enim se necessario morituros, possunt multa mala committere in eis, qui contra pugnant. Inde est, quod laudatur Scipionis sententia dicentis: numquam claudendos sic esse hostes, quod non pateat iis aditus fugiendi.[224] Nam fugientibus hostibus nullum est periculum, et in fuga periclitantur multi absque nocumento persequentium; sed cum se vident inclusos, quasi coacti feriunt includentes. Cum ergo supra diximus, formandam esse aliquando aciem sub forma forficulari, ut quando hostes sunt pauci, ad hoc quod melius

---

[224] Vegetius, III 21 (p. 111, 11): Ideoque Scipionis laudata sententia est, qui dixit viam hostibus, qua fugerent, muniendam.

includantur et circumdentur, non sic intellegendum est, quod ita debant circumdari, quod nullus pateat aditus abscedendi, nisi forte adeo essent pauci, quod quantumcunque rebellare vellent, nullum possent nocumentum efficere.

Ostenso itaque qualiter debeant stare pugnantes, si velint hostes percutere, et qualiiter eos debeant circumdare, restat nunc tertio declarare, qualiter sit declinandum a pugna, si non habeatur consilium, ut videatur bonum pugnam committere, eo quod hostes sint fortiores, et non possimus illis resistere. In quo, quantum ad praesen spectat, debet dux belli duplicem habere cautelam. Prima enim est quantum ad exercitum proprium. Nam etsi dux habeat consilium non esse pugnandum, debet hoc patefacere valde paucis, et non debet illud toti exercitui pandere, ne timentes turpiter fugiant et ab insequentibus hostibus occidantur. Taliter itaque dux se habere debet, quod non credit exercitus, quod velit fugere, sed alibi velit parare insidias, et quod contra hostes velit acrius dimicare.[225] Secunda cautela adhibenda est ex parte exercitus hostium. Nam sic debet inclinare bellum, ut hoc hostes lateat.[226] Ideo multi tempore nocturno potius quam diurno hoc agunt,[227] et plures hanc habuere cautelam, quod milites stantes in acie ex opposito hostium prohibebant eos, ne pedites videre possint, propter quod pedestris pugna latenter recedit, qua recedente equites postea melius possunt vitare hostium percussiones.[228] Est ergo advertendum, quod, quando sic declinatur pugna numquam acies se debent dividere, quia, si contingeret hostes insequi fugientes a bello, plures occident et magis nocumentum inferent fugientibus, quam si se verterent et

225 Vegetius, III 22 (p. 112, 8): ut tui nesciant, ideo te recedere, quia declinas inire conflictum, sed credant arte aliqua se ideo revocari, ut ad oportuniorem locum invitetur hostis ac facilius superetur aut cert insequentibus adversariis secretiores conlocentur insidiae.

226 Vegetius, III 22 (p. 112, 13): Illud quoque vitandum est, ne hostes te recedere sentiant et statim irruant.

227 Vegetius, III 22 (p. 112, 21): Aliquanti... noctu cum exercitu recedebant.

228 Vegetius, III 22 (p. 112, 15): plerique ante pedites suos equites posuerunt, ut discurrentes adversarios videre non sinerent.

bellarent. Debet etiam dux belli inquirere, utrum sit aliquis locus propinquus, ad quem posset confugere exercitus, si fugaretur ab hostibus.[229]

Cap. XVI. Quot sunt genera bellorum, et quot modis devincendae sunt munitiones et urbanitates, et quo tempore melius est obsidere civitates et castra.

Videntur autem omnia bella ad quattuor genera reduci, videlicet: ad campestre, obsessivum, defensivum et navale. Beelum autem campestre dicitur omnis pugna facta in terra, secundum quam bellantes ad invicem pugnant, absque munitione media; quanto tamen huiusmodi pugna magis est a munitionibus separata, tanto est magis campestris et magis perculosa. Secundum genus pugnae dicitur obsessivum, quando bellatores sunt tantae potentiae, quod non exspectant, ut hostes de munitionibus exeuntes vadant bellare ad campum, sed ipsi munitiones invadunt et obsident illas. Tale genus pugnae communi nomine dicitur obsessivum. Est autem et tertium genus pugnae, quod defensivum vocari potest. Nam sicut contingit pugnantes aliquos in tanta multitudine esse et tantam habere potentiam, ut non exspectent hostes exire ad campum, sed ipsas munitiones obsideant et invadant; sic contingit aliquos esse adeo paucos et tam debiles, ut non putent in campo posse resistere impugnantibus. Ideo se in munitionibus tenent clausos, et sufficit iis, quod possint munitiones defendere, si contingat eos ab hostibus impugnari. Tale genus pugnae, quo quis defendit munitiones et castra, defensivum dicitur. Nam etsi in omni pugna est aliquo modo invasio et defensio, attamen cum quis obsidet munitiones et castra, magis dicitur alios invadere quam se defendere: in pugna ergo obsessiva magis est invasio quam defensio; in bello vero, quo quis se tuetur in munitionibus et castris, magis est ibi defensio quam invasio: ideo tale genus

---

[229] Vegetius, III 22 (p. 113, 2): Praeterea levis armatura praemittebatur ad colles, ad quos subito totus revocaretur exercitus.

pugnae merito dicitur defensivum. Quartus autem modus pugnandi dicitur navalis, quia, sicut contingit esse pugnam in terra, sic contingit eam ese in aquis; immo horribiliores et periculosiores sunt pugnae aquaticae quam terrestres. Huiusmodi autem pugnae in aquis factae, cuiuscunque condicionis aquae illae exsistant, navales dicuntur.

Quare, cum sint quattuor genera pugnarum, postquam diximus de campestri, restat dicere de obsessiva, defensiva et navali; contingit enim aliquando reges et principes pugnare omnibus his modis pugnandi, nam aliquando committitur campestre bellum, aliquando vero obsidentur munitiones et castra, contingit etiam aliquando aliquos invadere aliquas munitiones eorum, propter quod oportet eos uti pugna defensiva. Amplius autem in principatu et regno contingit esse portus et terras maritimas, iuxta mare sitas. Propter quod, ne portus destruantur, et ne fiant per eos ab hostibus introitus in regnum, et ne terrae maritimae impugnentur, expedit regibus et principibus aliquando ordinare bella navalia. Dicto itaque de bello campestri, de aliis generibus bellorum est dicendum. Verum quia de campestri pugna diffusius diximus et de cautelis bellorum multa discussimus, cum per viam dictam circa omne bellum possint cautelae haberi, qualiter quis se debeat habere, non oportet circa alio bellorum genera diutius immorari. Primo tamen dicemus de bello obsessivo. Viso igitur, quot sunt bellorum genera, et dicto, quod post bellum campestre primo dicendum est de pugna obsessiva, cum per huiusmodi pugnam contingat obtineri et devinci muntiones et urbanitates, restat dicere, quot modis talia devinci possunt.

Est autem triplex modus obtinendi munitiones et castra, videlicet: per sitim, famem et pugnam. Convenit enim aliquando obsessos carere aqua; ideo vel oportet eos siti perire, vel munitiones reddere. Quare diligenter excogitare debent obsidentes munitiones aliquas, utrum per aliqua ingenia vel per aliquam industriam possint ab obsessis abripere[230] aquam; nam multotiens contingit aquam a remoto principio derivari usque ad munitiones obsessas. Quare, si in illo fontali principio destruatur fistula vel meatus, per quem pergit aqua ad obsessos, oportebit ipsos pati aquarum penuriam. Rursus aliquando munitiones sunt altae, et aqua non pervenit usque ad eas; quare, si sit a munitionibus remota, debent obsidentes adhibere omnem diligentiam, quomodo possint obsessis prohibere aquam.[231] Secundus modus impugnandi munitiones est per famem. Nam sine cibo durare non possumus, ideo obsidentes, ut munitiones obtineant, passus, vias et omnia loca, per quae possent obsessis victualia deferri, diligenter custodire debent, ne iis talia deferantur. In huiusmodi enim obsessionibus multotiens plus affligit fames quam gladius.[232] Inde est, quod multotiens obsidentes volentes citius obtinere munitiones, si contingat eos capere aliquos de obsessis, non occidunt illos, sed per mutilationem membrorum eos reddunt inutiles et postea eos remittunt ad munitiones obsessas, ut ibi una cum aliis comedentes apud ipsos obsessos maiorem famem et inopiam inducant. Tertius modus obtinendi munitiones est per pugnam, ut cum itur ad muros et cum per pugnam dimicatur contra obsessos. Sed qualiter et quot modis contingit talem pugnam committere, in sequenti capitulo ostendetur. Ostenso, quot sunt genera bellorum et quot modis devincendae sunt munitiones obsessae, restat ostendere, quo tempore melius est obsidere civitates et castra. Sciendum itaque, quod tempore aestivo, antequam sint recollecta blada, vina et alia, per quae subveniri potest inopiae obsessorum, est melius obsessionem facere; illo enim tempore omni modo devincendi melius devincentur obsessi. Nam si per sitim sunt munitiones obtinendae, est melius facere obsessionem tempore aestivo, eo quod tunc magis desiccantur aquae, nec sic abundent caelestes pluviae, ut possit per cisternas

---

[230] Translator's Note: Various copies differ as to this word. Schneider selected *abripere*, whereas some copies use *accipere*.

[231] Compare withe Vegetius IV 11 (p. 136, 7): Quodis hostis ab unda prohibeat, nam hoc accidit. Vegetius places these on the side of the defense, who must use all means at their disposal in order not to suffer from lack of water.

[232] Vegetius, III 3 (p. 69, 6): ferro saevius fames est.

subveniri obsessis. Rursus si per famem est castrum vel civitas obsessa obtinenda, melius est obsessionem facere aestivo tempore, antequam messes et vina sint recollecta, quia semper tali tempore consueverunt deficere fructus anni praeteriti. Quare, si obsessi non possunt gaudere fructibus anni advenientis, citius peribunt inopia. Amplius si per bellum et pugnam munitiones sunt obtinendae, melius est hoc agere aestivo tempore; nam tempore hiemali abundant pluviae, replentur fossae aquis, quare difficilius impugnantur obsessi; rursus incommoditates temporum magis molestant obsidentes et exsistentes in campis quam obsessos manentes in domibus. Vel igitur obsessiones fiendae sunt tempore aestivo, vel si per multa tempora obsessiones durare debent, saltem inchoandae sunt tempore aestivo, priusquam blada et vina et alios fructus terrae recolligere possint obsessi.

Cap. XVII. Quomodo se debent munire obsidentes, et quomodo per cuniculos impugnari possunt munitiones obsessae.

Si obsidentes neglegentes fuerint et non diligenter se muniant, ab obsessis molestari poterunt. Nam cum contingat obsessiones per multa aliquando durare tempora, non est possibile obsidentes semper aeque paratos esse. Ideo nisi sint muniti, contingit, quod exsistentes in castris, cum fuerint occupati obsidentes somno, cibo vel otio, aut aliqua necessitate dispersi, et repente prorumpunt in ipsos et succendunt tentoria, destruunt obsidentium machinas, et aliquando multi ex obsidentibus pereunt. Quare obsidentes, ut tuti permaneant, longe a munitione obsessa saltem per ictum teli vel iaculi debent castrametari et circa se facere fossas et figere ibi ligna et construere propugnacula, ut, si oppidani eos repente vellent invadere, resitentiam invenirent. Viso, quomodo se munire debent obsidentes, ne ab oppidanis molestentur, restat ostendere, quot modis debent impugnare obsessos. Est autem unus modus impugnandi communis et publicus, videlicet: per ballistas, arcus et per lapide emissos manibus vel fundis, vel etiam per appositiones scalarum. Nam multum enim industres in pugna,[233] si obsessi faciunt se ad muro et ad propugnacula, statim impugnant eos cum ballistis et arcubis, iaciunt contra ipsos lapides cum manibus vel cum fundis, apponunt scalas ad muros ut, si possint ascendere, sint pares illis. Praeter tamen hos modos impugnationis apertos est dare triplicem impugnationis modum, non omnibus notum: quorum unus est per cuniculos, alius est per machinas proicientes lapides magnos et graves, tertius est per aedificia implsa usque ad muros munitionis obsessae. De omnibus his itaque impugnationibus dicemus; sed primo de impugnatione per cuniculos. Primo igitur per cuniculos, id est per vias subterraneas, devincuntur muntiones. Debent enim obsidentes privatim in aliquo loco terram fodere, ante quem locum tentorium vel aliquod aliud aedificium debent apponere, ne obsessi videre possint, ubi incipiant fodere. Ibi enim fodiendo faciunt vias subterraneas, sicut faciunt fodientes argentum et invenientes venas metallorum; debent per vias illas, faciendo eas profundiores, quam sint fossae muntitionis devincendae, pergere usque ad muros munitionis praedictae. Quodsi hoc fieri potest, leve est munitionem capere; nam hc facto primo debent muros fodere et supponere ibi ligna, ne statim cadant, etcum omnes muros vel maximam partem murorum sic subfosserint et suppunctaverit, si viderint obsidentes, quod per solum casum murorum possint munitiones obtinere, statim debent apponere ignem in lignis sustinentibus muros et facere omnes muros vel magnam eorum partem simul cadere et replere fossas, quo quasi ex inopinato facto terreantur obsessi, ut facilius devincatur oppidum Est autem attendendum, quod viae subterraneae semper sunt muniendae tabulis et aliis artificiis, ne cadat terra et suffocet fodientes. Terra etiam quae extrahitur de dictis fossis, est taliter abscondenda, ne videatur ab obsessis; et rursus cum ignis apponitur ad ligna sustinentia murum, apponens huiusmodi ignem et exsistentes cum eo debent se ad locum tutum facere, ne laedantur per murorum casum.[234] Sic ergo agendum est in

---

233 Translator's Note: Some versions of the manuscript read as "*industres in pugna*"; other versions read as "*industris est pugna*".

impugnatione per cuniculos, cum ad munitionem obtinendam sufficit sola murorum ruina. Si tamen hoc creditur non sufficere, muris exsistentibus suffossis et suppunctatis nondum apponendus est ignis, sed procedendum est ad maiores munitiones et ad maiora moenia castri vel civitatis obsessae, et per similes vias subterraneas est similiter faciendum circa ea, quod factum est circa muros. Rursus procedendum est divertendo vias subterraneas, ut per eas possit habere ingressus ad civitatem et castrum, quae omnia latenter fieri possunt, absque eo quod sentiantur ab obsessis,[235] licet non sine difficultate et diuturnitate temporis possint haec omnia fini debito mancipari. His itaque sic peractis in aliquo tempore nocturno, vel in aliquo alio congruo ad pugnandum, per appositionem ignis debet fieri, ut simul cadant muri et munitiones suffossae, et per vias subterraneas fiat ingressus ad castrum vel ad civitatem, et per aditum factum ex muris cadentibus reliqui obsidentes ingrediantur castrum vel civitatem obsessam, et sic poterunt obtinere illam.

Cap. XVIII. Quae et quot[236] sunt genera machinarum eicientium lapides, per quae impugnare valent munitiones obsessae[237] et devinci possunt civitates et castra.[238]

Contingit autem pluries munitiones aliquas obsessas super lapides fortissimos esse constructas, vel esse aquis circumdatas, vel habere profundissimas foveas, vel aliquo alio modo esse munitas ut per cuniculos et per vias subterraneas[239] numquam vel

---

[234] Vegetius, IV 24 (p. 145, 18): cum ad murorum fundamenta pervenerint, suffodiunt eorum maximam partem appositis siccioribus lignis ruinamque muri tumultuario opere suspendunt; sarmenta insuper iungunt aliaque fomenta flammarum; tunc praeparatis bellatoribus operi ignis immittitur combustisque columnis ligneis atque tabulatis muro subito corruente irruptioni aditus reseratur.

[235] Vegetius, IV 24 (p. 145, 15): penetrant urbem et noctu non sentientibus oppidanis egrediuntur per cuniculum.

[236] Either "*Quae et quot*" or simply "*Quot*"

[237] Possibly also "*obsesse*".

[238] "*et devinci -- castra*" does not appear in manuscript B.

[239] *Subterraneas* vias in B.

valde de difficili obtineri possint.[240] Evenit etiam pluries, ut, si munitio obsessa per vias subterraneas capi possit, obsessi tamen, providentes fossionem, impediunt eam, ne per ipsam fraudulenter et per insidias devincantur; quod quomodo fierei habeat, ostendums, cum in sequentibus capitulis agetur de pugna defensiva. Cum enim tractabimus,[241] qualiter obsessi se defendere debeant, declarabitur, qualiter obsessi cuniculos et alia machinamenta obsidentium debeant providere. Quare: si modus artis debet imitari naturam, quae semper faciliori via res ad effectum producit,[242] cum per cuniculos non ita de facili munitiones impugnari possunt sicut per machinas lapidarias vel per aedificia propulsa usque ad moenia castri vel civitatis obsessae, oportet talibus uti argumentis, ut habeatur intentum. Videndum est igitur, quot[243] sint genera machinarum lapidariarum, et quot[244] sint modi aedificiorum, per quae munitiones impugnantur.

Machinae autem lapidariae quasi ad quattuor genera reducuntur. Nam in omni tali machina est dare aliquid trahens et elevans virgam machinae, ad quam coniuncta est funda, qua lapides[245] iaciuntur. Haec autem elevatio virgae aliquando fit per contrapondus; aliquando vero non sufficit contrapondus, sed ulterius[246] cum funibus[247] elevatur virga machinae: qua[248] elevata iaciuntur lapides.

Si ergo per solum contrapondus fit huiusmodi proiectio, contrapondus illud vel est fixum, vel est mobile, vel est[249] compositum ex utroque.

---

[240] Manuscript B reads *possunt.*

[241] The words "*obsessi tamen -- tractabimus*" do not appear in B; it simply reads "*obsessi tabimus.*".

[242] B reads *perducicit.*

[243] A reads *quot* while B reads *qd'.*

[244] A reads *quot* while B reads *qd'.*

[245] A read *lapides*, whereas B reads *lapides rapides.*

[246] *Ulterius* in A, *ultius* in B.

[247] A reads *cum funibus*, whereas nothing of the sort appears in B.

[248] A reads *qua* while B reads *que.*

Dicitur autem contrpondus esse fixum, quando in virga infixa[250] est quaedem cassa, immobiliter adhaerens virgae, plena lapidibus et arena, vel plena plumbo, vel aliquo alio gravi corpore, quod genus machinae vateres Trabucium vocare voluerunt. Inter ceteras autem machinas haec rectius proicit, eo quod contrapondus semper uniformiter trahat; ideo semper eodem modo impellit, cum signum percutiendum est[251] per ipsam, si nimis proicit ad dextram vel ad sinistram, vertenda est ad locum, erga quem iaciendus est lapis, si vero nimis alte proicit, vel elonganda est machina a signo, vel in funda eius[252] apponendus est lapis[253] gravior, quem non tantum elevare poterit; si vero nimis basse,[254] appropinquanda est machina, vel alleviandus[255] est lapis. Semper enim ponderandi sunt lapides machinarumm, si determinate sit proiciendum ad aliquod[256] signum.

Aliud genus machinae habet[257] contrapondus mobiliter adhaerens circa flagellum vel virgam ipsius machinae, vertens se circa huiusmodi virgam; et hoc genus machinae Romani pugnatores appellaverunt Biffam.[258] Differt autem haec a trabucio. Nam qui contrapondus mobiliter adhaeret virgae machinae, licet plus trahat ratione motus,[259] non tamen sic uniformiter trahit; ideo plus proicit, non tamen sic recte et uniformiter percutit.

---

[249] *Est* only appears in B. It is missing in A.

[250] B reads *infixa*, but A only reads *fixa*.

[251] A reads *est*, but this is missing from B.

[252] *Eius* is only present in A. Nothing is present here in B.

[253] *Lapis* is only present in A. Nothing is present here in B.

[254] A reads "*nimis basse*". B, however, has the longer "*nimis hme vel nimis vasse*".

[255] *Aleviandus* in A; *ille viandus* in B.

[256] A is the only version that reads *aliquod*. This word is absent in B.

[257] A reads *habet*, whereas B reads *habent*.

[258] B reads *Biffam*, but A reads *Byffam*.

[259] *Motus* is used in A, but B uses the word *notus*.

Est autem etiam tertium genus machinae, quod Tripantum nuncupant, habens utrumque contrapondus: unum infixum virgae, et aliud mobiliter se vertens circa ipsam. Hoc enim ratione ponderis infixi rectius proicit quam biffa,[260] ratione vero ponderis mobiliter se vertentis longius emittit lapidem quam trabucium.

Quartem ver genus machinae est, quod loco contraponderis habet funes,[261] qui trahuntur per vires et manus hominum. Huiusmodi enim[262] machina non[263] proicit lapides ita[264] magnos sicut praedicta tria genera machinarum, tamen non oportet tantum tempus apponere ad proportionandum huiusmodi machinam sicut in machinis praefatis; ita quod pluries et spissius proicit haec machina quam praedictae.

Ille igitur, qui obsidet castrum aut civitatem aliquam, si vult eam impugnare per machincas lapidarias, diligenter considerare debet, utrum magis possit munitionem illam impugnare proiciendo rectius, vel longius, vel medio modo inter utrumque, vel etiam magis possit obsessos[265] offendere proiciendo spissius et frequentius. Nam prout viderit expedire, omnibus praedictis machinis,[266] vel omnibus praefatis modis proiciendi vel aliquibus, sive aliqua praedictarum machinarum castrum vel civitatem obsessam poterit impugnare. Si enim plena notitia habeatur de machinis, de quibus mentionem fecimus, sufficienter scietur, quomodo per machinas lapidarias[267] poterit quaelibet munitio impugnari.

---

[260] B spells this word *biffa*, but A spells it *byffa*.
[261] B spells this words as *fines*, but A uses the word *funes*.
[262] *Enim* only appears in B. The word is absent in A.
[263] *Non* only appears in B, while it is absent in A.
[264] The word *ita* only appears in manuscript B. There is nothing there in manuscript A.
[265] *Obsessos* in B, and *obsessas* in A.
[266] B, however, reads *machinis praedicits*.
[267] A reads *lapidaria* instead.

Nam omne genus machinae[268] lapiilidariae vel est aquod praedictorum, vel potest originem sumere ex praedictis. Est etiam advertendum, quod die et nocte per lapidarias machinas[269] imugnaris possunt munitiones obsessae. Tamen ut videatur, qualiter in nocte percutiunt lapides emissi a macinis, semper cum lapide alligandus est ignis, vel titio ignitus;[270] nam per titionem ignitum lapidi alligatum apparere poterit, qualiter machina proicit, et qualis sive quam ponderosus lapis est in funda machinae imponendus.

Cap. XIX Quomodo per aedificia lignea impulsa ad muros civitatis vel castri impugnari possunt munitiones obsessae.

Tangebanur autem supra tres modi impugnandi munitiones obsessas, quorum unus erat per cuniculos, alius per machinas lapidarias, terius vero per aedificia lignea impulsa ad muros munitionis obsessae. Dicto ergo de impugnatione facta per cuniculos et per lapidarias machinas, restat dicere de impugnatioone, quam fieri contingit per aedificia impulsa ad muros vel ad moenia castri vel civitatis obsessae. Huiusmodi autem aedificia quasi ad quattuor genera reducuntur, videlicet: ad arietes, vineas, turres et musculos. Vocatur autem aries testudo quaedam lignorum, quae, ne igne comburatur, crudis coriis cooperitur. Sub hav enim testudine sic cooperta coriis et fortiter contexta, ne lapidibus obrautur, intrinsecus ponitur trabs, cuius caput ferro vestitur; ideo appellatur aries, quia ratione ferri ibi appositi durissimam habet frontem ad percutiendum. Huiusmodi enim trabs funibus vel catenis ferreis alligatur ad testudinem factam ex lignis; ad modum arietis se subtrahit et postea muros munitions obsessae percutit et dirumpit. Cum enim per huiusmodi trabem sic ferratam multis ictibus percussus est murus, ita quod iam lapides existentes in ipso incipiunt commoveri, in capite eius infigitur

---

[268] A uses the phrase *machinae genus*.

[269] A uses the word *machinas* while B substitutes the phrase *et machinas*.

[270] *Vel titio ignitus* only appears in A. It is missing in B.

quoddam ferrum retortum ad modum falcis, per quod lapides commoti et conquassati evelluntur a muro, ut citius perforetur.[271] Valet autem huiusmodi aedificium ad impugnandum munitionem aliquam, dato quod quis non possit pertingere usque ad muros eius. Nam quia huiusmodi trabs habens caput sic ferratum retrahitur et impungitur, poterit percuti murus munitionis obsessae, dato quod textura illa, sub qua sunt homines impungetntes trabem, non pertingat usque ad muros. Est autem huiusmodi textura, sub qua sunt homines impungetntes arietem sive trabem, optime munienda, ne viri illi sagittis vel lapidibus vel aliquo alio modo ex aliqua parte possint offendi.

Aliud autem aedificium est ad impugnandum munitiones obsessas, quod vocant vineaml quidam autem huiusmodi aedificium alias cattum[272] nominant. Fit autem hoc, cum tabulae grossae et fortes optime colligantur et duplicantur, ut sit duplex tabulatum, ne lapides emissi possint tale aedificium frangere; cooperitur etiam crudis coriis, ne ab igne possit offendi. Consuevit autem tale aedificium fieri in latitudine VIII pedum et in longitudine XVI, in altitudinem ver tot pedum, quod homines competentes ibi possint exsistere.[273] Huiusmodi enim aedificium tantae quantitatis vel etiam maioris est optime undique muniendum et impellendum usque ad muros munitionis obsessae, sub quo homines exsistentes fodiunt muros illos. Est autem hoc aedificium utile,

---

[271] Vegetius, IV 14 (p. 137, 10): Haec (tetsudo) intrinsecus accipit trabem, quae aut adunco praefigitur ferro et falx vocatur ab eo, quod incurva est, ut de muro extrahat ;apides; aut certe caput istius vestitur ferro et appelatur aries, vel quod habet durissimam frontem, qua subruit muros, vel quod more arietum retrocedit, ut cum impetu vehementius feriat.

[272] Potentially also *cautum.*

[273] Vegetius, IV 15 (p. 137, 20): Vineas quas veteres dixerunt, nunc militari barbaricoque usu *causias* vocant. E lignis levioribus machina colligatur, lata pedibus VIII, alta pedibus VII, long pedibus XVI. Huius tectum munitione duplici tabulatis cratibusque contexitur. Latera quoque vimine saepiuntur, ne saxorum telorumque impetu penetrentur. Extrinsecus autem, ne immisso concremetur incendio crudis ac recentibus coriis vel centonibus operitur. Istae cum plures factae fuerint, iunguntur in ordinem, sub quibus obsidentes tuti ad subruenda murorum penetrant fundamenta.

cum talis est munitio obsessa, quod usque ad muros eius potest tale aedificum impelli.

Tertium genus aedificiorum sunt turres vel castra. Nam si nec oer arietes nec per vineas capi possunt munitiones obsessae, accipienda est mensura murorum munitionis illius, et secundum huiusmodi mensuram vel secundum altiorem constituendae sunt ligneae turres vel castra, quae tegenda sunt crudis coriis, ne succendantur ab igne. Cum his quidem ligneis castris dupliciter impugnantur munitiones obsessae: primo iaciendo lapides. Nam si altitudo castrorum excedit altitudinem murorum et etiam turricularum et propugnaculorum exsistentium in ipsis, sic se habebunt exsistentes in castris ad exsistntes in munitionibus quodammodo, sicut exsistentes <in munitionibus> ad eos, qui sunt in basso vel in terra. Rursus in huiusmodi castris ordinantur pontes cadentes, per quos itur ad muros munitionis obsessae.[274]

Altitudo autem murorum dupliciter potest accipi. Primo per umbram; nam leve filum, cuius nota sit quantitas, ligandum est ad sagittam et proiciendum usque ad muros munitionis, secundum quantitatem cuius sciri poterit quantitas umbrae. In illa ergo hora, in qua accipitur umbrae quantitas, erigendum est aliquod lignum in altum, faciens tantam umbram, et secundum altitudinem ligni illius erit altitudo murorum. Verum quia non semper sol splendet et facit umbram, sed aliquando tegitur nubibus, dabimus alium modum accipiendi altitudinem cuiuslibet aedificii et quorumcunque murorum.[275] Accipiatur autem aliquod lignum vel tabula aliqua ad

---

[274] Vegetius, IV 17 (p. 139, 19): diverso genere conatur irrumpere. Nam in inferioribus habet arietem, cuius impetu destruit muros; circa mediam vero partem accipit pontem... in superioribus autem turris illius partibus contati et sagittarii collocantur, qui defensores urbis ex alto contis missilibus saxisque prosternunt.

[275] Vegetius, IV 30 (p. 149, 5): Mensura autem colligitur duplici modo; aut enim linum tenue et expeditum uno capite nectitur in sagitta, quae cum ad muri fastigia directa pervenerit, ex mensura lini murorum altitudo deprehenditur; aut certa, cum sol obliquus umbram turrium murorumque iaculatur in terram, tunc ignorantibus adversariis umbrae illius spatium mensuratur itemque decempeda

quantitatem alicuius hominis, et ille homo, ad cuius quantitatem accepta est tabula illa, iaciat se in terram, et ad pedes eius ponatur praedicta tabula et adspiciat per summitatem illius tabulae; et si visus eius protenditur magis alte quam sit aedificium, cuius est altitudo sumenda, trahat se magis prope aedificium illud; si vero visus protendatur nimis basse, cum tabula sic exsistente ad pedes et sic iacens in terra elonget se ab aedificio praedicto, donec per summitatem tabulae punctaliter videat summitatem eius. Nam ut probari potest geometrice: quanta erit distantia a capite hominis sic iacentis usque ad aedificium illud, tanta erit aedificii altitudo. Possent etiam menurae talium altitudinum accipi per regulas traditas in astralabio et in quadrante; sed de hoc nobis non sit curae, sufficiat autem de talibus ad praesens tanta dicere, quanta sufficiunt ad propositum.

Quartum geuns aedificiorum vocant musculos. Sunt enim musculi quadam aedificia, sub quibus tegeuntur homines trahentes vel impellentes castra usque ad moenia munitionis obsessae.[276] Possent autem per huiusmodi musculos quasi continuari castra usque ad munitionem obsessam. Quod cum factum est, tripliciter est impugnanda munitio. Nam in castro sic aedificato ad munitionem impugnandam est tria considerare, videlicet: partem superiorem excedentem muros et turriculas munitionis capiendae, partem quasi mediam, ad quam applicantur pontes cadendi super muros illos, et partem infimam, ad quam applicantur musculi, sub quibus sunt homines trahentes vel impellentes castrum. Cum ergo castrum illud appropinquaverit, quantum debuit, ad muros munitionis obsessae, illi, qui sunt in parte superiori, debent proicere lapides et fugare eos, qui sunt in muris; qui autem sunt in parte intermedia, debent pontes dimittere et invadere muros; sed qui sunt in parte infima et sub musculis, si

---

figitur et umbra ipsius similiter mensuratur.

[276] Vegetius, IV 16 (p. 138, 18): musculos dicunt minores machinas, quibus protecti bellatores sudatum auferunt civitatis, fossatum etiam apportatis lapidibus lignis ac terra non solum complent sed etiam solidant, ut turres ambulatoriae sine impedimento iungantur ad murum.

possint, ad muros accedere et eos suffodere, ut et etiam sic obsidentes intrare possint obsessam munitionem. Sunt etiam ballistae, arcus, machinae lapidariae et omnia talia congreganda, ut, quando haec fiendae sunt, munitionem percutiant; quanto enim pluribus modis simul munitio impugnatur, tanto plus terrentur obsessi et citius capitur.

Cap. XX. Qualiter aedificanda sunt castra et civitates, ne per pugnam ab obsidentibus faciliter devincantur.

Postquam diximus de bello campestri et determinavimus de bello obsessivo, docentes obsidentes munitiones et castra, qualiter debeant ea obsidere et debellare, in parte ista determinare volumus de bello defensivo; vel postquam docuimus obsidentes, qualiter se debeant invadere obsessos, volumus docere ipsos obsessos, qualiter se debeant defendere ab obsidentibus. Primum autem, quod maxime facit, ne obsessa civitas devincatur ab obsidentibus, et quod maxime facit, ut obsessi faciliter possint defendere munitionem aliquam, est scire, qualiter aedificanda sunt castra et civitates et munitiones ceterae, ne faciliter impugnentur. Sunt autem quinque in huiusmodi aedificatione consideranda, per quae munitiones fortiores exsistunt et difficiliores ad capiendum. Primo quidem fortificantur munitiones et sunt difficiliores ad debellandum ex natura loci; secundo ex angularitate murorum; tertio ex terratis, quarto ex propugnaculis; quinto ex fossatis.

Ex natura quidem loci urbes et munitiones fortiores exsistunt, si editae sunt in praeruptis rupibus vel locis eminentibus et inaccessibilibus, aut si mare est circa eas, vel paludes aut flumina circumdant ipsas.[277] A principio igitur quando aedificandae sunt munitiones defendendae ab exteriori pugna et ab obsidentibus, consideranda est natura loci, ut in tali loco aedificentur, quod ex ipso situ fortiores exsistant; vel si non vacat

---

[277] Vegetius, IV 1 (p. 129, 15): urbes... muniuntur... natura: aut locorum edito vel abrupto, aut circumfuso mari sive paludibus vel fluminibus.

munitiones de novo aedificare, et aliqui timentes iram dominorum aut domini metuentes furorem populi volunt se in munitione aliqua tueri, si adsit facultas, quaerenda est munitio talis, quae ex ipsa natura loci fortior exsistat et difficilior ad impugnandum. Secundo urbes et munitiones sunt difficiliores ad impugnandum ex angularitate murorum. Nam si munitio muros habeat angulares, si contingat obsidentes ad muros accedere, ut munitionem devincant, obsessi facilius se tuentur ab illis et levius offenndutntur obsidentes. Nam propter angularitatem murorum non solum ex parte anteriori, sed etiam a tergo et quasi ex parte posteriori percutiuntur impugnantes munitionem illam.[278] Fiendi itaque sunt muri angulares, ut munitio facilius defendi possit. Tertium autem quod reddit munitionem difficiliorem ad capiendum, dicuntur esse terrata vel muri ex terra facti; nam in munitione fienda non solum quaerenda est bonitas situs et angularitas murorum, sed circa munitionem illam aedificandi sunt duo muri aliqualiter distantes, et intra spatium, quod inter illos duos muros includitur, ponenda est terra, quae fodienda est de fossis, quae fodiendae sunt circa munitionem illam, vel est aliunde terra apportanda et ponenda in illo spatio intermedio. Est etiam huiusmodi terra intra tale spatium posita ita densanda, quod ad invicem conglutinetur et efficiatur quasi murus.[279] Contingit enim etiam turres ex terra facere, si bene condensetur, propter quod non est inconveniens, constituere huiusmodi muros ex terra densata; valet quidem constiutio talium murorum ad defendendam munitionem, ne devincantur per machinas lapidarias. Nam dato quod per huiusmodi machinas totus murus exterior rueret, murus constitutus ex terra, quasi

---

[278] Vegetius, IV 2 (p. 130, 7): sinuosis anfractibus iactis fundamentis clausere urbes, crebrioreque turres in ipsis angulis reddiderunt propterea, quia, si quis ad murum tali ordinatione constructum vel scalas vel machinas voluerit admovere, non solum a fronte sed etiam a lateribus et prope a tergo velut in sinu circunclusus opprimitur.

[279] Vegetius, IV 3 (p. 130, 14): Intervallo vicenum pedum interposito duo intrinsecus parietes fabricantur. Deinde terra, quae de fossis fuerit egesta, inter illos mittitur vectibusque densatur... quia nec murus ullis potest arietibus rumpi, quem terra confirmat, et quovis casu destructis lapidibus ea, quae inter parietes densata fuerat, ad muri vicem ingruentibus moles obstitit.

absque laesione suscipiet ictus machinarum, quia, cum lapis eiectus a machina perveniret ad huiusmodi murum, propter mollitiem eius cederet terra et reciperet lapidem illum, quasi ac si sibi esset fabricatus. Expertum enim est, muros ex terra densata constitutos minus laedi a machinis lapidariis quam muri alii. Debet quidem talis murus ex terra factus esse grossus, quia tunc quasi absque laesione suscipiet lapides emissos a machinis. Quartem autem, quod facit munitiones fortiores, sunt turres et propugnacula, nam in ipsis muris constituendae sunt turres et propugnacula, ut munitio levius defendi possit, maxime autem ante portam quamlibet ipsius munitionis, de qua timetur, ne ad eam accedant obsidentes, fiendae sunt turres et propugnacula. Et ante huiusmodi portam ponenda est cataracta pendens anulis ferreis, undique etiam ferrata et prohibens ingressum hostium et incendium ignis. Nam si obsidentes vellent portas munitionis succendere, cataracta, quae est ante portas, prohibet eos. Rursus super cataractam debet esse murus perforatus recipiens ipsam, per quem locum poterunt proici lapides et emitti poterit aqua ad exstinguendum ignem, si contingeret ipsum ab obsidentibus esse appositum.[280] Quintum, quod facit munitiones magis inaccessibiles et fortiores, est latitudo et profunditas fossarum, quae, si adsit facultas, replendae sunt aquis.[281]

His ergo modis sunt munitiones difficiliores ad capiendum; ideo videndum est a principio ab his, qui volunt munitiones defendere ab obsidentibus eas, ut in munitionibus illis omnia haec vel plura ex istis concurrant ad hoc, quod facilius defendantur.

---

[280] Vegetius, IV 4 (p. 131, 3): Cavetur praeterea, ne portae subiectis ignibus exurantur Propter quod sunt coriis ac ferro tegendae; sed amplius prodest, quod invenit antiquitas, ut ante portam addatur propugnaculum, in cuius ingressu ponitur cataracta, quae anulis ferreis ab funibus pendet, ut, si hostes intraverint, demissa eadem exstinguantur inclusi. Ita tamen supra portam murus est ordinandus, ut accipiat foramina, per quae de superiore parte effusa aqua subiectum restinguat incendium.

[281] Vegetius, IV 5 (p. 131, 11): Fossae autem ante urbes latissimae altissimaeque faciendae sunt... et, cum aquis coeperint redundare, ab adversario cuniculum continuari minime patiantur.

Cap. XXI. Quomodo muniendae sunt civitates et castra et universaliter omnes munitiones, ut ab obsidentibus difficilius capiantur.

Non sufficit scire, quomodo aedificandae sunt munitiones, et quales muros debent habere, et quomodo debent esse sitae, nisi sciatur, quomodo sunt muniendae, ut non de facili devinci possint. Dicebatur autem supra, triplicem esse modum devincendi munitiones, videlicet: per famem, sitim et pugnam. Sic ergo muniendae sunt munitiones obsessae, ne aliquo horum modorum possint devinci. Ne enim fame devincantur, tria sunt attendenda, videlicet: ut frumenta, avena, hordeum et cibaria singula et universa pabula, quae possunt deservire ad victum, deportanda sunt ad munitionem obsessam, priusquam obsideatur ab extraneis; et, si timetur de opbsessione ante recollectionem frugum, ex aliis locis propinquis sunt talia acquirenda, ne munitio obsessa ad carentiam victus possit pati defectum. Quidquid autem non potest ad munitionem deferri, vel si deferreretur, non multum esset utile castro vel civitati obsessae, totum est igne comburendum, ne obsidentes supervenientes inde capiant emolumentum, et ex bonis propriis munitionis obsessae impugnent ipsam.[282] Si autem timeatur de diuturnitate temporis, vel quod per multa tempora debeat obsessio perdurare, maxime munienda est civitas vel castrum obsessum milio; nam milium inter cetera minus putrescit et diutius durare perhibetur. Copia enim carnium salitarum non est praetermittenda; salis etiam multitudo multum est expediens munitioni obsessae, eo quod ad multa sit utilis. Secundo in muniendo castrum vel civitatem aliquam obsidendam, quantum ad victum, non solum attendendum est, ut magna copia victualium deferatur ad munitionem obsessam, sed etiam ut victualia delata per temporatos erogatores per familias dispensentur.[283] Verum sic fieri posset: si civitas obsessa esset

---

[282] Vegetius, IV 7 (p. 133, 4): quae apportari nequiverint, exurenda... nihilque, quod usui proficiat, hostibus relinquendum.

magna et non posset aliunde recuperare victum, in qualibet contrata civitatis victualia reduci deberent ad horrea publica. Et parce et temperate per viros providos dispensari; quodsi munitio obsessa modici esset ambitus, hoc efficere non esset difficile. Quasi enim nihil prodest praeparatio multa victualium, nisi parce et cum temperamento dispensetur.

Tertio est in talibus attendendum, ut personae debiles et inutiles, non valentes proficere ad defensionem munitionis obsessae, si commode fieri potest, sunt ad partes alias transmittendae; tales enim consumunt et comedunt, quae deberent bellatoribus erogari.[284] Rursus, si timeatur de inopia victualium, bestiae, quae sunt in munitione obsessa, a quibus obsessi possunt commode abstinere, sunt occidendae vel saliendae, si esui sint aptae; immo in tali casu comedenda sunt multa, quae ad esum vetat communis usus.[285] Viso quomodo munitio obsessa vitat, ne capiatur fame, de levi potest videri, qualiter se debeant habere obsessi, ne devincantur per sitim. Nam antequam aliqui eos obsideant, providere debent, quod ad talem munitionem pergant, in qua sit aquarum copia; quodsi vero ibi non sunt fontes, fodiendi sunt putei; quodsi etiam locus sit siccus, ut ibi nec putei fieri possint, fiendae sunt cisternae, ut caelestium aquarum superabundantia suppleat aliarum aquarum defectum;[286] quodsi munitio sit obsessa circa mare, et non possint habere aquam nisi salitam, eo quod dulcem aquam habeat distantem, ad

---

[283] Vegetius, IV 7 (p. 133, 8): Parum autem proficit plurimum collegisse, nisi ab exordio dimensione salubri per idoneos erogatio temperetur.

[284] Vegetius, IV 7 (p. 133, 12): Imbellis quoque aetas ac sexus propter necessitatem victus portis frequenter exclusa est, ne penuria opprimeret armatos, a quibus moenia servabantur.

[285] Vegetius, IV 7 (p. 132, 16): Non solum autem porcinum sed et omne animalium genus, quod inclusum servari non potest, deputari oportet ad laridum.

[286] Vegetius, IV 10 (p. 135, 12): effodiendi sunt putei. (p. 135, 21): praeterea in omnibus publicis aedificiis multisque privatis cisternae sunt diligentissime substruendae, ut receptacula aquis pluvialibus, quae de tectis effluunt, praestent.

quam capiendam prohibent obsidentes, tunc mediante cera poterit dulcificari. Nam secundum philosophum in II metaphysicorum:[287] quidquid ex aliqua salita per poros cerae transit, totum in dulce convertitur. Deferendum est etiam ad munitionem obsidendam in magna copia acetum et vinum, ne ex potu solius aquae bellatores adeo debilitentur, quod non possint viriliter resistere obsidentibus.

Ostenso quae sunt remedia adhibenda contra famen et sitim per quae obsessa munitio devinci consuevit, restat videre, quae sunt remedia adhibenda, ne per pugnam obsessa munitio devincatur. Debet ergo ad civitatem vel ad castrum obsessum deportari in magna copia sulphur, pix, oleum ad comburendum machinas hostium;[288] ferra etiam et ligna sunt ad munitionem obsessam in debita abundantia deportanda, ut per ligna hastae sagittarum et telorum et etiam aedificia necessaria munitioni fieri possint; per ferra vero reparari possunt arma et tela et sagittae et alia per quae impugnari valeant obsidentes.[289] Est enim multitudo ferri utili ipsis obsessis ad destruendum aedificia et machinas ipsorum obsidentium, ut in sequenti capitulo apparebit. Saxa etiam torrentium in maxima copia sunt ad munitionem deportanda, quia talia sunt solidiora et aptiora ad iaciendum; ex iis ergo replendi sunt muri et turres munitionis obsessae.[290] Calcem etiam pulverisatam deferendum est ad ipsam munitionem in magna abundantia, et ex ea replenda sunt multa vasa; et cum obsidentes appropinquant muris munitionis, iacienda sunt vasa illa, quibus fractis pulvis ille subintrat obsidentium oculos et adeo offendit eos, ut quasi caeci et non videntes percuti possint. Nervorum etiam

---

[287] Aristotle. *Meteorology*. II 354 17: διηϑούμενον γὰρ γίνεσϑαι τὸ ἁλμυρὸν πότιμον.

[288] Vegetius IV 8 (p. 133, 14): Bitumen sulphur picem liquidam oleum, quod incendiarium vocant, ad exurendas hostium machinas convenit praeparari.

[289] Vegetius, IV 8 (p. 133, 17): ad arma facienda ferrum utriusque temperaturae et carbones servantur in conditis; ligna quo que hastilibus sagittisque necessaria reponuntur.

[290] Vegetius, IV 8 (p. 133, 19): Saxa rotunda de fluviis, quia pro soliditate graviora sunt et aptiora mittentibus, diligentissime colliguntur; ex quibus muri replentur et turres.

copia et funium utilis est munitioni obsessae propter ballistas et arcus et alia praeparata; quodsi nervi deficiant, loco eorum adhiberi poterint crines equini vel capilli mulierum.[291] Recitat etiam Vegetius, quod cum Romanis nervorum copia defecisset, et non possent machinas reparare ad resistendum bellatoribus, muliere Romanae abscisis crinibus eos suis maritis tradiderunt, per quos machinis reparatis adversariorum impetum reppulerunt. Maluerunt enim, ut ait Vegetius, illae pudicissimae feminae cum maritis convivere deformato capite quam servire hostibus integirs crinibus.[292] Sunt etiam ad munitiones deportanda cornua bestiarum ad reformandum ballistas et arcus, et coria cruda ad tegendum machinas et alia aedificia, ne ab adversariis per incendia comburantur.[293] His enim cautelis et per ea quae dicta sunt, resistere poterunt obsessi, ne eorum munitiones per pugnam ab obsidentibus devincantur.

Cap. XXII. Quomodo resistendum est impugnationi factae per cuniculos, et qualiter machinis lapidariis et aliis aedificiis obsessi debeant obviare.

Enumerabantur supra tres speciales modi impugnandi munitiones obsessas, quorum unus erat per cuniculos et vias subterraneas, alius per machinas lapidarias, et tertius per aedificia impulsa usque ad moenia castri vel civitatis. Quare, si docuimus per praefatos modos obsidentes invadere obsessos, reliquum est, ut declaremus, quomodo obsessi a praedictis impugnationibus

---

[291] Vegetius, IV 9 (p. 134, 12): Nervorum quoque copiam summo studio expedit colligi, quia onagri vel ballistae ceteraque tormenta nisi funibus nervinis intenta nihil prosunt. Equorum tamen saetae de caudis ac iubis ad ballistas utiles asseruntur. Indubitatum vero est crines feminarum in eiusmodi tormentis non minorem habere virtutem Romanae necessitatis experimento.

[292] Vegetius, IV 9 (p. 135, 2): Nam in obsidione Capitolii corruptis iugi ac longa fatigatione tormentis, cum nervorum copia defecisset, matronae abscisos crines viris suis obtulere pugnantibus, reparatisque machinis adversariorum impetum reppulerunt. Maluerunt enim pudicissimae feminae deformato ad tempus capite libere vivere cum maritis, quam hostibus integro decore servire.

[293] Vegetius, IV 9 (p. 135, 8): Cornua quoque vel cruda coria proficit colligi ad catafractas texendas aliaque machinamenta sive munimina.

contra obsidentes se defendere valeant. Primo igitur dicemus de remediis contra impugnationem per cuniculos. Possumus autem circa haec duo remedia adsignare: unum est per profunditatem fossarum repletarum aquis.[294] Nam si circa munitionem obsessam sunt profundae foveae aquis repletae, impediuntur obsidentes, ne obsessos impugnare possint per cuniculos et vias subterraneas. Dato tamen quod fossae aquis repleri non possint, si vint valde profundae, peramplae, sufficienter impediunt subterraneas vias, quia hoc genere impugnationis impugnari non possunt munitiones obsessae, nisi dictae viae subterraneae profundiores sunt fossis. Munitio igitur defendenda vel est supra petram firmam, et tunc propter duritiem lapidis non est facile per cuniculos debellare eam; vel est supra petram de facili dolabilem aut supra terram, quae de facili fodi potest, et tunc per profundas foveas est fortificanda munitio, ne per cuniculos devincatur. Secundum remdium contra cuniculos et vias subterraneas est, facere in munitione obsessa viam aliam correspondentem viae subterraneae factae ab obsidentibus. Si enim obsessa munitio foveas non habet profundas, nec habet eas repletas aquis, propter quod timetur de impugnatione per cuniculos, diligenter considerare debent obsessi, utrum ab aliqua parte videant terram defrri, et utrum per aliqua signa cognoscere possint obsidentes inchoare cuniculos; quod cum perceperint, statim debent viam aliam subterraneam facere correspondentem illis cuniculis, ita tamen, quod via illa tendat contra obsidentes. Et per viam illam sic perforatam, cuius partem fecerunt obsidentes et partem obsessi, debet esse bellum continuum, ne obsidentes per viam illam munitionem ingrediantur; debent etiam obsessi iuxta inchoationem viae subterraneae habere magnas tinas plenas aquis vel etiam urinis, et cum bellant contra obsidentes, debent fingere se fugere et exire foveam illam, quo facto totam aquam aut urinam sic congregatam effundere debent supra obsidentes exsistentes in cuniculis. Temporibus enim nostris multi obsidentium sic periclitati sunt. Quare si hoc

---

294 Vegetius, IV 5 (p. 131, 15): Nam duplici modo opus subterraneum peragi, earum (fossarum) altitudine et inundatione prohibetur.

aliquando factum fuit, non debemus reputare impossibile, ne iterum fieri possit.

Viso quomodo resistendum sit debellationi factae per cuniculos, restat videre, quomodo obsessi debeant obviare impugnationi factae per lapidarias machinas. Contra has autem quadrupliciter subvenitur. Primo, quia aliquando subito ex munitione obsessa exit magna multitudo armatorum et invadunt machinam, et priusquam exercitus possit succurrere ad defendendum eam succendunt ipsam.[295] Sed si munitionem ipsam obsessi exire non audeant, tunc clam de nocte per muros aliqui ligati funibus emittuntur, qui absconse ignem portantes, absque eo quod alii percipiant, machinam incendunt; quo peracto trahuntur superius per funes ad munitionem ipsam.[296] Est etiam tertius modus destruendi machinas faciendo sagittas, quas appellant colos.[297] Est autem sagitta illa in medio quasi habens quandam caveam, in qua ponitur ignis fortis, factus ex oleo, sulphure, pice et resina, quem ignem cum stuppa convolutum bellatores antiqui 'incendiarium' vocaverunt.[298] Huiusmodi autem sagitta per ballistam fortem emissa usque ad machinam multotiens succendit ipsam. Quarto etiam modo resistitur machinas lapidariis faciendo alias machinas interius, percutiendo eas et destruendo ipsas.[299] Inter cetera autem summum remedium est, postquam constituta est machina interius, facere ei fundam ex catenis ferreis vel textam ex ferro et iuxta machinam illam construere fabricam, in qua aliquod magnum ferrum bene igniatur, quod bene ignitum

---

[295] Vegetius, IV 18 (p. 140, 10): eruptione facta globus egreditur armatorum et vi hostibus pulsis machinamentum illud ingens dereptis coriis de lignis exurit.
[296] Vegetius, IV 18 (p. 141, 2): Depositi quoque homines funibus, cum hostes dormiunt, in lanternis portant lucernas et incensis machinis rursum levantur in murum.
[297] Vegetius, IV 18 (p. 140, 8): ad maiores ballistas malleolos vel falaricas cum incendio destinant.
[298] Vegetius, IV 18 (p. 140, 17): inter tubum etiam et hastile sulphure resina bitumine stuppisque convolvitur infusa oleo, quod incendiarium vocant.
[299] Vegetius, IV 22 (p. 143, 11): Adversum haec obsessos defendere consueverunt ballistae onagri scorpiones arcuballistae fustibali fundae.

apponatur super fundam ex ferro textam et proiciatur ad machinam aliam vel ad quodcunque aedificium ligneum. Contra hoc enim coria cruda non valent, ligna non habent resistentiam; omne enim aedificium ligneum hoc modo comburi potest. Sunt autem et multae aliae particulares cautelae valentes ad defensionem contra lapidarias machinas; sed quia talia complete sub narrationem non cadunt, prudentis iudicio relinquantur.

Ostenso quomodo resistendum sit cuniculis et lapidariis machinis, reliquum est declarare, quomodo obviari debat aedificiis allis impulsis ad moenia munitionis obsessae. Ad hoc autem valent, quaecunque diximus circa resistentiam machinarum. Nam sicut destrui possunt lapidariae machinae per improvisum insultum obsessorum, et per homines latenter de nocte emissos, et per sagittas deferentes ignem fortem, et per machinas alias emittentes lapides, vel per fundas ex ferro textas iacientes ignita ferra, sic omnibus his modis possunt huiusmodi aedificia lignea impugnari; immo expertum est, contra singula huiusmodi aedificia maxime valere, si per alias machinas vel aliquo alio modo ferra ignita iaciantur in ipsa. Possumus tamen specialia remdia contra huiusmodi aedificia adsignare, ut contra arietem construatur lupus.[300] Dicebatur enim trabem ferratam percutientem muros munitionis obsessae propter duritiem capitis vocari arietem. Contra hoc autem construitur quoddam ferrum curvum, dentatum dentibus fortissimis et acutis et ligatum funibus, cum quo capitur caput arietis vel caput illius trabis ferratae, quo capto vel omnino aries ad superiora trahitur, vel ita suspenditur, ut muris nocere non possit. Unde et bellatores antiqui huiusmodi ferrum vocaverunt lupum, eo quod acutis dentibus arietem caperet. Contra castra vero multum valent ferra ignita. Adhibetur tamen speciale remedium contra ipsa, quia fiunt cuniculi et viae subterraneae et clam suffoditur terra, unde debet transire castrum; qua suffossa et castro demerso

---

[300] Vegetius, IV 23 (p. 144, 19): Plures in modum forficis dentatum funibus inligant ferrum, quem lupum vocant, apprehensumque arietem aut evertunt aut ita suspendunt, ut impetum non habeat feriendi.

in ipsam, propter magnitudinem ponderis, oportet castrum iterum construi, eo quod non possit ex fovea integrum removeri.[301] Contra vineas vero et musculos etiam multum valent ferra ignita; quodsi tamen contingeret, per huiusmodi aedificia perforari muros munitionis obsessae, cum de hoc dubitatur, antequam hoc fiat, iuxta illos muros eriguntur aedificia lignea, vel, si sit possibile, aedificentur muri lapidei, ut, si contingeret obsidentes intrare munitionem, retinerentur clausi inter muros illos; et non valentes se defendere propter murorum inclusionem lapidibus obruuntur[302]. Est tamen diligenter advertendum, quod aliquando obsidentes fingunt se fugere et sic per insidias invadunt munitionem obsessam; ideo non statim post resessum hostium sunt munitiones dimittendae et est custodia neglegenda;[303] immo investigandae sunt condiciones hostium, ut, quod palam habere non potuerunt, per insidias et astutias obtineri non possint.

Cap. XXIII. Qualiter constituenda est navis, et qualiter committendum est navale bellum; et ad quid singula bella ordinantur.

In hoc ultimo capitulo tractare volumus aliqua de navali bello; non tamen in hoc oportet circa hoc tantum insistere, quia multa; quae dicta sunt in aliis generibus bellorum, applicari poterunt ad navalem pugnam. Circa hoc autem pugnandi genus primo videndum est, qualiter fabricanda sit navis. Nam navis male fabribata ex modica hostium impugnatione de fecili perit.

---

[301] Vegetius, IV 20 (p. 141, 20): mechanici ingenio inventum est tale remedium. Per noctem sub fundamenta muri cuniculum fodit et illum locum, ad quem die postero turris fuerat promovenda, nuullo hostium sentiente egesta terra cavavit intrinsecus, et cum rotis suis moles fuisset impulsa atque ad locum, qui subtercavatus fuerat, pervenisset, tanto ponderi solo cdente subsedit nec iiungi muris aut moveri ulterius potuit.

[302] Vegetius, IV 23 (p. 145, 3): Quodsi tanta vis fuerit, ut murus arietibus perforetur et, quod saepe accidit, decidat, salutis una spes superest, ut destuctis domibus alius intrinsecus murus addatur hostesque intra binos parietes, si penetrare temptaverint, perimantur.

[303] Vegetius, IV 26 (p. 146, 19): Propter quod maior est adhibenda custodia, cum hostis abscesserit.

Sciendum ergo, quod secundum Vegetium ligna ex quibus constituenda est navis non sunt quolibet tempore incidenda. Nam tempore Martii et Aprilis, in quo umor incipit in arboribus abundare, non est bonum incidere arbors, ex quibus fabricanda est navis, sed tempore Julii et Augusti, vel etiam aliquo alio tempore, in quo umor arborum desiccetur, ad huiusmodi fabricam incidenda sunt ligna.[304] Rursus non statim lignis incisis est ex iis fabricanda navi, sed primo arbores sunt dividendae per tabulas et per aliquod tempus dimittendae, ut desiccari possint. Nam si ex lignis viridibnus construatur navis, quando naturalis eorum umor exspiraverit, contrahuntur ligna et faciunt navibus rimas, quibus in navibus quasi nihil periculosius esse potest.[305] Durum est enim intendere simul bellis navalibus et exponere se periculis, ne puppis per rimas naufragium patiatur. Viso qualiter incidenda sunt ligna et quomodo reservanda, ut ex iis navis debite valeat fabricari, videre restat, quomodo in navi bene fabricata committenda sunt bella. Habet autem navale bellum, quantum ad aliqua, similem modum bellandi cum pugna terrestri. Nam sicut in pugna campestri oportet pugnantes bene armatos esse, et bene scire se a percussionibus protegere, et hostibus vulnera infligere, sic et haec requiruntur in bello navali; immo in huiusmodi pugna oportet homines melius esse armatos quam in terrestri, quia, cum pugnatores marini quasi fixi stent et modicum se moveant, melius sustinere possunt armorum pondera; quare eorum armatura gravior esse debet.[306] Possumus tamen, quantum ad praesens, decem enumerare, per quae marini pugnatores hostes impugnares debent. Primum est ignis, quod incendiarium vocant; expedit enim iis habere multa vasa plena pice, sulphure, resina, oleo, quae omnia sunt cum

---

[304] Vegetius, IV 36 (p. 152, 18): Caeduntur autem trabes utiliter post solstitium aestivum, id est per mensem Julium et Augustum et per autumnale aequinoctium usque in Kal. Januarias.

[305] Vegetius, IV 36 (p. 153, 7): Nam quae virides compinguntur, cum nativum umorem exsudaverint, contrahuntur et rimas faciunt latiores, quo nihil est periculosius navigantibus.

[306] Vegetius, IV 44 (p. 162, 12): De onere namque armorum nemo potest conqueri, qui stans pugnat in navibus; scuta quoque validiora propter ictus lapidum et ampliora sumuntur.

stuppa convolvenda. Haec enim vasa repleta sunt succendenda et proicienda ad navem hostium, ex qua proiectione vas frangitur et illud incendiarum comburitur et succendit navem. Sunt vero enim multa talia in navem proicienda, ut ex multis partibus possit navis succendi; et cum proiciuntur talia, tunc est contra nautas committendum duurum bellum, ne possint succerrere ad exstinguendum ignem. Secundo ad committendum marinum bellum multum valent insidiae. Nam sicut un terra ponuntur insidiae militum, qui ex improviso invadentes hostes eos terrent et de facili vincunt, sic in mari post aliquas insulas fiunt insidiae, ut marini pugnatores ex improviso irruentes in hostes eos facilius vincant.[307] Tertio circa marinum bellum est attendendum, ut semper pugnantes navem suam faciant circa profundum aquarum et navem hostium impingant ad litus, quia pugnandi impetum perdunt, qui detruduntur ad terram.[308] Quarto ad arborem navis suspendendum est lignum quoddam longum, ex utraque parte ferratum, quod ad percutiendum tam navem quam nautas se habeat quasi aries, cum quo conteruntur muri civitatis obsessae. Debet autem sic ordinari lignum illud, ut ligamentum retinens ipsum possit deprimi et elevari, quia hoc facto maior habebitur commoditas, ut cum ipso percuti possit tam navis quam et exsistentes in ipsa.[309] Quinto in bello navali habenda est copia ampularum sagittarum, cum quibus scindenda sunt vela hostium. Nam velis eorum perforatis et non valentibus retinere ventum, non tantum possunt ipsi hostes impetum habere pugnandi, nec etiam possunt sic faciliter receder, si velint declinare a bello. Sexto

---

[307] Vegetius, IV 45 (p. 163, 9): Ad instar autem terrestris proelii superventus fiunt ignorantibus nauticis vel circa oportunas insularum angustias collocantur insidiae.

[308] Vegetius, IV 46 (p. 164, 3): Praeterea utile est, ut alto et libero mari tua semper classis, utatur, inimicorum vero pellatur ad litus, quia pugnandi impetum perdunt qui detruduntur in terras.

[309] Vegetius, IV 46 (p. 164, 10): Asser dicitur, cum trabes subtilis ac longa ad similitudinem antemnae pendet in malo, utroque capite ferrato. Hunc, sive a dextra sive a sinistra parte adversariorum se iunxerint naves, pro vice arietis vi impellunt; qui bellatores hostium sive nautas sine dubio prosternit ac deprimit ipsamque navem saepius perforat.

consueveretunt nautae habere quoddam ferrum corvatum ad modum falcis incidens, quod applicatum ad funes retinentes vela statim incidit ipsa. Velus autem sic incisis et cadentibus ab arbore, subtrahitur ab hostibus, ne sic pugnare possint, quia per talem incisionem velorum redditur navis pigrior et quodammodo inutilior ad pugnandum.[310] Septimo consueverunt etiam nautae habere uncos ferreos fortes, ut, cum vident se esse plures hostibus, cum illis uncis capiant eorum naves, ut non permittant eas discedere.[311] Octavo in navali bello est haec cautela attendenda, ut de calce alba pulverisata habeant multa vasa plena, quae ex alto sunt proicienda in naves hostium. Quibus ex impetu proiectis et fractis elevatur pulvis, ut supra diximus in bello terrestri, et subintrat hostium oculos et adeo offendit eos, ut quasi caeci videre non possint; quod in bello navali est valde periculosum, quia ex omni parte bellantes in tali bello vident sibi imminere mortem, quare, si oculi bellantium in tali pugna ex pulvere calcis sic offenduntur, ut videre non possint, de facili vel perimuntur ab hostibus, vel submerguntur in aquis. Nona cautela est, habere multa vasa plena ex molli sapone, quae cum impetu proicienda sunt ad naves hostium, et hoc super loca illa, in quibus contingit hostes exsistere ad dendendum naves. Nam vasis illis confractis in huiusmodi locis, loca illa per saponem liquidum redduntur adeo lubrica, quod hostes ibi ponentes pedes statim labuntur in aquas. Est autem et decima cautela quasi perniciosior omnibus. Nam reperiuntir aliqui marinarii, qui diu sub aquis durare possunt. Nautae ergo debent se serie ordinare contra navem hostium, et clam post tergum debent aliquem emittere diu valentem durare sub aquis. Qui, accepto penetrali, sub aquis debent accedere ad hostilem navem et eam in fundo perforare faciendo ibi plura foramina, quae foramina ab

---

[310] Vegetius, IV 46 (p. 164, 15): Falx autem dicitur acutissimum ferrum curvatum ad similitudinem falcis, quod contis longioribus inditum chalatorios, quibus antemna suspenditur, repente praecidit collapsisque velis liburnam pigriorem et inutilem reddit.

[311] Vegetius, IV 44 (p. 162, 18): qui de virtute praesumunt, admotis liburnis iniectis pontibus in adversariorum transeunt naves ibique gladiis manu ad manum, ut dicitur comminus dimicant.

hostibus reperiri non poterunt, cum per ipsa coeperit abundare aqua, qua abundante et hostes et navem pariter periclitabit. Sunt autem in bello navali alia observanda, ut sit ibi copia lapidum et etiam ferrorum acutorum, quae quasi lapides iaciuntur, cum quibus hostes nimium offenduntur. Sed cetera talia, quia nimis particularia sunt, sub narratione nan cadunt; sufficiant ergo cautelae, quas tradidimus, erga navale bellum. Ostenso qualiter incidenda sunt ligna, ex quibus construenda est navis, et quomodo bellandum est in navali bello, reliquum est ut declaremus, ad quid bella omnia ordinentur.

Sciendum igitur, quod secundum philosophum[312] non bellamus, ut bellemus, sed ut pacem habeamus. Possunt ergo bella ex nequitia hominum et ex cupiditate eorum ordinari ad lucrum vel ad aliquam satisfactionem irae vel concupiscentiae, bella tamen si iuste gerantur et debite fiant, ordinanda sunt ad pacem et ad quietem hominum et ad commune bonum. Nam sic se debent habere bella in societate hominum, sicut se habent potiones et phlebotomiae in copore humano. Nam sicut in humano corpore plures sunt umores, sic in conversatione et societate hominum est dare plures personas et plures homines. Et sicut, quamdiu umores sunt aequati in corpore et non est ibi umorum excessus, non indigemus nec potione nec phlebotomiam et potionem superfluitas umorum est eicienda, per quam turbatur sanitas corporis, sic per bella sunt hostes conculcandi et occidendi, per quos impeditur commune bonum et pax civium et eorum, qui sunt in regno. Supposito ergo reges et principes iustum habere bellum, et hostes eorum iniuste turbare pacem et commune bonum, non est inconveniens, docere eos omnia genera bellandi et omnem modum, per quem possint suos hostes vincere, quod totum debent ordinare ad commune bonum et ad pacem civium. Nam si intendant commune bonum et pacem civium,

---

[312] Aristotle. *Politics*. VI 1333 35: εἶναι… πόλεμον μὲν εἰρήνης χάριν, ἀσχολίαν δὲ οχολῆς.

merebuntur pacem illam aeternam, in qua est summa requies, quam deus ipse suis promisit fidelibus, qui est benedictus in saecula saeculorum. Amen.

6: Itinerarium Peregrinorum et gesta Regis Ricardi

(W. Stubbs, Chronicles and Memorials of the Reign of Richard I. London, 1864 Vol. I)

Itin. III cap. 7:

Rex Franciae citius convaluit de infirmitate et machinis intendebat conficiendis et petrariis locis aptis applicandis, quas nocte dieque incessabiliter instituit iaculari. Quarum unam habuerat peroptimam, quam vocavit Malam Vicinam. Turci vero infra civitatem alteram habebant, quam vocabant Malam Cognatam, quae vehementibus iactibus frequentius dissipare solebat Malam Vicinam: quam rex reaedificabat, quousque iugiter iaciendo principalem civitatis murum in parte diruit et Turrim Maledictam conquassavit. Hinc et petraria ducis Burgundiae non in vanum iaciebat: illinc Templariorum petraria Turcos vastabat egregie, et Hospitaliorum quoque Turcis metuenda nequaquam cessabat a iactibus. Praeter has quoque fuit quaedam petrariam Dei. Iuxta illam praedicabat presbyter assidue, vir magnae probitatis, multum conquirens monetam ad eam iugiter restaurandam et ad conducendum, qui lapides congregarent iaculandos. Per ipsam demum ad aestimationem duarum perticarum iuxta Turrim Maledictam conquassatus est murus. Comes Flandriae petrariam habuerat electam, quam post eius mortem habuit rex Richardus, et praeterea minorem electam. Hae duae sine intermissione iaciebant versus turrim iuxta portam quandam, quam Turci frequentabant, donec turris medietatem diruerunt. Et praeter has fecerat rex Richardus alias novas duas, operis electi et materiae, ineffabiliter destinatam percutientes quorumcunque metam locorum. Aedificaverat etiam machinam firmissimis compactam compagibus, gradibus ad ascendendum dispositis, vulgo dictam Berefredum, sese nexibus arctius complectentibus, coriis opertam et funibus et solidissimis ligneis tabulatis, nec petrariarum iactibus dissolvendam, nec ignis Graeci perfusione, nec cuiuscunque materiae cessuram iniuriis. Duos etiam praeparaverat mangunellos, quorum unus tante fuerat agilitatis et vehementiae, quod iactus eius pervenirent in interiores macelli civitatis plateas. Petrariae itaque regis Ricardi die nocteque iugiter iaciebant, de quorum una certissime constat, quod unius lapidis ictu prostraverit in mortem duodecim homines. Idem lapis ad Salahadinum transmissus est videndus per nuntios dicentes, quod ille diabolus rex Angliae attulerat illuc a Messana civitate, quam ceperat, tales silices marinos et limpidissimos lapides ad puniendos Saracenos, quorum ictibus nihil potuisset resistere, quin quassaretur vel in pulverem minueretur.

Drawings

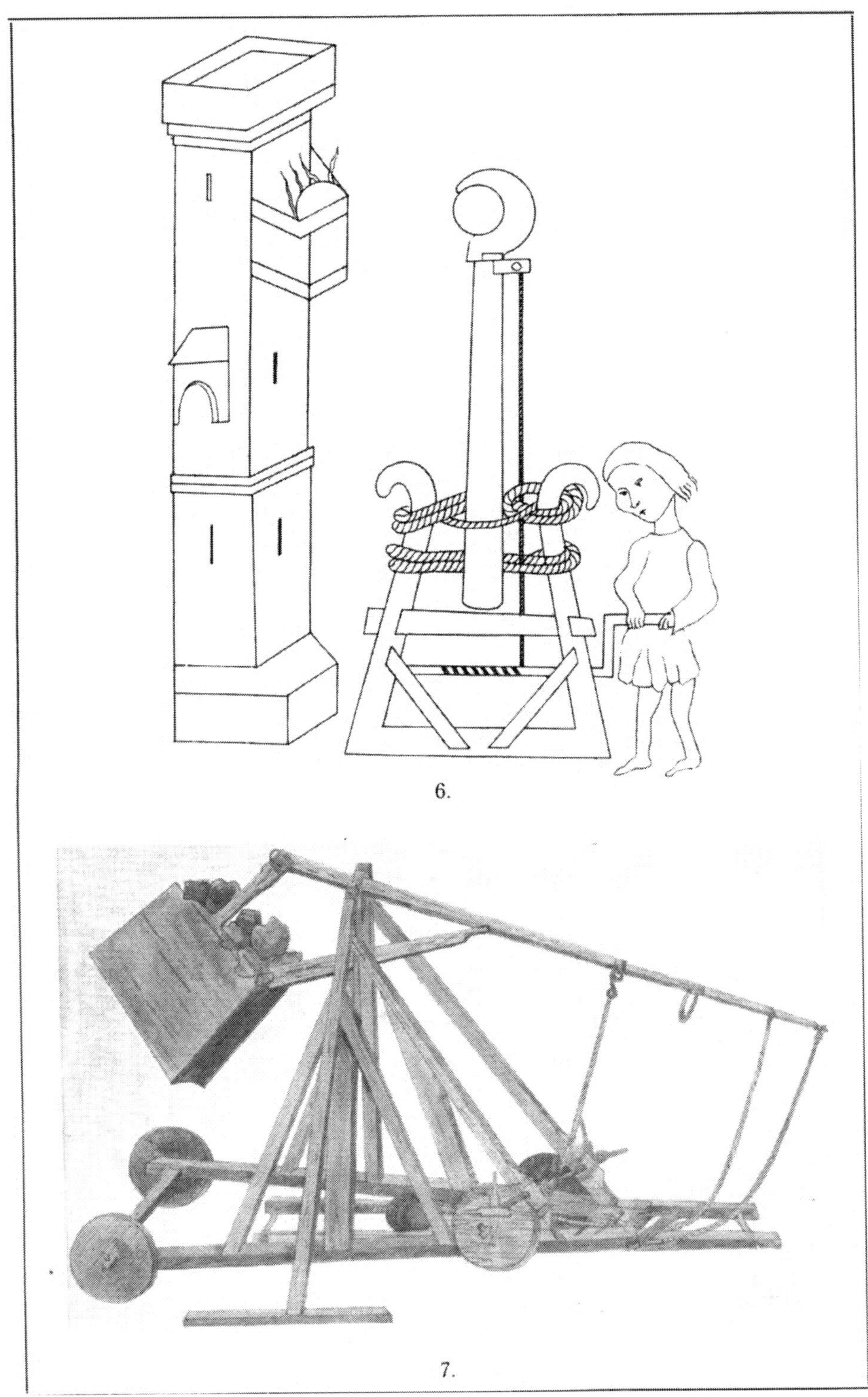

6.

7.

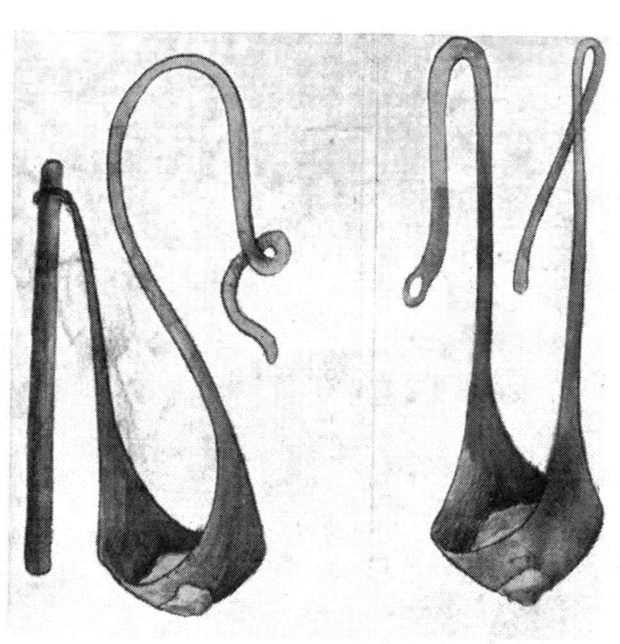

8.

9.

10.

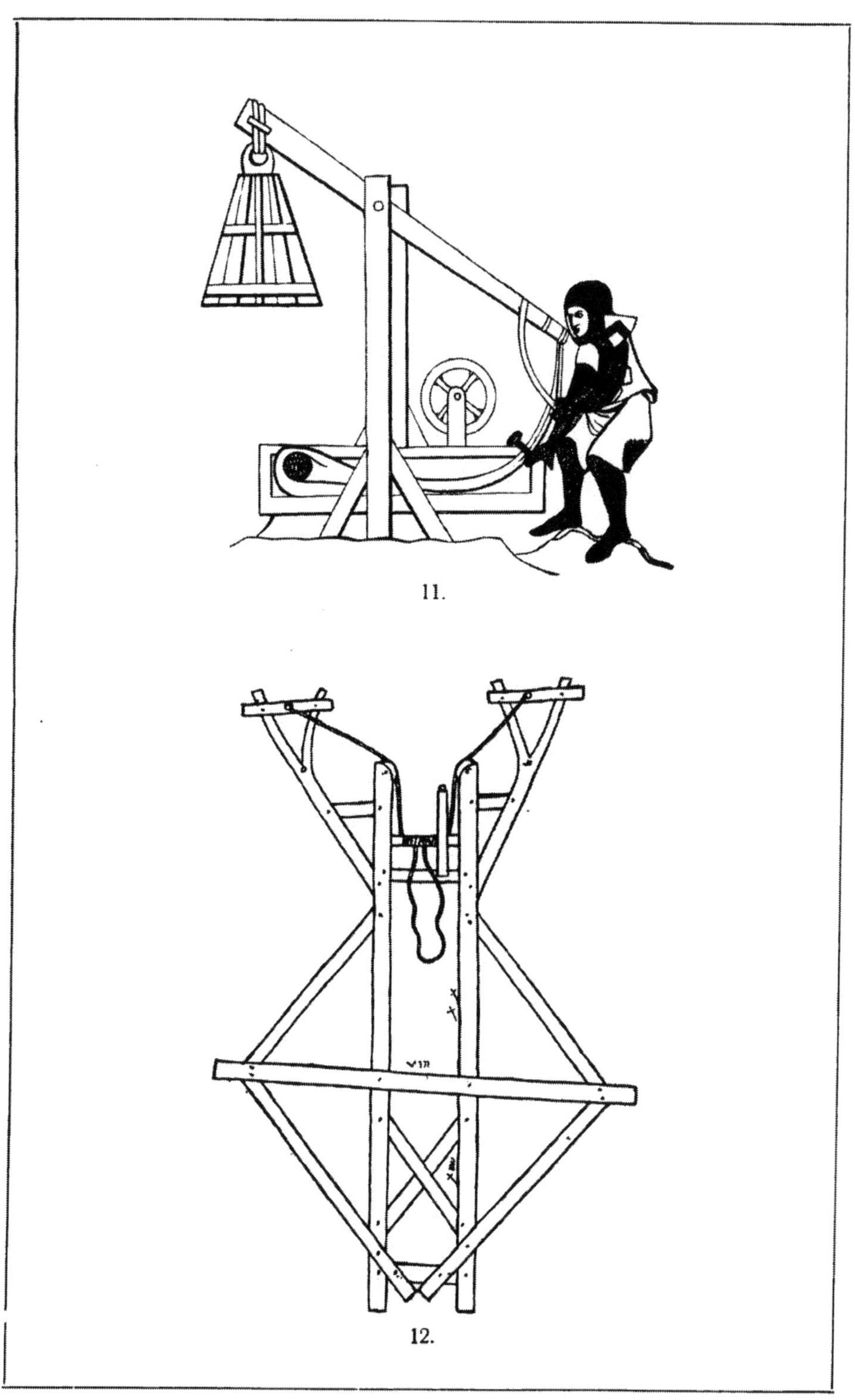

11.

12.

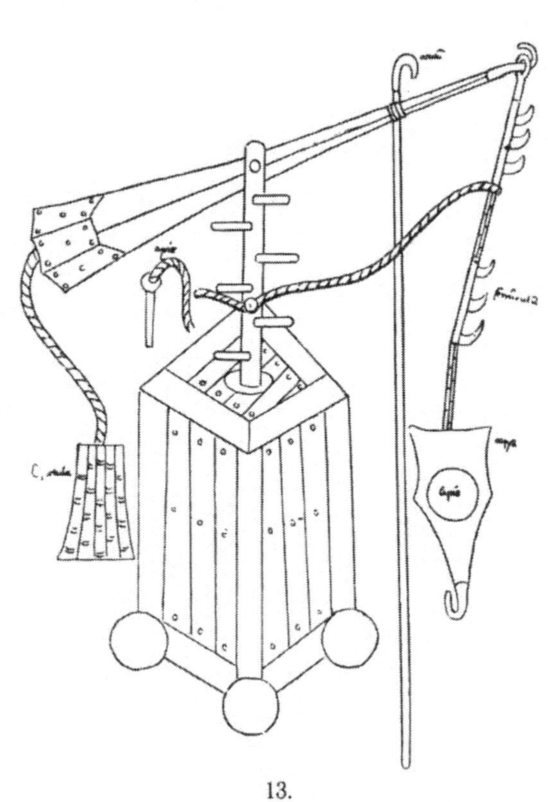

13.

14.

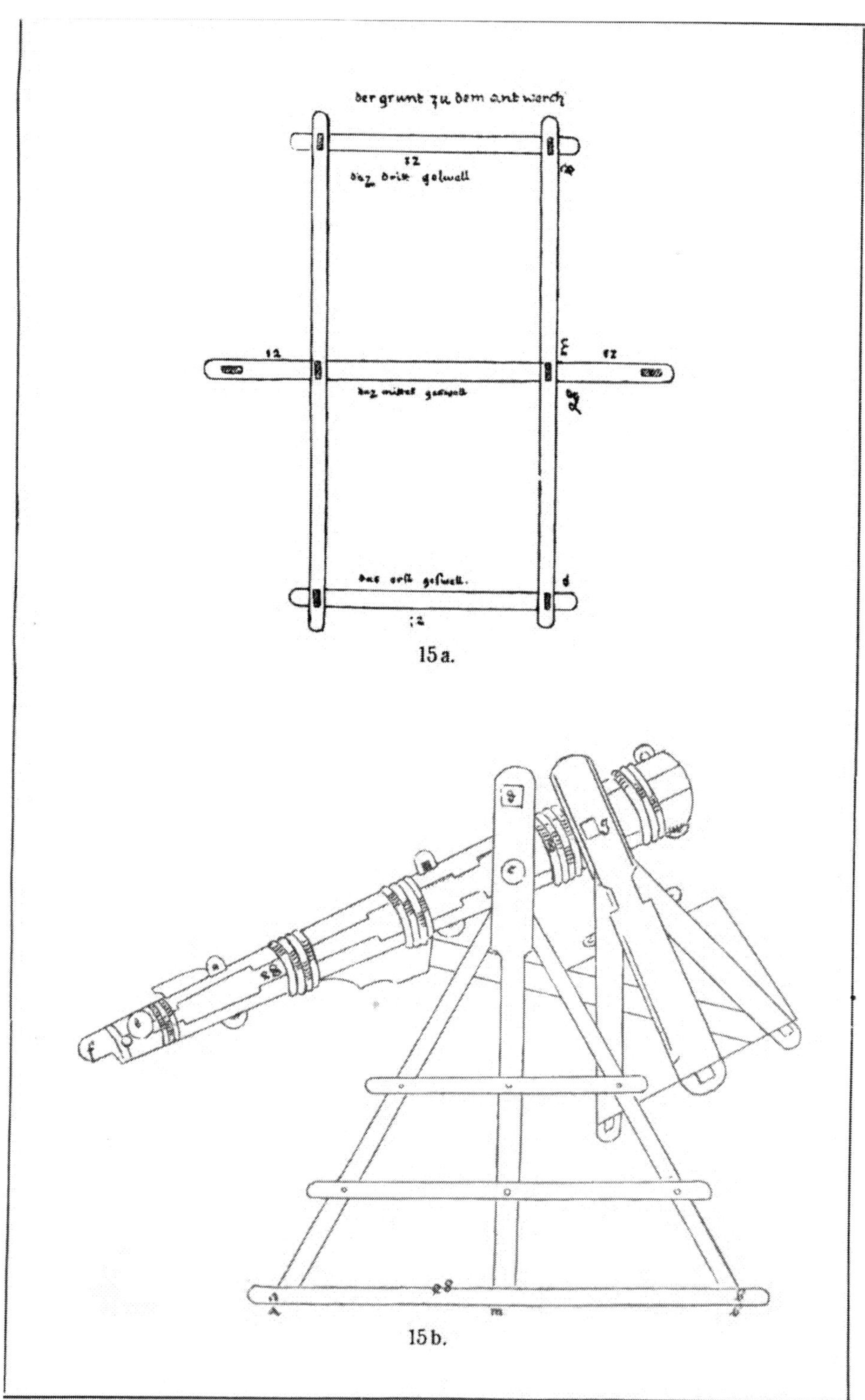

15a.

15b.

16.

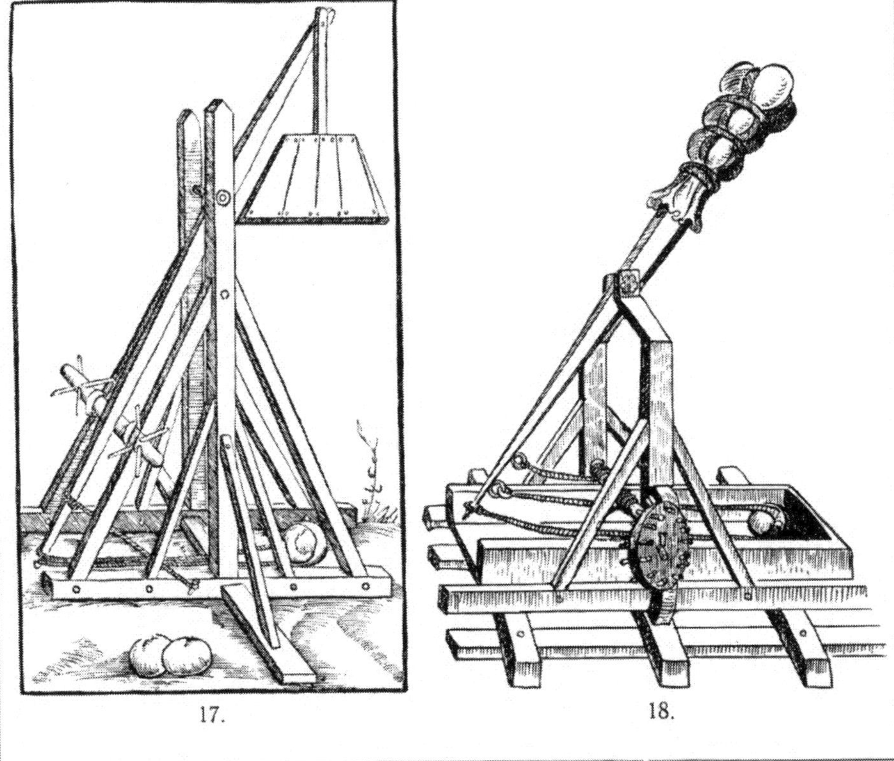

17. 18.

45441563R00129

Made in the USA
San Bernardino, CA
29 July 2019